MARK GERARDOT

IRREPARABLE

*Three lives. Two deaths. One story
that has to be told.*

ISBN 978-0-578-66562-7

M,

Your heart. Your voice. The way you could light up a room. The world is a far less special place without you in it.

TABLE OF CONTENTS

CHAPTER 1

THEY'RE GONE

I don't want to write this book. What I want is for none of this to have happened, to have the chance to go back and change history. But I can't. So, for this to have happened, it must have meaning. It must have purpose. It has to be talked about, not forgotten, not silenced, not scandalized as if it's something that could only happen to bad people, people so outside normal codes of conduct that they must be set aside, as if they're somehow not quite human nor worthy of compassion. Yet I know I am as much a part of the audience and judge as any reader, for I have not stopped condemning my own actions that set these events in motion. It's difficult to dig it all up again and easy to want to forget it happened. But it did happen. I don't want to write this book. I have to.

Now that it's all over, the events tucked into the tidy corners of countless news reports about yet another human tragedy, the people involved transformed to characters whose only mark on this earth will be their culpability in life or their finality in death, I'm left trying to understand why. And trying to pick up the pieces of what's left of my life. Still, one year later, I am tirelessly searching for and discovering new clues to the events of that otherwise ordinary day. Searching for how I am supposed to feel about the past. Searching for what I am supposed to do tomorrow. Searching for the meaning of a

1

tragedy in which I know my actions played a part and yet I never once imagined was a possibility. But possibility, I've discovered, is sometimes limited only by the boundaries of our sanity.

April 23, 2018

I left our apartment to drive the forty-minute commute to my new job. Before the door closed, I looked back at my wife to tell her I loved her, because I did. Even though Jennair and I were in the early stages of a divorce, I repeatedly reminded her that I would always love her. Those simple words exchanged countless times in our near three decades together now had a different meaning. Often, they would bring tears to her eyes, because she couldn't comprehend how I could still love her and yet want to start a new life without her. This time, however, she just stared back at me without any expression at all. I then added, "See you tonight," prompting a barely discernible nod.

We had plans to meet for dinner that evening in Newtown Square, a burgeoning suburb west of Philadelphia. She had an appointment nearby with her divorce coach in the afternoon and planned to stay in the area so we could talk. She was scheduled to have exploratory surgery and a possible hysterectomy the following day, so our dinner would have to be an early one, and I wanted it to be especially comforting because I knew the pending surgery was causing her some stress, and Jennair had certainly had her share of stress in the last few months.

As I drove to work to start the second week of my new job as the creative director for an international luxury resort company, I decided to make a slight detour and surprise Meredith with her favorite drink from Starbucks—a venti blonde roast with extra soy. Getting each other coffee was a favorite morning ritual we had started while working together at the University of Delaware. It was sort of an unspoken rule. Whoever got to the office first bought the other one coffee. I'm sure our coworkers noticed the routine, but no one said a word. Everyone knew we worked closely together, so morning closed-door meetings weren't out of the ordinary. While I had been her direct report, she had considered me her partner and treated me as such.

Now she too was starting the second week of her new job at Villanova University as the assistant vice president of marketing. Serendipitously, we had both gotten our new employment offer letters the same day and started our new jobs the same day. Both our careers were taking us in new directions and giving us a chance for new lives. Together.

As had become my habit over the past few months, I turned off the location services on my iPhone so Jennair wouldn't know where Meredith lived. With my phone still in my hand, I sent Meredith a text:

Mark: *Morning babe. On the way with SBUX*

Meredith: *Huge boyfriend points. Love you. Can't wait to see you.*

Two days earlier, I had spent all day with Meredith, helping her move from the house she'd shared with her then-husband in Newark, Delaware, and arranging the furniture in her new home, just off campus in Bryn Mawr. But I still couldn't wait to see her before she left for work. We were both so head-over-heels in love it literally hurt for us not to be together. Meredith and I had not yet spent a night together, but she frequently talked so lovingly about what it would be like to wake up in my arms and experience our morning routine together. I shared her dream and couldn't believe it was so close at hand.

By some standards, Meredith and I were practically strangers. Yet somehow, just seven months after I had first sat across from her in her office for a job interview, I found myself in the most intense romantic relationship I had ever experienced. I felt like a forty-nine-year-old teenager—giddy, in love, and resolved to end my twenty-four-year tumultuous marriage. In a way Jennair never could or would do, Meredith had a way of challenging me. Encouraging me. Inspiring me. Without even looking, I had found the woman who was everything I wanted and needed in my future.

But happiness wouldn't come without a price. After six exhausting months of secrecy, stolen moments, and enduring Jennair's endless inquisitions, I felt like I had no other choice. I was leaving my wife. Our marriage had been reduced to an endless game of cat and mouse and a series of malicious attacks from Jennair, and I couldn't take it anymore.

It was a painful but necessary decision wrought with guilt and uncertainty, but after telling my divorce attorney about what we had been through, she became concerned for my safety. My wife, I discovered, had not just been interrogating me about my relationship with Meredith. She had been stalking me. I do not use that word lightly. Certainly she felt betrayed and had a right to seek answers she felt were hidden from her. But what ensued went far beyond simple investigative work to the level of menacing.

My privacy, I discovered, was not private. I had to get out. But unknowing at the time the full extent of her surveillance and her actions, my concern wasn't for my safety. I'd known Jennair over half my life. She was distraught, but not crazy, the kind of woman who would nurse an injured animal back to health, campaign for gun control, and fix an amazing dinner, all before sundown. I knew I had hurt her, profoundly. I also knew that, for so many reasons, I needed to leave our marriage. I wanted so much for Jennair to land on her feet, stronger and in a better place, and I was confident she would do so. Now, just weeks away from filing an official petition for divorce, we had finally come to a difficult but civil decision to end our marriage.

While Jennair had reluctantly accepted that I was in love with Meredith, it still wasn't public knowledge. Meredith and I had worked hard to keep our relationship a secret from friends, coworkers, and family. If anyone had found out about our relationship, we feared we would have lost our jobs. But now, with new positions, we were both excited at the prospect of starting a new life together. When enough time had passed, we intended to let everyone know about us. It would be easy to explain how, living only fifteen minutes apart from each other, we spent time together and just fell in love. That was the story we had hoped we could tell.

That morning's visit would be a short one, but one I will never forget. Meredith came to the door in a colorful silk bathrobe, looking as beautiful as ever. I handed her the coffee and we exchanged "I love yous" before she gave me a hug and lingering kiss, and I left, the memories of that kiss following me throughout the day. Just after noon, as I joined my new colleagues for a long lunch to welcome me to the team, Meredith added to my anticipation when she sent me a selfie, sitting in her Audi A3 Cabriolet, convertible top down, wearing that signature smile that turned me inside out. My heart soared at the thought of spending my life with this amazing woman, who somehow was even more intelligent and charismatic than she was beautiful.

As lunch wrapped up, one of my colleagues told me about a rooftop bar in Philly that was about to open again for the spring season. It sounded like a great spot for a date. I shot Meredith a quick text with a link to the website.

Mark: *What do you think?*

Meredith: *Looks amazing. I'll put it on our calendar.*

Meredith and I shared a Google calendar where we kept important dates and plans. Within minutes I received a calendar invitation for Saturday, May 19. It was less than a month away, the day she would pick me up from the airport after my trip to Costa Rica and take me to my new apartment, just blocks from her new home. For the rest of the afternoon it was all I could do to keep from smiling, daydreaming about our future.

After an afternoon of back to back meetings, I left my office just before 5:30 p.m., and Jennair and I exchanged text messages.

(5:28 p.m.)

Mark: *So where did you decide for dinner?*

Jennair: *The new place—Firepoint*

Mark: *K. See you there*

Jennair: *K*

(5:45 p.m.)

Mark: *Here. Sitting at bar outside. Get you a glass of cab?*

Jennair: *Sure*

(5:50 p.m.)

Jennair: *I'm running late. I made a wrong turn.*

Mark: *K. I'm ordering food*

(6:00 pm)

Jennair: *Where is Huck?!!*

Mark: *What?*

Jennair: *Where is Huck? You took him. I knew you would do this. I asked Alicia to let him out, but he's not there.*

Mark: *I didn't take him. He's there. Have her check again.*

Five minutes later, Jennair sent me a reply.

(6:05 p.m.)

Jennair: *She found him. But now I'm too upset. I'm turning around. Just go home.*

Mark: *Can't. I ordered food*

Jennair: *Go home now!*

Mark: *No. I'm going to finish*

(6:10 p.m.)

Jennair: [sends photo of a small pile of trash on the ground.]

Jennair: *You fucked her.*

Mark: *I don't know what you're talking about. This photo is disturbing in so many ways.*

Jennair: *Then she was cheating you*

(6:15 pm - 6:20 pm)

Jennair: *You ruined my life*

Jennair: *I hope you never find happiness*

Jennair: *Bye Mark*

During the course of this thirty-minute exchange with Jennair, I became increasingly confused. Why was she panicking about our dog, and why was she ordering me to go home? But with the photo of the used condom, my confusion turned to shock, disgust, and anger. She was going through the trash outside Meredith's home.

7

I tried again and again to call Meredith and sent her several text messages. She didn't reply, which almost never happened. Like me, Meredith always carried two iPhones with her — one for work, the other for personal use. Unless she was in a meeting or at the gym (and sometimes that didn't even stop her), she usually replied immediately. Radio silence for thirty minutes really concerned me, especially with the knowledge that Jennair was going through her trash. I thought, *My God, now she's found out where Meredith lives and she's going through her garbage cans. Jennair's out of control.*

Had she gone home? Or was she still there? Oh my God, if she's there, what has she said to Meredith? And why isn't Meredith returning my calls? My thoughts ran wild as I imagined maybe they were in the middle of a screaming fight, and who knows what Jennair would say. She could say the most terrible things when she was angry. I thought maybe Jennair had confronted Meredith and filled her head with all sorts of awful lies about me. I had to do damage control. As quickly as I could, I paid my bill and rushed to Meredith's house, just fifteen minutes from the restaurant. But fifteen minutes is a long time when your mind is racing with worry.

On the way there, my phone rang. *Thank God,* I remember thinking. But it wasn't Meredith. It was Jennair's mother. Why is she calling me? I can't talk to her now. I let the call go to voicemail. I didn't know it then, but it would be the first of several panicked calls from Jennair's mother and sister that evening.

When I arrived at Meredith's home, I could see her car parked in its usual spot behind the house. I knocked on the front door, standing where we had shared a goodbye kiss just ten hours before.

8

She didn't answer. I walked to the back of the house and before knocking on the glass-paneled door, I hesitated for a moment and peered inside. And what I saw in that moment triggered the state of shock and disbelief I still find myself suspended in today.

Meredith was lying face down in the doorway between the kitchen and the dining room, her phone in one hand, her keys in the other. Thinking she had passed out, I rapped on the glass door and yelled her name, "Meredith! Meredith!" She didn't respond. Knocking on the door more forcefully, it moved, and I realized it wasn't latched. As I ran to her I noticed small flecks of red on her calf and more of the same on the white wall just above her. *What?* I was so confused. I rubbed her back, calling her name, "Meredith. Meredith." No response. I ran outside to get help from her neighbor, who by this time was standing on his porch.

"Tim, call 911!" I screamed. "Meredith is down. She isn't responding!"

Within seconds Tim came running over and into the house with his phone in his hand, already talking to 911 dispatch. I stood there, so confused, as the voice on the other line told him to check for Meredith's pulse.

"No pulse," he said.

I went to my knees by her side and rubbed her back. "No, wait. She's still warm! She's alive! Somebody help her! Please, God, call an ambulance! *Help her!*"

The 911 dispatch told us to get out of the house. The police were on their way. Tim walked outside, but I couldn't leave her. I sat there on the floor, talking to her, touching her, feeling her warmth through the silk floral blouse I recognized from the selfie she had sent me at lunch. Her soft brown hair covered her face and flowed beautifully onto the floor.

It was then I saw her head was surrounded in a pool of blood. In my shock, it hadn't registered at first. This was the most grisly and gruesome thing I had ever seen. I should have been repulsed, shaken to my core. And yet, somehow, I wasn't. This halo of dark red blood, as still as a pond in the night, was once coursing through this amazing and energetic woman. It was all a part of my sweet Meredith and I loved every part of her. So full of life. So full of promise. I wanted so much to lay down next her and envelope her in my arms.

Abruptly the dispatch again instructed us to get out of the house. Stunned, confused, and still not comprehending what was happening, I stood up and slowly turned to leave. Then, out of the corner of my eye, I saw her. Across the room was a dark figure lying face down on the floor. It was a woman. She was wearing a black hoodie, black running pants, and black Nike running shoes, her head turned to the side. I remember vividly how the dark clothes starkly contrasted with the blonde hair and light complexion. As I knelt, I saw that she was facing me, eyes closed. The face, the body, the clothes, it didn't register at first. Then it hit me.

"*FUCK! NO! NO! NO! JENNAIR!*"

I ran to her and touched her hair and neck. She was warm, too.

"Tim! My wife is in here! Please tell them to hurry!"

I struggled to comprehend what I was seeing when I noticed a small wound just behind her right ear. As I stroked the back of her head, I said softly to her, "Oh baby, baby, baby, what did you do? What did you do?"

The police arrived and forced me to leave the house. Outside, I saw the backyard was filling up with police cars and curious neighbors. Yellow police tape had been strung around trees to set up a perimeter. A policeman took me behind a garage and started asking me questions. I was shaking uncontrollably and could barely speak coherently. The only thing I remember saying with any clarity was repeating, "Fuck! Fuck! Fuck!"

I know I talked to the police, but I don't remember anything I told them. Then I found myself in the back of an ambulance surrounded by paramedics. I didn't understand. Why were they concerned with checking my vitals? "I'm fine!" I yelled at them. "Who cares how *I* am? Somebody needs to save *them*. Please, go in the house and save *them!*"

And then one of the paramedics, a motherly figure in her late fifties, looked me in the eye and told me, "They're gone."

"What? They're gone? *No! Fuck! Fuck! Fuck! No!*"

I sat there shaking, crying and yelling. I turned angry and agitated and wanted to leave, but they wouldn't let me. The paramedics asked the police if they could release me. The answer was no. Finally, after half an hour or longer, two detectives ushered me into the back of a police car and drove me to the Radnor Township Police Station. Now, on top of the blur of everything I had just experienced, the nightmare was about to get worse. Two detectives took me into a windowless room and closed the door. I was completely and utterly alone, the prime suspect in a double homicide.

CHAPTER 2

DON'T DO THIS

I first met her in 1986. When I walked up to the counter and got my first glimpse of those iridescent blue eyes framed by the longest natural eyelashes I'd ever seen, I couldn't look away. I was mesmerized. On reflex, I smiled. She smiled back. But I couldn't find any words to say. After a few awkward seconds, I realized I was literally just staring at her. *Say something,* I thought. Embarrassed, I shifted my focus to the menu board behind her. "I need a few seconds," I managed to say, and then stepped to the side.

It's not just anyone who could make a brown polyester Taco Bell uniform look that good, I thought. But I could tell this girl wasn't just anyone. That huge beaming smile. Her kinky blonde hair pulled into a ponytail that poked out over the back of her visor. I was lovestruck. But it was my friend Rick, standing behind me, who made the first move.

"Jennair, what a beautiful name," he said suavely, stepping up to the counter and staring at her employee name tag in a not-so-subtle way. I caught her eye again, and we both smiled, rolled our eyes and chuckled under our breath. We would later laugh about that summer day in 1986 in Fort Wayne, Indiana, telling everyone how we first met. But it really wasn't until several years later that our paths would officially cross again.

I would see her from time to time at football and basketball games when our respective high schools would play each other, and at city and regional choir competitions in which we both competed. But I never approached her, nor did I think she would remember me and our brief encounter. Then on a brisk fall day in 1990, I needed to replace the battery in my 1980 Pontiac Firebird Esprit. It didn't quite have the muscle or allure of a *Smokey and the Bandit* type Trans Am that was the object of every hormone-crazed teen male's affection at the time, but short of a giant, fire-breathing bird on the hood, it looked pretty much the same and I thought every bit as cool.

As I walked into the waiting room at Sears Auto Center, my heart skipped a beat. Like a bombshell right out of a movie, there she sat, in a brown leather bomber jacket and that unmistakable kinky blonde hair. I instantly knew who she was, but I definitely didn't think she would remember me. Yet after a few silent minutes of stealing glances at each other, she looked me straight in the eye and asked, "Are you a Gerardot?"

I nodded and replied, "You're Jennair, aren't you?" And that was the spark that lit a fire that would burn on and off again for the next twenty-eight years.

One problem though—I had a girlfriend. Nothing serious, but I knew I had to be honest with her. When I told Jennair she insisted I break it off or not bother calling her. She had no intention of being "the other woman." Within a week, I ended things amicably with my then girlfriend and Jennair and I began dating.

From the start I knew she was out of my league. Jennair was way hotter and way cooler than I even pretended to be. Sporting a mullet, a leather jacket and my Francisco red Firebird, I may have dressed the part of a card-carrying member of the cool crowd, but deep down I knew I was just a dork, a kid from the sticks who went to a high school surrounded by corn fields on all sides. I was a straight-A student, a rule follower and not once from kindergarten through high school did I miss even a day of school. Not that I didn't dream about it, but it simply wasn't allowed.

I was the tenth of eleven children, sheltered, shy and controlled by much older socially awkward parents who would have been happy if I and my siblings had never left the safety of home. They didn't seem to comprehend what the world outside had to offer us, or more likely they were afraid we might like it. Unlike most of my friends, I was constrained by a strict curfew. Going to a school dance was a rare treat and parties were simply out of the question.

In stark contrast, Jennair was a shooting star. Fearless. Independent. She didn't play by anyone else's rules—the same rules I was always afraid to break. Like me, Jennair grew up in a blue-collar household, in a less than great inner-city neighborhood. But wanting more and better for their two daughters, both her parents worked hard to send Jennair and her sister to private Catholic schools.

From an early age, however, Jennair told me she felt like she never fit in with her more affluent classmates, the sons and daughters of doctors, lawyers and local business owners. Instead, she found refuge in her identity as a rebel. While many of her classmates were classically trained musicians, Jennair listened to heavy metal, went to Kiss concerts, and despite her parents' objection, she proactively challenged the idea that she was limited to only dating Caucasian boys.

She was a free-spirited thinker and simply didn't care what everyone else thought of her. Jennair didn't need anyone's approval, and as someone who was raised Catholic, she reviled against her mother because she told me her mom was a hypocrite for not living out her supposed Christian values, and thus did everything she could to mock those values. Fed up with her home life, by the age of seventeen Jennair moved in with her grandparents.

But more than just a rebel, Jennair had an unstoppable drive. She was a cheerleader, a thespian, a singer and a serious student. She had a handful of people she considered friends, but she said she didn't really need them. Instead, she took her lunches in the library, reading, doing her homework and studying for exams. She always held down at least one, sometimes two, part-time jobs. Jennair was going places, and my attraction to her on so many fronts was too strong to ignore. She was like no other girl I had ever known. I was hooked.

As our dating relationship became more intimate, some of our greatest differences became more apparent. I had grown up the son of a Catholic father and an awkwardly shy mother and was taught that sex was a vile, disgusting act, the mere mention of which was met with disapproval, scorn and often admonishment. When I discovered how babies came into this world, I was convinced for a short time that I and my ten brothers and sisters must surely be the product of an immaculate conception. How else? In the bookshelves of our formal living room was a set of health encyclopedias, including Volume 12, *Sex and Your Body*. At around age eleven or twelve, as I hit puberty, I naturally became curious and found myself flipping through that book, mouth wide open, astonished as I learned about human reproduction and all the parts that make someone uniquely male or female. Suddenly my mother walked in.

15

"What are you doing?" she asked angrily. "Put that back. What are you, sick?"

Ashamed and mortified at her reaction, I promptly put the book back on the shelf. Days later, as I walked past that bookshelf again, that volume had mysteriously disappeared.

Ten years later, at the age of twenty-two and dating one of the most enlightened people I had ever known, I discovered I had a lot of baggage around sex. Suffice it to say, when I met Jennair, my sexual experience was very limited—to once, to be exact. But here was this beautiful person, open and free, wanting to share something amazing with me. Not to imply that Jennair was wildly promiscuous, but clearly she had had more experience. But to her surprise, when she wanted to have sex with me, I rejected her, afraid I was going to get in trouble, I suppose. My repudiation hurt her at first, but she didn't give up on me.

"Mark, sex is supposed to be fun," she told me, which was a foreign concept at first. It was hard to let go of the guilt from so many years of parental programming. But soon I began to let my guard down. I was in awe of her experience, her appetite for intimacy and her initiative to make sex a healthy, normal part of our relationship. She completely changed my outlook.

This was my senior year as an art and design student at the University of Saint Francis, a private Catholic university. Jennair was a sophomore at nearby Indiana University Fort Wayne, where she majored in broadcast media. We dated for the next few months and I introduced her to my circle of close friends. To be honest, she wasn't an immediate fit with the group, but I didn't care. That was probably my greatest attraction to her. She wasn't like anyone I knew. Unlike me, Jennair was outspoken and strong-willed. She always said what was on her mind with very little filter.

It was off-putting to many at first and it took some getting used to her direct, brutally honest way of communicating. But for me, at least early on, it was far from off-putting. Instead, I saw her outspoken honesty as part of her allure.

In addition to being one of the most beautiful people I knew, Jennair was absolutely fearless. As the spring semester began, a spot opened up as a model for one of the life drawing classes and the pay was great for a college student. As a senior in the art department with some pull, I told Jennair about it, letting her know that being fully nude was optional. She didn't give it a second thought. Without hesitation she disrobed and stood confidently, completely nude in front of dozens of art students three times a week for an entire semester. By no means was she an exhibitionist, but she truly enjoyed seeing how art students interpreted her in their work. I was in awe of the beauty of her body and even more so her fearlessness to be so free with it.

With just weeks to go in the semester, walking to and from class in the frigid air, snow and ice, it seemed to me the Indiana winter would never end. But then spring break finally arrived. Jennair and I had planned separate trips with our respective group of friends, but at the last minute, Emily, supposedly her best friend at the time, had uninvited her. It would be the last time she spoke to Emily and the last time she ever planned much of anything with friends. To this day I still don't know exactly what happened between them, and Jennair never wanted to talk about it, so I respected her silence on the matter.

All I knew was that my girlfriend had been hurt, and she was alone. We briefly discussed how great it would be for her to join me and my friend Mike in Florida, but it just didn't seem right to spring her on my friend at the eleventh hour. Jennair agreed. But

17

undeterred, she made the bold decision to plan a romantic evening for the two of us the night before I departed for Florida. With her own money she surprised me by renting the best hotel room in town, complete with a jacuzzi, champagne, room service and a night of passion I would never forget.

But young love can be fickle. We were in college. She was just twenty and I was twenty-two. I hadn't dated that many women seriously, so at the time it seemed way too soon to settle down. Jennair had an emotional intensity about her that I just couldn't seem to match. Then, just after spring break, I met Jamee, a bright, beautiful film and broadcast media student who had just transferred from nearby Ball State. We talked and flirted back and forth with notes in class. It didn't take long before I fell for her. I knew I had to break it off with Jennair, but that's not something they teach you how to do in school. I took her out for a date, nervously waiting for just the right opportunity to tell her. I brought her home and before she opened her car door, I found the courage to just say it.

"I want to see other people."

Tears came streaming down her face. I didn't know what to do. I tried to apologize, but she opened her door and ran from my car and into the wooded area next to her parents' house. I felt awful. *What an awful thing to do to someone,* I thought. As I would soon come to learn, however, being rejected by someone you love is one of the most painful human experiences possible. Three months later, Jamee absolutely crushed me. I don't think she even actually broke up with me. She just stopped seeing me and returning my calls. I found out she was dating a tennis pro at the club her family belonged to and I was devastated. But that's young love. You date. Fall in love. Fall out of love. Break hearts and get your heart smashed to smithereens. It's a rite of passage. And it's how you eventually find the person you want to spend the rest of your life with.

After a month or so of licking my wounds, I ran into Jennair at the mall. She looked and smelled absolutely amazing. Her perfume, an intoxicating combination of black currant, jasmine and orange flowers that I still recall to this day. A familiar feeling came rushing back to my heart. We made small talk for a few minutes and then walked in different directions. I knew in that moment I wanted her back.

On Sundays, Jennair worked part-time at the Sears Telecatalog call center. So that Sunday, I sat on the bumper of her red Pontiac 1000 in the parking lot, waiting for her to come out. When she saw me, she looked stunned, and clearly not happy to see me.

"What are you doing here?" she asked defensively.

"Hoping for forgiveness for being a complete idiot," I replied.

While I could tell she was fighting her emotions, her wary look of concern slowly melted away to the sweetest smile, rolling her eyes and shaking her head.

"Jerk," was all she said, and then I folded her into my arms, and laid a gentle kiss on her closed eyelids, feeling the tickle of her eyelashes on my lips. An hour later, standing on a miniature golf course, I promised Jennair I would never hurt her again. It was a promise I intended to keep.

We spent an amazing summer together, including a drive up to visit a good friend of mine in Chicago with whom I had planned to spend a few weeks. Jennair agreed to tag along but only stay a few days so she could get back to Fort Wayne for work. We spent days on the beach, exploring art museums, eating at restaurants and watching the Fourth of July fireworks over Navy Pier. We truly enjoyed being a couple, holding hands wherever we went. I didn't even realize how much I actually cared for her until it was time for her to go. After driving her to the Greyhound station and putting her on a bus, I stood there struggling to make her out through the dark tinted windows. I couldn't find her, but the memories of our time together raced through my mind. "Dammit," I said out loud. "I love you, Jennair." I didn't know it then, but she later told me she was looking right at me, waving through the dark smoky window. I wasn't sure if she could tell what I had said out loud that afternoon, but she knew. She knew.

While Jennair and I were dating that summer, I was still living with my parents, who had never approved of anyone I had dated, a goal so unattainable I had given up trying. I didn't need their approval. Nor did I want it. No one was ever going to make them happy, because they were so painfully shy, and people with strong, outgoing personalities especially made them feel uneasy. I knew there was no way they'd approve of Jennair.

One evening I invited her over to watch television. As it got to be later, my father walked in, saw us snuggling closely on the couch and then announced it was time for her to go home. I was mortified. After walking her to her car and returning to the house, I was met by my mother in the hallway.

"Never bring that hussy into this house again," she said sternly.

"What did you call her?" I asked.

"You heard me," she replied.

"Yes, I did," I said, closing my bedroom door. Right then and there I packed a bag and quietly left the house, never to return. Nobody was going to talk that way about someone I loved. And I truly loved her. Jennair was my future.

We dated seriously for a year, and after my roommate took a job in Indianapolis, Jennair moved into my apartment. We both had part-time jobs and she continued to take classes at IU. Life was good. Sex was great. We took up playing tennis, although we were both terrible at it, and we just had a blast spending time together. We were just enjoying being in love.

It was a tough job market for college graduates in 1991. But after a year of trying, I finally landed a job as a graphic designer with a magazine publisher in Indianapolis. Jennair and I knew a long-distance relationship would be a challenge, but we were committed to trying. Every other weekend, I drove the 110 miles back to Fort Wayne to see her, but it wasn't enough to sustain a relationship. And I didn't want to lose her.

Before I knew it, I found myself at a jewelry store, over-whelmed by the choices presented to me. I was a twenty-two-year-old kid. I didn't know the first thing about buying a diamond or what she would like. Jennair's style and taste in clothing and especially jewelry were difficult for me to nail down. As I had learned from birthdays and Christmases, when it came to giving her gifts, her honesty could be beyond brutal. She wouldn't just tell me she didn't like it; she would chastise me for not knowing better. And that petrified me. Spending thousands of dollars on a diamond ring with the chance that she wouldn't like it was more risk than my young heart and small budget was willing to take. In the end I decided to buy her a modest promise ring so she could have the fun of picking out her own engagement ring.

That weekend I was sweating bullets, waiting for just the right moment to ask her to marry me. Finally, after dinner one evening Jennair was acting strange. She started crying and looked up at me with those big blue eyes.

"I can't do this anymore," she said. "I want more. I need more. I think we need to break up."

Without saying a word, I reached into my pocket and pulled out the ring, holding it up for her to see.

"Is that—?" she said puzzled. "What is this? What does it mean?"

"Will you marry me?" I asked simply. Then the tears really started. I think she said yes, but she really didn't need to.

The next morning we announced our news to her parents, and soon thereafter I proudly made the announcement to my friends, family and everyone I knew at work. But while I was outwardly excited, internally the enormity and the finality of our engagement scared the bejesus out of me.

Everyone, including my family, offered us the obligatory congratulations, but it wasn't long before even that slim support started to crumble. One of my oldest friends and designated best man, Mike, took me to a late lunch. It was a Friday and before long, drinks were flowing.

"Haven't seen you in a while, man," he said. "Why didn't you come out with us the other night?"

"Because Karen and Lori were there," I replied, gulping my second beer. "Jennair doesn't exactly like them."

"Dude," Mike scoffed, shaking his head.

"There's a lot she doesn't like," I continued. "Stults. How I drive. The art I put up. The clothes I buy. The stuff I decide to get rid of—"

"Don't do this," he said, interrupting me.

After spending time with us as a couple and interacting with Jennair, he and my friends were concerned that Jennair wanted to control everything I did. She dictated when and with whom I could go out. She called me when it was time to come home and insisted I get ready for work in the dark so I didn't wake her up in the morning. Given my upbringing, being controlled seemed commonplace and bearable at the time. I thought they were being ridiculous. I was too in love to even consider listening to their cautionary pleas. So on October 23, 1993, I replaced the promise ring with a wedding ring and vowed to love her through sickness and in health, until death do us part.

I'll be the first to admit, my friends and family never really "got" us. She was so different. *We* were so different. They could never see what Jennair and I felt—a deep friendship, knowing we were different from each other, but also knowing we had so much to learn from each other. We also shared a unique, sometimes bizarre sense of humor and a private language of inside jokes. With each other we could just be our silly selves like we could with no one else, not caring about the rest of the world.

As young naive honeymooners without a lot of money, we got suckered into a "free cruise" to the Bahamas. All we needed to do was tour a timeshare and listen to an hour-long sales pitch. For us, that was easy. We couldn't have afforded to do this any other way, so we made the most of it. Before long we were sitting around a large round dinner table with other couples, sipping champagne and wine at sunset, about to set sail for a week-long cruise. Then suddenly my head began to spin.

"Oh, God," I said. "I've only had two drinks, but I don't feel so good."

Then over the speaker, the captain made an announcement. "Well folks, if you hadn't noticed, we pushed off a few minutes ago and by the time you awake in the morning, we'll be at port in

Grand Bahama Island. We hope you enjoy dinner and the rest of your evening."

"Jennair," I whispered in her ear, "I think I'm seasick and I'm going to throw up. I'm going back to the room to lie down."

"Okay," she said, disappointed. "But I'm not going back with you. This is my honeymoon. I'm going to enjoy it."

"Do whatever you want," I pleaded, "I'm sorry." I stumbled my way back to our room, and not even bothering to turn on the light, I fell into the bed and turned on the TV to watch a movie. Enduring the next few hours of nausea, bed spins and cold sweats, I felt like I was going to die. Then around 10 p.m. I heard Jennair come into the room and I instinctively rolled over to shield my eyes when she flipped on the lights.

"How are you do—?" she started to ask and then in a panic, she screamed "Oh, God! No, honey! No. No. You didn't!"

"Didn't what?" I said groggily.

"You shit the bed!" she said.

"I what? I did? Holy shit!" I said in shame, looking down at the sweaty brown stains on the duvet cover I had been rolling around in, smearing up my backside for hours.

"Wait," Jennair said abruptly, and then leaned in to get a closer look and better smell, like you could only do for your child or someone you truly loved. She then reached down and carefully picked up a piece of shiny green foil.

"Andes mints!!!" she announced in a loud bellowing laugh. And we both began to laugh and cry, not being able to stop for hours. And then days. Then months. Over the next twenty-four years, we must have told that story more than a hundred times, and it never got old.

When we returned from our honeymoon in the Bahamas, we were riding a high. Jennair took a job as a waitress and transferred to Butler University in Indianapolis, while I paid my dues at my first job. Money was tight. We subsisted on ramen noodles and spaghetti and watched a twelve-inch television from a twin bed that served as our couch. We didn't care. We were in love.

Twenty-four years later I was looking in the rearview mirror from the back seat of a police car. The scene behind me was lit up like a circus with police cruisers, emergency vehicles and hordes of media already descending on the quiet neighborhood. I sat quietly shaking.

Minutes later, when we reached the Radnor police station, the detectives asked me to hand over my phone for evidence, then escorted me into an eight-by-ten-foot interrogation room complete with one-way mirror, cameras and a small table and chairs, and closed the door.

It was all so surreal, and I truly expected I would wake up any second. As I sat there alone, the thoughts and images of what I had just experienced hit me like bolts of lightning. I stood up and began pacing the tiny room. Suddenly I became aware that I was being watched. Of course, I was. I had seen it a hundred times on TV and in movies. Put the suspect in a small room all alone and watch him squirm.

What if I didn't act like I was supposed to? How is someone whose life was just destroyed expected to act? Should I be crying? Should I be sitting stone-faced in a chair? For the next forty-five minutes, I was all over the place. I sat. I stood. Crying, curled up in a ball on the floor like a child, I screamed, cursed and begged,

"Please don't let this be real. Please don't let this be real." I felt like I was losing my grip on reality and my own sanity.

When the two detectives finally came in, I was so relieved to see and talk to other human beings that I would have told them anything. I didn't even think to ask for an attorney. I spent the next hour telling them everything I knew. And then they asked the question.

"Did you shoot these two women?"

"Shoot them? They were shot?" I asked, stunned.

It sounds ridiculous now, but finding their bodies had been such a shock that *how* it happened hadn't clicked in my head until that moment.

It all sank in like a heavy stone.

Jennair and Meredith had been shot. Dead. And so was the life I had known.

CHAPTER 3

ALL TO HERSELF

Our first place together was a tiny one-bedroom apartment, horrifically outdated, but perfectly located on the burgeoning north side of Indianapolis. I had lived most of my life in a small rural Indiana town near the Ohio state line, and Jennair was a city girl from Fort Wayne. Like a lot of young couples just starting out, neither of us could wait to escape from where we had grown up. To us, Indianapolis was the big city, full of opportunities and things to do. But money was scarce. So aside from the rare indulgence of a pizza or an occasional beer, when Jennair wasn't in class or we weren't working, we spent most of our time at home or finding inexpensive things to do. On the weekends, one of our favorite pastimes was to go to the bookstore down the street and spend hours drinking coffee and looking through magazines and books we couldn't afford to buy. We were poor, but what we lacked in money, we made up for with the love we had for each other. We had just started our life together and we just knew it was going to be great.

It wasn't long, however, before we began having occasional arguments about spending time with my friends. They wanted to go out or come over. But Jennair wanted to spend time with me—alone. She felt like there was something wrong with me or with us that I needed friends outside of our relationship. I encouraged Jennair to make friends of her own and have interests outside of me, but, except for the occasional casual drink with coworkers after a shift at an Italian restaurant where she had started working after classes, she didn't want any part of it.

"I don't have time for friends," she told me. "I just want to spend time with you. Why can't it just be us?" I was torn. On one hand, I guess I was flattered, but on the other, not having friends felt strangely familiar yet smothering, as it had when I was growing up and couldn't bring friends over. But what did I know? My parents never made time to go out with friends. I thought maybe this was what married life was *supposed* to be like.

I tried to keep in touch with my closest circle of friends, but it was a common source of disputes between me and Jennair that I finally learned to succumb to. So, for most of our marriage, sadly, we didn't really have friends. Early on it seemed like a small price to pay to keep the peace and be with the woman I loved.

Then one evening while she was at work, I unknowingly made one of the biggest mistakes of our budding relationship—I decided to clean our apartment. When we began living together, I had noticed she had stacks and stacks of magazines and catalogs, many of which were three, even five years old. While she was at work that evening, I took it upon myself to reduce the clutter in our tiny apartment and threw many of the outdated magazines in the dumpster.

When she arrived home after work, I was so proud to tell her about the hard work I had done that evening, including helping her part with lots of unnecessary clutter. Her unexpected reaction would be a harbinger for the next twenty-plus years. My good deed was met with screaming and rage. After a heated exchange,

Jennair spent the next hour knee-deep in the dumpster, angrily digging through garbage to retrieve dozens and dozens of dusty, outdated magazines, which she would keep for years to come.

It's a common argument among couples. There always seems to be one person who saves everything and the other who wants to purge. Our differences in this area, however, were on an entirely different level. While I hate the reality TV image that the word "hoarder" conjures up, Jennair definitely had an issue distinguishing between which possessions were important and which were not. Her inability to part with stuff was a compulsion I didn't understand, and I admittedly had very little patience for it. Throughout our twenty-four years together, we spent tens of thousands of dollars on storage, moving, and houses with bonus rooms, garages and basements to keep boxes of knick-knacks, magazines, empty wine bottles, and countless other useless things. We even had boxes full of empty boxes.

Seldom did I ever say anything about it because I knew it was a powder keg ready to go off at even the slightest mention. But every time we packed to move, an argument was simply unavoidable. She staunchly defended what I considered irrational behavior, and I knew I could never win. So I learned to live with, rationalize and, I suppose, enable a growing habit of accumulating things we weren't allowed to part with. Back then it seemed like a small price to pay for happiness. I loved her and so much else in our life together was so good.

Buying our first house in 1998 was one of the greatest highlights of our life together. We finally felt like grownups and as if we could do anything. It took five years of hard work and saving money, but we finally had amassed enough for a down payment on a modest starter home in a great neighborhood. The house and the yard had been neglected for years, but we saw it as a blank canvas and a chance to make something great together. Most of all, it was ours.

We would spend the next seven years fixing, updating, and giving our home the character we felt it deserved and we needed. We had so much fun doing it together. Jennair learned to cut tile with a wet saw and run electrical wiring. I replaced every bit of cedar trim, refurbished a worn deck and built a pergola from scratch. We painted every room and replaced every stitch of carpet and every brass fixture. We made great memories, and took vacations to New York, Vegas and the Grand Canyon. Looking back at it now, we were the consummate happy couple, living the American dream.

From the beginning Jennair and I had always planned on making the leap to have kids. At ages twenty-eight and thirty respectively, it seemed like the natural next step as a couple in fulfilling that American dream. We had even gone so far as talking about baby names. For a girl, Audrey, after Jennair's grandmother, who she felt especially close to. And for a boy, Jackson, because, well, how cool was the name Jack Gerardot. We were just waiting for the right time, we told ourselves, or maybe even a sign. A little less than a year after moving into the labor of love that was our first home, that sign came. A single mother and her two young girls moved in two doors down. Something about Jennair and me attracted kids in the neighborhood to come visit. We didn't have kids of our own, and maybe they felt sorry for us. I don't know. But something in these two young girls, ages seven and four, stirred something in us both. One summer evening as we sat on the grass in the front yard of our home, we had one of the sweetest and most charming discussions with these two girls. Jennair and I locked eyes and without saying a word, I know we were both thinking, *How amazing would this be?*

But that's as close as it ever came. As each year went by, we found a new excuse. Career. Money. Health concerns. But there was something else, an uneasiness about children she didn't want to talk about. Having kids wasn't some deep-seated desire for me at the time, so I didn't push it. Instead, we decided to channel our parental instincts into a new golden retriever puppy. Mésa, or Mésa Girl as she was affectionately known, became our first-born child and the center of our universe. We poured every bit of love we had into raising her, and for the next fourteen years of our lives, our vacations, our everything, revolved around her.

During this period of our lives, things were great financially. Jennair had a good job working as a marketing coordinator for a successful publicly traded commercial real estate firm. She travelled all over the country on the company jet and coordinated the setup of industry trade shows. Occasionally, she'd invite me to go with her and we'd spend a few days after the show enjoying a romantic getaway vacation in Vegas or an exclusive club wherever the company had properties. Those were wonderful times. Except for having a boss who she swore was bipolar, she loved that job, because she felt needed and important. And because of her success, in 2001 I was able to quit my job at an advertising agency and take the risk of starting my own design firm. It was a scary decision, so we both worked around the clock, terrified to fail.

Our hard work started to pay off. The work just kept coming and I soon realized that after three years of running the business out of the house, I needed to hire employees and move the business into an office.

Gerardot & Company's first office was no more than six-hundred square feet. How we squeezed three employees, me and an intern into that space is now hard to imagine. But somehow we made it work, because we were a close team. Then it all changed.

One day, Jennair called me at the office, sobbing. She had just lost her job as a result of downsizing. My immediate instinct was to make her feel better. Without thinking I said, "Don't worry about it. You can work here." And that was that.

When Jennair came to work for my company, the biggest mistake I made (as she would tell me often) was not clearly defining her role. Without specific boundaries, Jennair had a license to do and say whatever she wanted. She was a smart and talented marketer. I thought she would find her spot and help elevate the company to the next level. She did, but at a cost.

Jennair had always been a force to be reckoned with. Again, her independent thinking and outspoken demeanor were attractive to me from the start. And in the right setting, those characteristics are potentially assets to a company. But as part of a larger team, she lacked the soft skills to earn the heart and respect of my employees. To them, she was the owner's wife who just did and said whatever she wanted, regardless of how it affected others. In hindsight, I failed her and the entire team.

Within six months, it all came to a head. My employees asked to meet with me outside of the office, so we walked across the street to Starbucks. They told me that either she goes or they all go. At first I was shocked. Then I was pissed. Who did they think they were to ask that my wife be removed from the company? I would not respond to ultimatums nor give in to their demands.

More than a reflection of Jennair's people skills, I think this fiasco was actually a referendum on my own ability to lead people and create a clear vision for them to follow. Over the course of the following two weeks I took a hard look at what I wanted the company to be and where I wanted it to go. In the end, one employee quit. Another one I fired. What shook out was a team that included my strongest designers and Jennair. I believed in Jennair and I wanted her to be a part of the company. Employees come and go, but Jennair was my life and my future.

In 2005 the real estate market continued its unprecedented climb. After just seven years, our modest first home appraised for sixty-thousand dollars more than we had paid for it. As we saw everyone else making a killing in the housing market, it just seemed stupid not to take advantage of it.

"If we can make sixty-K in seven years on an eighteen-hundred-square-foot home, just imagine what we could do with a house three times that size," I remember us musing together.

The thought of us owning six-thousand square feet of house in Carmel, the most affluent city in Indiana, scared the hell out of us, but in many ways we felt this decision was the jolt our relationship needed. We wouldn't be just doubling down, we'd be tripling down. After all, the business was doing well, money was great and we could afford it.

It had always been Jennair's dream for us to work out of our home, so we began looking for a house with a barn or out-building to retrofit into offices. But after a few months of not finding what we wanted, we hired a custom home builder and spent even more months planning and designing a beautiful French provincial home with a private entrance for the business. We came very close to buying a plot of land to put it on, but when the deal fell through, we threw up our hands, exhausted. Instead we decided to buy an existing home in a well-established Carmel neighborhood.

It was way more grandiose than any house I thought I would ever own, complete with a three-car garage, beautifully landscaped fenced back yard, and an arched two-story entrance that opened to a sweeping stairway. I never expected to, nor really wanted to live this way, but Jennair was convinced we had earned it. "Never be afraid to buy the very best," she told me. "Because we'll always be happy with it."

In most respects, I was the one who tended to pay top dollar for the very best, and Jennair was the one to badger me about saving money. But when it came to this house, I could tell right away she envisioned herself in it, enjoying a life neither of us had ever known. It was massive. Light filled. And every room with a feature or two we hadn't even known existed—remote control window blinds, two Jenn-Air ovens, and bonus storage space in the unfinished portion of the basement, which eventually became my photo studio. We were finally breaking free of the financial struggles we'd known, ascending to a status of luxury living. Yes, we could do this. Yes, we wanted to do this. Yes, we'd always be happy with it. Together we signed mortgage papers that would seal our fate for the next seven years.

On the day we took possession of the house, we ordered Chinese takeout and camped out with cozy blankets in the cavernous two-story living room, complete with cathedral ceilings, gas fireplace and giant windows that towered from floor to roofline. In so many ways, we both knew we had gotten in over our heads, but once we were actually in the house, its size made us feel silly for just two people and a dog. Four bedrooms, formal dining room, a beautiful kitchen full of top of the line appliances and a full basement that seemed to have no end. But to us it wasn't just our home. It was an investment, a business venture, and we were up for the challenge.

Our new home was only ten years old, but as we soon learned, a lot can happen to a house in a short period of time when you don't take care of it. Over the next three years, we poured our hearts and souls (and dollars) into that house. While our much more affluent neighbors, who were doctors, lawyers and the occasional professional athlete, hired contractors to work on their homes, Jennair and I had no choice but to take it on ourselves. Relying on the skills we had learned from our first home, we replaced or repaired almost every window, reseeded the three-quarter-acre yard, finished the unfinished basement, replaced carpet with hardwood on the first floor, and upgraded every cheap light fixture, brass door hardware and bathroom faucet. After investing close to a hundred thousand, this house had never looked better. Then, the bubble burst.

We heard it on the news, but what did it really mean? They said the markets were in freefall, but it wasn't the first time we had heard Wall Street cry the sky was falling. When they reported home values were depreciating in a matter of months, however, they had our attention. We had never even considered the value of a home could go down. It was unthinkable. Our grand vision of flipping our investment in this gargantuan house was about to come to a screeching halt. We decided to just ride out what we thought would be a small blip in the market.

While we didn't immediately feel the effects of the housing bubble and credit crisis at home, by 2009 we started to feel it in the business. We had already moved out of our tiny office and into a much larger studio space in downtown Indianapolis. We had been riding a wave of success for eight years and we were positioning ourselves for more growth. But seemingly overnight, the phones just stopped ringing, our largest client stopped paying, and our oldest client filed for bankruptcy. Suddenly it felt like the weight of the world was on our shoulders.

Jennair and I started to take out our stress on each other, having huge shouting matches in front of staff, and it didn't stop when we left the office. Because we worked together, we took every bit of that stress home with us and most nights we dragged out those arguments into the wee hours of the morning. It was taking a toll on our marriage. We needed help.

For as long as I had known her, Jennair was my biggest critic. She told me I wasn't a good manager of people. That I was disorganized. That I didn't take care of nice things. But the thing that drove her up a wall daily was my attention span. She would call me on my way home to pick something up from the store, and fifteen minutes later I would walk in the door empty-handed. It was true. My short-term memory was a challenge and often a source of arguments. I likened it to having an astigmatism or not being able to hear well. I had a disability. But out of frustration, Jennair continually mocked and ridiculed me for it. She called me "A-D-D boy" and told me I had early stages of Alzheimer's disease, because it was hereditary. That cut deep. My mother had just passed away after suffering from Alzheimer's for ten years. Jennair was convinced that half our problems would be solved if I would just seek help for my memory problems.

After mounting pressure from Jennair and a suggestion from a colleague, I made an appointment to see a therapist about Attention Deficit Disorder. Since childhood, I found it difficult to focus on one thing at a time—especially reading. I constantly juggled a half-dozen thoughts in my head at one time. Reading a restaurant menu or dialing a phone number from a phone book were daily challenges for me.

When the therapist prescribed me Adderall, I was skeptical that medication would solve anything, but out of respect for our marriage and the health of the business, I was willing to at least try it. I learned Adderall was a prescription amphetamine—in other words, it was speed. Taking an amphetamine seemed counterintuitive for someone who was supposedly scatterbrained. But just two hours after taking it the first time, I spent the night powering through a lengthy, boring client contract—something I had never experienced before. To me, Adderall was a miracle drug—or so it would seem.

While the drug did give me the focus I needed, the side effects started to become apparent. I took it in the morning and by lunch I could feel it working at its peak. But by dinner I could feel it wearing off, and I'd feel utterly exhausted. More troubling still, it made me feel foggy and agitated. I could practically feel my blood and the meds coursing through my veins.

Far worse, I became argumentative and occasionally enraged by even the simplest things. Normally I avoided conflict and arguments, especially with Jennair. I had learned early on that was the best way to keep the peace, because nobody ever won an argument with her, and all her arguments had to be won. It's probably going too far to say that she enjoyed confrontation, but in the heat of battle, she seemed to be in her element. If she was going to engage in an argument, she would have the last word. Always. And not just with me—with anyone.

"It was just too easy," she would tell me, when bragging about the epic fights she had growing up with her father. "I knew exactly what to say and what buttons to push to get him going," she said with pride, more than once. Mocking him, she'd even perform their battles for me. 'You wanna go? Come on, bring it,' I'd taunt him. And that would just piss him off even more." Then she'd laugh that beautiful, engaging laugh, made all the more unsettling given the context in which she'd say it. She viewed her role as antagonist as a strength but my reaction to her antagonism as a weakness.

"You're just like my dad," she would say to me. "You can't have a fucking argument without losing your shit and screaming like a howler monkey. Oooh-oooh-ahh oooh-oooh-ahh!" she mocked me. The look in her eyes during those confrontations was such a far cry from the iridescent eyes that had seduced me all those years before that I sometimes felt as if I had married two different women—one the exciting free-spirit I'd fallen in love with and who made me feel loved in return, and the other a bitter and angry woman who constantly reminded me of how much I disappointed her.

She was right about one thing, though. I was losing my temper, and I was becoming perpetually angry with Jennair, just as her dad had been. But that wasn't who I was before I met her. What she failed or refused to recognize was that she was the common denominator in the two relationships. In any argument she had with anyone, her father, her sister, a neighbor or me, she was the one who poured the gasoline on the fire. Resolving a conflict was never her goal; destroying her opponent was what mattered.

As much as I instinctively avoided conflict, however, I had to admit that Adderall took me to a place where I couldn't walk away from an argument. And she knew it. Jennair and I went head-to-head with epic shouting matches almost every night. Occasionally, one of us would slam a door or even throw something across the room, but neither of us ever let our anger become physical toward each other. I have never had the capacity or tolerance for physical violence, and neither had she. But the verbal abuse we subjected each other to took a dramatic toll on our day-to-day happiness.

This madness went on for three months before I decided to stop taking the Adderall. I wasn't myself on the drug and the negative side effects far outweighed the benefits. But once I'd stopped the medication, the drama didn't stop. Our arguments frequently became more and more histrionic and public. Once content to argue in private, now Jennair seemed to like our arguments on display for all the neighbors and others to see and hear.

One evening, we were enjoying dinner at our favorite Italian restaurant when a seemingly innocuous disagreement came up. But instead of waiting until we got home or at least to the car to discuss it, Jennair ratcheted up the argument right there in the restaurant. Once she had everyone's attention, she threw an entire glass of red wine in my face. I stood up, walked out and walked home. Nothing made her more angry than when I walked away from an argument, but most of the time it was the only way to diffuse the situation. I refused to play her game because I knew I couldn't win it.

A few weeks later we had another argument, this time at our home. It got loud and verbally abusive, and I felt that familiar need to walk away. But she wasn't having it.

"We're not finished," she snapped. The argument continued for another hour, and every time I tried to walk away, she got louder. With no escape, I finally reciprocated. I was seething. I had reached the breaking point and smashed a dinner plate on the tile floor in front of me, sending the shards flying across the floor. That was the opportunity she was looking for. She picked up the phone and dialed 911. "My husband is out of control and threatening me," she told the dispatcher.

"What did you just do?" I said in disbelief. I walked out, slammed the door and jumped on my bike for a ride. Within minutes a police car and two officers were talking with my wife in the driveway for all the neighbors to see. She had gotten what she wanted—another public spectacle.

Eight years later, sitting in a tiny room at the police station in Radnor, Pennsylvania, I was flanked by two detectives who were prepared to give me a gunshot residue test. As they continued their barrage of questions, I couldn't help but play back the vivid details of the brutal crime scene in my head.

Jennair was lying on her stomach, her head turned toward the right as if looking directly at Meredith who lay not less than ten feet from her in the doorway between the kitchen and the dining room. I didn't recognize the black running pants, hoodie and shoes Jennair was wearing, and yet as that image burned into my mind, I was taken back to the summer of 2010 in Carmel.

On what seemed like the hottest day of the year, Jennair and I were walking our dogs through the neighborhood. As we passed a neighbor's house, we heard a metallic scratching sound. We stopped to listen closer and looked to determine the source. Sitting in the mulch bed, directly in the midday sun, we could see a metal cage with a small animal trapped inside. It was a chipmunk. We could tell by its deep, rapid breathing that it had been in there a while, trying in vain to claw its way out of the hot metal box.

We considered knocking on the door and asking our neighbors nicely to release the poor distressed animal. However, it was unlikely they would oblige us, given that they had purposely set the trap. We decided to come back after the sun went down and steal the entire cage. That way not only would the chipmunk be free, but they would not be able to reset the trap the next day.

At around 9 p.m., Jennair walked into my basement office where I was working.

"Are you ready?" she asked. "Let's do this."

When I looked up, I couldn't believe what I was seeing.

"Holy shit!" I said. "Are you crazy?"

Jennair was dressed head to toe in black—black running pants, black shoes, black hoodie and a black baseball cap. Maybe she was just being overly cautious, but it seemed like she was actually enjoying the excitement and the risk of this clandestine mission. But it wasn't a risk I wanted to take.

"It's the middle of summer," I said. "You're going to draw even more attention to yourself. I'm not going."

"Fine," she said, "I'll do it myself, you pussy." Lifting the hood over her head to conceal her face, she walked out the door and rode off into the darkness on her bike. In the morning I found the metal cage on a workbench in the garage. Mission accomplished.

Later that month, at a meeting of the homeowners' association, of which we were both board members, the secretary read the neighborhood police report out loud. At the top of the list, she described an incident a neighbor had reported about a metal cage being stolen from their front yard. Other neighbors reported seeing a kid dressed all in black, riding a bike down the sidewalk that same evening.

I looked up at Jennair and shook my head. She was absolutely beaming with pride for what she had done. And I have to admit, I felt some pride for her as well, for standing up to animal cruelty.

But I also couldn't shake this strange feeling that the adventure and the risk of getting caught had thrilled her even more than the reward.

Just then, one of the detectives slid a consent form in front of me to sign. "This form allows us to search your apartment," he said. "Is there anything you want to tell us about what we'll find before I send detectives in there?"

"I don't know," I said nervously, holding the pen in my hand, hovering over the consent form in front of me. "I haven't been there since I left this morning. Who knows what she—

I don't know what she's capable of."

As much as I thought I knew my wife, after the horrific thing she had just done, I obviously didn't know that woman lying dead in Meredith's house. What surprises had she left behind? A letter? A stash of weapons? A faked confession somehow manipulated to frame me? As I speculated the worst of the worst-case scenarios, I could sense a growing concern and suspicion from the detectives for my hesitation to voluntarily allow them access to my home. But not seeing I had much of a choice, I reluctantly signed the form, slowly expelling my concerns in a deep cleansing breath.

As I watched the detectives hurry out the door with the signed form, I spotted a small white dog in the hallway. Almost instantly I recognized her. "Indy!" I called to her. She turned, and with a look of joy, she was clearly happy to see someone she knew. It was Meredith's dog.

"Can I?" I asked the female officer who was restraining Indy with a leash.

"Sure," she said.

I reached for her and picked her up, hugging her tightly. "Thank God, you're alive." Then it hit me. Huck. Gypsy. My dog and cat. Jennair knew how much they meant to me. *Oh, God,* I thought in horror. *What if . . .*

CHAPTER 4

ANOTHER DEEP BREATH

I'm far from a recluse, but like most everyone I have always valued my alone time, running, biking or just sitting silently in nature with my own thoughts. But I have never felt more alone than sitting for more than seven hours in an eight-by-ten interrogation room at the Radnor police station, a nightmare that seemed to have no end. I waited in that room for close to an hour, still taking in the shock of finding my wife and girlfriend dead, before the two detectives who had driven me to the station finally came back in.

Adding to the surrealness of the situation, Detectives Santoliquito and Metzler looked like they had come from Central Casting, dressed up to look like TV detectives. Both men were in their fifties with thinning hair and thick bristly mustaches and donning sport coats and thick striped ties.

"Do you know where you are?" Detective Metzler asked, pulling out a chair and sitting down next to me at the table.

"No, not really? Bryn Mawr?" I guessed.

They looked over at each other like I was a complete idiot.

"No," he corrected. "You are at the Radnor Township police station. We oversee the unincorporated communities of Garrett

Hill, Rosemont, Strafford, Villanova and Wayne and parts of Bryn Mawr."

"Okay, sorry," I said. "I'm not from here."

Detective Santoliquito gripped a pen and steno pad and asked sternly, "Why don't you just tell us what happened this evening?" He set a digital recorder in front of me and pushed the button.

From that moment on, I held nothing back, nervously spewing everything about my twenty-four-year marriage and every intimate detail about my relationship with Meredith over the past six months. I had nothing to hide and I wanted to know as much as they did how it had all come to this tragic end, however damaging or embarrassing the circumstances.

After I'd finished, the interrogation began. One after the other, the questions came at breakneck speed, as if they hadn't heard a word.

Q: "What was your relationship with Ms. Chapman?"

A: "It's Sullivan. Chapman was her married name. She was divorced. We were……. dating. She was my girlfriend. My wife and I, we were divorcing, too."

Q: "Had your wife ever had contact with Ms. Sullivan before this evening?"

A: "No. Actually, yes. Kind of. There was sort of a confrontation. Back in March. The twenty-second I think. A month ago."

Q: "What kind of confrontation?"

A: "Meredith and I were at a wine bar. Jennair showed up and said something to Meredith and told me to come home."

Q: "What did she say to her?"

A: "I don't know. Don't quote me. Something about going to hell. Then she left."

Q: "Who left? Meredith or Jennair?"

A: "Jennair. She just seemed to show up out of nowhere, ordered me home and then stormed out. Later we found out she keyed Meredith's car. It was crazy. But it wasn't violent."

Q: "Had your wife ever been violent or threatened violence?"

A: "No. Absolutely not."

Q: "Do you or your wife own any firearms?"

A: "Absolutely not. We both hated guns. We've never owned one. Ever."

The interview went on for at least another hour. When it was finally over, my brain and my entire body were utterly exhausted, gasping for every precious breath as if I had just finished running a marathon. But to my horror, it wasn't over. As both detectives stood up from the table, Santoliquito handed me a pen and a sheet of paper.

"We need a written statement from you." he said. "Write down everything you just told us and anything else you can remember."

"Seriously?" I said in disbelief. "I can't. I couldn't possibly. Look at me." I said, holding out my half-clenched hands, shaking uncontrollably. "Why do you need a written statement? You just recorded everything I said."

They both looked at each other and shrugged, as if this was the first time anyone had ever refused them. "Fine," one of them said. "We'll be back," and then walked toward the door.

Before the door slammed shut, I yelled out loud. "Wait! I need to use the restroom." I didn't really, but I couldn't spend another minute alone in that life-sucking claustrophobic beige room.

"Okay," Santoliquito said, motioning with one hand for me to come.

As I stood up and tried to take a step, my legs, bent slightly at the knee, failed me. My back hunched over, my hands turned inward, stiff and trembling. My motor skills just weren't there. Finally I willed my legs to move, but as I shuffled out of the room and down the hallway I looked and felt like an elderly man or someone suffering from cerebral palsy.

Bracing myself with one hand on the bathroom sink, I splashed water on my face with the other, waiting, hoping to vomit. But it just wouldn't come. I stood in front of the mirror, wiping my face with a paper towel, but I couldn't bring myself to look up. I didn't want to see myself. I couldn't bear it.

When I walked out the door, I was immediately met by an officer who escorted me back to the interrogation room. As I shuffled past an open door, I saw the detectives and a group of uniformed officers talking, huddled around a table in a room crowded with computer equipment. Spotting me as I walked by, one of the detectives came out and stopped me.

"We have your wife's phone and iPad," he said. "We need the passcodes to get in. Do you know them?"

Looking back over my shoulder and then turning to face him, I looked up toward the ceiling, scanning my brain for the six-digit codes. "No," I said. "I don't have a clue. I've never known any of her login passcodes. Why would I?" While I never seemed to be able to keep Jennair from one way or another hacking my passwords, I didn't share her obsession or the need to invade her privacy. But in that moment, I regretted not knowing, not being more invasive about what she was doing with her free time these past few months. She was always sitting at her computer when I left for the day, and right there when I returned. She would tell me about the jobs she'd applied for, the professional connections she'd reached out to. When in the world had she found time to get a gun? How did she even know how to use it? She had been tracking us for weeks. It was annoying but harmless, I thought. How could I ever have guessed she'd go this far?

Back in the room, I took a seat at the table, and then the officer began to close the door. "Can we please leave it open?" I pleaded "Please? I can't."

Giving me a look of pity, the officer held up one finger, "Let me check."

He walked back down the hall. I assumed it was okay because he never came back to close it.

With the door open I could at least breathe again, filling my lungs with sweet oxygen from the cool breeze coming from the hallway. As the minutes and then another hour passed, I inched my chair closer and closer to the door, eventually taking the bold step into the hall and sitting down on the floor against the wall, hugging my knees, rocking back and forth like a scared child. "My God, how much longer is this going to take?" I grumbled to myself.

Sitting there on the carpeted floor, I started thinking about my drive to see Meredith that morning and the thoughts that had been running through my head. Jennair and I had agreed to an amicable split. Within days I would meet Delaware's six-month residency requirements and file the official petition for divorce. It was a huge step and I hoped I had the courage to actually go through with it. Jennair had told me she'd been looking for jobs and reaching out to family for a place to stay in Indiana or with my friends back in South Carolina. With the lease ending the following month, we'd agreed to both leave the apartment and Jennair didn't want to stay in the area. She was upset but seemed prepared to accept the challenges of the next chapter of her life. God knows she had the talent and drive to do anything she set her mind on.

Still, I knew the free-spirited determination and fire that had once burned inside her just weren't there anymore. Sadly, that fire had started to burn out long before our marriage did.

That next chapter in our lives—her future—is what we had planned to discuss at dinner that night after she met with her divorce coach. I had told her I would support her as much and for as long as she needed, just as I planned to be there during her pre-hysterectomy exploratory surgery that was scheduled for the next day and to take care of her as she recuperated. I mean, for all we had put each other through in the last months of our marriage, I still loved this woman. I wanted to do anything I could to help her. But I just had to get out, and she did, too. Our marriage, for all its blessings, had turned into a battleground that kept us both from living better lives. I so wished she had been able to see that.

I was deep in thought about how the past decades could have come to such a violent end when Detective Santoliquito came down the hallway. "You can't be out here," he said forcefully. "Look, we let you keep the door open, but you need to stay in the room."

"Can I please have someone to talk to? I just can't be alone anymore. I'm losing my mind," I begged.

"Let me see what I can do," he said in a more sympathetic tone.

Forty-five minutes later, I was greeted at the door by the detective and a large teddy bear of a man, dressed all in black, looking like a nightclub bouncer. "Hello, Mr. Mark" he said with a deep velvety soft voice, shaking my hand. "I'm Chaplain Manuel. I'm here to keep you company. How are you doing?"

"I've been better," I said. "How are you?"

"I'm doing great," he replied jovially. "I was just celebrating my daughter's eighth birthday tonight."

"Oh wow. That's great," I said. "I'm so sorry they called you in for this."

"No," he replied, "This is what I do. I'm here to serve. Serve people. Serve you."

"Do you know? Did they tell you?" I asked.

He closed his eyes and gave me a slight nod. "They told me a little," he said softly.

I was just so glad to talk to someone again. As he took a seat in the corner of the room and folded his arms in front of his enormous chest, I began telling him everything, pausing only long enough for him to acknowledge me with the occasional "uh-huh" or "hmmm," letting me know he was still listening. Otherwise, he didn't offer a word.

"She killed her," I said bluntly, and then began to well up. "She killed herself. Because of me. I loved them. I loved them. My wife, she and I were happy once. Not that long ago, actually."

"Mm-hmm," he said slowly through pierced lips, nodding.

"We're not from here. We're from Indiana. We just moved here a few months ago," I told him. Then I told him how it had all come to pass, how we'd ended up in Pennsylvania, and I ended up in an interrogation room, and the women I loved had ended up dead beside each other.

The recession had hit our business hard. We had negotiated our way out of our office lease and let our last remaining employee go. It was a tough decision, but one that needed to be made. And while it was a tremendous cost savings for us, we were still paying for a six-thousand square foot house we didn't want, nor did we need.

By the summer of 2011, Jennair and I had settled into our new reality and a new calm. I was working out of the basement of our house, while she took on contract marketing projects with a local insurance company. We were still riding out the recession, barely making ends meet. But because we weren't working together, we weren't arguing as much. Then one day, I got a call that neither of us expected.

A friend and colleague who Jennair and I had met and worked with in the Bahamas had recommended me to a small web development firm in Greenville, South Carolina. They needed a creative director to build their creative team and help shape the company into a digital agency. After ten years of being a business owner, I had never seriously considered the idea of working for someone else again, but I took a phone meeting with the owner as a courtesy to our friend. After our thirty-minute conversation, I was surprised to feel so much alignment with the company. Later, sitting at our favorite Mexican restaurant we visited at least once a week for burritos and Negro Modelos—my favorite Mexican beer—I told Jennair I seriously wanted to pursue it.

"South Carolina?" she questioned. "Why the hell not?" Her smile spread across her face as if I'd suggested we vacation in Paris. "We've lived in Indiana all our lives and I've always wanted to get the hell out. Let's do it!" Without wavering she had given me her full support. This was the life change we needed, but there was so much to consider.

During the recession, the business had taken on a substantial amount of debt, for which I had personally signed. I knew others who had filed for bankruptcy and several people told me I should seriously consider it. I'll never know how my decision not to file might have changed our lives. Call it pride. Call it ignorance. I just couldn't walk away from that obligation. We also had to consider the loss we might take with the house. The real estate market had bottomed out and we prepared ourselves for the worst. But we needed so badly to get out from under the weight of that home.

After a face-to-face interview with the owner of the web development firm and meeting their team, Jennair and I sat together next to a fountain in downtown Greenville, South Carolina, pondering what a new life in the South would look like. We were both emotionally battered and bruised from years of stress and fighting. We needed this. We needed to rebuild *us*. We decided right then and there to make it happen. If an offer was extended, I would take it. We had nothing to lose. But what I didn't know then was that something else was on Jennair's mind.

A pinging sound suddenly rang out from inside the room. Startled, Chaplain Manuel hurriedly and clumsily reached into one coat pocket, and then another, and pulled out his phone. It was a text message from his wife, he told me. It was just past midnight.

"They took my phone," I told him. "They won't let me call anyone. I've got to call my friends. I need someone to check on my cat and dog. And I have to tell Jennair's mother. She tried to call me earlier. I'm sure they're freaking out. I don't want them to get a call from the police."

"Oh, you need to talk to them," Manuel said, as he stood up and walked toward the door. "Let me see what I can do."

Five minutes later, he was back. "They said you can use the landline phone there on the desk. Go ahead. Call them," he urged.

I picked up the receiver and dialed nine for an outside line. When I heard the dial tone in my ear, I just froze. What was I going to say? I had just spent six hours of captivity in this room with nothing to do but think. And now I didn't know what I was going to tell her mother? How do I begin to explain the awful thing that had taken place when I barely understood it myself?

I took a deep cleansing breath and dialed the number. It rang just once. "Hello?" the voice on the other end of the line said with an audibly urgent sense of dread. It was Jennair's father.

"It's Mark," I said calmly.

"Mark! Becky is on the phone talking to the police right now," he said nervously.

I pounded the table in frustration. *Dammit? Why didn't they let me tell them first?*

"We heard about Meredith," he said. "I'm sorry. What about Jennair?"

I took another deep breath.

CHAPTER 5

DEATH AND MERCY

When I first met Jennair shortly after she had turned twenty, she had just moved back home with her parents after living with her grandparents for over a year. Describing her father as a verbally abusive alcoholic, she recounted epic shouting matches with her dad as a child and teenager, arguments where she learned to never back down, but to win at all costs. The full nature of these "arguments" I only recently discovered since speaking to childhood friends of hers after her death. What Jennair hadn't revealed to me was the many years of horrible name-calling, shaming and put-downs from her father—words a daughter should never hear, and possibly the worst rejection a child can experience—creating an environment that undoubtedly wounded her young mind and heart.

By the time she was a teenager, she had found her limit. "I told him I wasn't taking his shit anymore," she boasted to me. And not taking his shit meant never standing down. Never losing an argument, no matter the cost. The years of enduring verbal battles with her father were just one of the many revolving reasons Jennair gave for ultimately deciding she didn't want to have kids. She said she refused to subject them to the same trauma she had endured as a child.

She also resented her mother for telling her who she could and could not date and, as Jennair put it, for not living up to the Christian values her mother espoused. Jennair had little tolerance for hypocrisy and for people with whom she didn't agree and, like any teen, she didn't agree with her parents, nor with their rules, so she moved out.

Personally, I had never seen nor experienced that side of her parents she so resented. Her father had long since quit drinking, so I never witnessed any alcoholic outbursts. From the beginning, they had been nothing but welcoming and kindhearted to me, and also to Jennair in all their interactions I saw, even when Jennair wasn't as kind in return. While it seems commonplace for people to joke and complain about their in-laws, I had nothing to complain about. I always loved and respected Jennair's parents. And I still do.

Perhaps my attachment to them stemmed from my own alienation with my parents. I had never been particularly close to them, especially my mother. By the time I had moved out of the house and started to actively seek an adult relationship with them, my mother was suffering from early stages of Alzheimer's disease, which lasted for more than fifteen years. Yet even before the tragic diagnosis, with eleven kids to care for, she had never truly been there for me emotionally while I was growing up. And now the disease was taking her away from me permanently. It was sad, but I didn't have the emotional intelligence to deal with my mother's illness the way I now wish I had. Instead, I looked to Jennair's mother, Becky, to fill that void. And she did.

Admittedly, Jennair's father and I had very little in common, but we both tried. He was a former marine who had fought in Vietnam and he had seen more than his share of wartime atrocities, but that wasn't something we talked about. Instead, we would shoot the breeze about sports and occasionally watch a game together. He and I went golfing once, but because I wasn't much of a golfer, I felt embarrassed and intimidated by his much more advanced skill at the game. While I'm sure I wasn't the son-in-law he had probably hoped for, he never had a harsh word for me. In many ways, while we never compared notes, I suspected he understood more than anyone the difficult challenge I had dealing with Jennair's headstrong resolve, a challenge we both shared.

While we never gave them grandkids, we did give them plenty of opportunities to fawn over their "granddogs." Raising and rescuing golden retrievers for most of our marriage, Jennair's parents graciously agreed to watch our dogs and put up with all their fur and affection whenever we traveled for work or took vacation.

But life with my in-laws wasn't necessarily idyllic. While I always looked forward to visiting with them during holidays or on special occasions, I also learned to dread the inevitable conflicts that seemed to happen without fail. Whenever we drove to their home, just as we pulled in their driveway, I made it a habit to remind Jennair to try to keep her cool.

"Please don't start an argument with your parents or your sister this weekend," I would ask, which usually prompted one of two typical responses. 1.) "Shut up. Don't tell me what to do." Or 2.) "I'll try, but if they start something, I'm going to finish it."

I couldn't begin to understand Jennair's relationship with her family. Despite her repeated harsh words about them to me, I know she loved her parents. But it was her unapologetic disdain for her younger sister Jill that made me so uncomfortable and flummoxed at times.

Jennair's mother once asked me privately, "Why can't Jennair get along with her sister?"

"I don't know, Becky," was all I could tell her. "But I wish I did."

In at least one way, however, I suppose I did know, though I didn't offer her my theories or gut hunches. For our entire marriage, Jennair and I had always lived at least a hundred miles away from where she and I had grown up. So, when we wanted to see her family, we understood it was on us to do the traveling. On the rare occasion when her parents would travel to visit us, however, Jennair would look forward to the visit, clean for days, plan activities and make reservations at local restaurants. Occasionally, she would even paint the walls, buy new pillows, sheets, and even furniture, and pull out all the stops to make them feel like important guests. But as excited as she got, she would just as quickly become distraught and disappointed if she discovered her parents had invited her sister along.

Like a spoiled teenager, Jennair would complain, "Why does she have to come? She always ruins everything."

To me it seemed like a case of pure jealously. She wanted her parents' love and time all to her own. She wanted so much to be the center of attention and to be the sole recipient of their loving adoration. Despite the planning, the cleaning and looking forward to the visit, it almost always ended in a war of words, hurt feelings and utter disappointment for Jennair. After they would leave, I would spend hours listening to her vent and then consoling her. What I really wanted to say to her was, "You brought this on yourself." But I knew she didn't want to hear that, nor would she accept it.

After a blowup with her father during a visit at our home in Indiana one time, he felt the need to confide in me his feelings for

Jennair. "I love Jennair," he told me. "But I don't like her very much." I understood. While I both loved and liked Jennair for her free spirit, I knew how demoralizing it felt to be on the receiving end of her judgments. Whatever her father's failings, Jennair made sure he was aware of them. What she couldn't see were her own failings and how they damaged the people who loved her most.

Now, years later, standing there on the phone in the police station with Jennair's father at the other end of the line, it was my unenviable duty to tell him the tragic news.

"She's gone," I told him.

What came next was a guttural howl of grief unlike any sound I had ever before heard a human make. His pain shot through me in a wave of sorrow, a sorrow far beyond even my own indescribable pain. I had lost a wife and lover. He had lost a child.

"She shot and killed Meredith and then shot herself in the head," I said bluntly. "I'm sorry. I'm so sorry. I wanted to call earlier, but the police took my phone."

"You broke her, Mark" he said. "You just broke her."

Staring at the wall, I didn't say a word. Those words pierced like daggers.

After a few seconds, I heard him talking in the background to his wife. "Here, Becky wants to talk to you," he said, his voice so broken and strained.

"Beck? I'm so sorry," I said. "Jennair and I, we, we've been drifting for a while now, and…"

"I know you have," she said, holding back her tears.

"I told her to go back to Indiana for a while," I said. "But she wouldn't. She refused to go."

"I know. She could be so stubborn," Becky said, now crying.

Just a month prior, I had heard Jennair talking to her parents on the phone, begging them not to come to Philly after she had sent them a troubling email the night before. They were on their way to the airport to come and take their daughter home.

"Please don't come. I'm fine," I heard Jennair tell her mother. "Go back home, Mom. I'm fine."

When Jennair hung up, she seemed put out and frustrated that her parents were so worried and insistent about her going back home to Indiana.

"Mom said you never treated me right, and I never should have followed you to South Carolina," Jennair had told me. "She thinks you took me from home. From Indiana. From them. But I told them it was my decision, too. I wanted to leave. And I'm not going back to Indiana now."

It was true, it had been as much her decision as mine. How I was made into the bad guy who took her away from home hurt and baffled me. But I'd become accustomed to being baffled by Jennair's conflicts with her parents.

Landing that job with the digital agency in South Carolina in 2011 had been the opportunity we didn't expect, nor did we realize just how badly we needed it. And yet Jennair saw the opportunity differently, I would eventually discover. Rather than viewing it as a chance for a new life together, as I did, she would later tell me that to her, it was a chance for a clean break from each other. But as with so many things, she didn't tell me what she was thinking at the time. Those, and other thoughts and acts she kept concealed, would later be revealed.

When the job offer officially came, I asked Jennair one last time. "Are you sure this is what you want?"

Without hesitation she said, "Yes. Definitely. I think we have to."

It was a leap of faith, but with Jennair's full support, I gladly accepted the job offer, and we both began planning the next chapter, whatever it may bring. As we prepared to officially close the business and put the house on the market, we were also prepared to lose every bit of money and hard work we had put into it over the previous seven years, including most of our down-payment. The realtor we had spoken to told us we needed to list the house for fifty-thousand less than we had paid for it. He said the housing market was still bottoming out and it was a buyer's market, while the most expensive houses, like ours, just weren't selling at all. We were told it might take a year or more to sell it, a year when we still had to come up with the hefty mortgage we'd once easily afforded when the business had been doing so well. It was a tough pill to swallow, but it seemed like we didn't have much choice.

While Jennair put the finishing touches on the house in Indiana, I moved to South Carolina, taking a cheap studio apartment in the basement of a couple's home. Still paying the mortgage, it was all we could afford and we were buckling down to spend up to a year apart if necessary.

At the last minute, however, Jennair and I decided not to sign with the realtor who had tried to convince us to short-sell the house. Our instincts told us to get a second opinion, so we contacted the realtor who had originally sold it to us. He was convinced we should sell it for no less than what we paid for it. That was what we wanted to hear—and we prayed he was right. So, on the day before Thanksgiving, we crossed our fingers, put the sign in the yard and then waited. And on the day after Thanksgiving we were beyond shocked and ecstatic to get an offer for exactly what we had asked. Crisis averted. Our prayers had been answered. Someone, it seemed, was looking out for us. And then, just as we were relaxing into our newfound luck, a crisis of a different order struck.

For more than fourteen years of our marriage, one of the things that had bonded Jennair and me together was our first beloved golden retriever, Mésa. As I prepared to make the long drive back to South Carolina, Mésa didn't seem herself. She was listless and didn't want to eat. Hoping it was minor, I left her in Jennair's hands.

The next day Jennair took her to the vet and we learned Mésa was dying of kidney failure. Without question, I dropped every-thing to drive the ten hours back to Indy to spend three days with her before putting our girl down in the comfort of her own back-yard. To parents and non-pet people, it might sound silly, but los-ing her devastated both of us. We had poured every bit of our parental instincts into raising her. We didn't just lose a family pet. It felt as if we'd lost our first child.

For me, it was the third death in two years, including both my parents. After a long-fought battle with Alzheimer's, my mother finally succumbed to a stroke. I hadn't shed a tear for her since the day of her diagnosis. As the illness slowly progressed, I just gradu-ally ceased to know her anymore. In the latter stages of the disease, she had become as much a stranger to me as I was to her, a child trapped in the body of a frail, eighty-two-year-old woman. On her death bed, which had been wheeled into the living room of my father's house, I handed her a wind-up musical teddy bear that had been my favorite toy as a small boy. I wound him up and as the melodic tune began to play, she smiled and gave it a hug, as though she understood the deeper meaning and symbol of the gesture. She died later that day and I took solace in having made her smile one last time.

My father, who had spent the better part of the prior fifteen years taking care of her, didn't know what to do with himself anymore. His identity had been that of her caretaker. He told me he felt guilty because he finally felt free, free to do whatever he wanted. And that included writing his own memoir, a tale that included his time as a sailor in the US navy during World War II. But a little more than a year after my mother's passing, my father also suffered a massive stroke and later died the day after Thanksgiving 2010.

My parents had both been in their eighties, and as they aged each year, I must have unknowingly galvanized my heart, preparing for the pain of losing them. While I ultimately felt sadness for their loss, I actually took it in stride at the time. But losing our first dog that Jennair and I had raised together from a pup was a pain that neither of us had expected. Mésa was fourteen years old and her body had been slowly deteriorating for years. We knew she wouldn't last much longer, but we still weren't prepared for the deep, immobilizing sorrow we felt with her loss. She had bonded our little family together. And while it could have just as easily ripped us apart, the day before our nineteenth wedding anniversary, Mésa's sickness and death actually brought us closer together, even though we were still living five-hundred miles apart. "Are you sure you want to go back to work so soon?" she asked, concerned about my state of mind. "Are you even going to be able to function at work?"

It was true. To some, Mésa may have been just a dog, but to me, losing her was like losing a part of my life. I had felt her pain as if it was my own. I felt her love, as if it were the love of a child for her father. And I had felt helpless to prevent her death, which came far too early in my mind. I was an emotional wreck, and Jennair understood like no one else could, how and why I hurt so much—and it was a pain she shared, as well.

"I need to do something to keep me busy," I told her, appreciative of her concern for me. When we needed it most, Jennair and I were reminded that life and love are fragile and not to be taken for granted.

A few months later, I lost my older brother Ernie to lung cancer. Seven years my senior, Ernie had been my idol growing up. When I was twelve he went to college to be an architect. So, I wanted to be an architect. A year later he changed his major to graphic design. So, I wanted to be a graphic designer. He bought a brand new car when he graduated college and got married at twenty-five. Everything he did I followed suit. Growing up, he was my model for how to live life. But that soon changed. Ernie had always dealt with the stress of living with my parents differently than I had. He smoked at least a pack of cigarettes a day. He got divorced by the age of thirty, became a raging alcoholic with multiple arrests for DUI, and ultimately lost his job because of it. Divorced, bankrupt and jobless by 2005, I hired him to join Gerardot & Company, despite warnings and protests from Jennair.

"He's going to embarrass you," she warned me. "He isn't the person you idolized anymore."

But I didn't listen. I wanted to give him a second chance. He was my brother and I thought he deserved at least that much from me, so Ernie joined our staff. But after multiple comments and complaints from clients, his continued alcohol dependency and other questionable behavior, I knew Jennair was right. I had to let him go. It was the hardest choice I had ever had to make. But it was the right choice for the company and for my marriage. After a year of trying to help him get back on his feet, I fired my brother. And six years later he was dead.

I had never once told Ernie or any of my siblings I loved them, nor had we ever shown each other any kind of physical affection. But as I stood at the side of his hospital bed and told him I would be back in a couple days, he grabbed my arm, pulled me toward him and planted a huge kiss on my cheek.

Neither of us said a word. And that was the last time I ever saw my brother.

A month later, Jennair and I sat in silence, driving through the foreign landscape of South Carolina. For miles and miles we saw nothing but thick stands of Carolina pine, towering magnolia trees with white flowers the size of dinner plates and dense webs of Spanish moss hanging like decorative tinsel from the lush green canopy. A far cry from the corn fields and flat plains of the Midwest, this world was a completely new and enchanting place for us to have a new start.

When we arrived at the house we had rented on Kiawah Island, an hour south of Charleston, Jennair walked straight to the beach and sat down on the warm white sand. After carrying a load into the house, I followed and sat down beside her, enjoying the breeze and the roar of the incoming tide that came closer and closer to us as we playfully dug our feet into the wet sand.

Then Jennair dropped the bombshell she had been holding back for weeks.

"I wanted to leave you," she said. "I didn't want to move down here. I almost didn't."

"You what?" I said, surprised by her candor. She'd expressed nothing but agreement, even excitement, at the prospect of moving to South Carolina.

"I didn't think I could take it anymore," she said with tears in her eyes. "The fighting. You. I just wanted to leave and start over. But you've changed."

The truth was, we had both changed. There had been so much death. The sale of the house. The move. An unknown future. It had humbled us both. We didn't know what was going to happen next, but we still had each other, and we were in it together. There was no longer any pressure to work together, to manage employees or to operate a business. We no longer owned a home we had to fix up or had a mortgage to pay. But we also didn't have a dog to welcome us when we walked in the door, a feeling we both sorely missed, and left an emptiness that ached to be filled.

Three days later, on the drive back home from the beach, we agreed it was time to change that. We decided to get involved with two different Golden Retriever rescues in nearby Atlanta. And after months of being scrutinized, multiple adoption day visits and impatiently waiting, we met probably the only dog that could have possibly filled the gaping hole Mésa had left in our hearts. Huckleberry (aka Huck) was a six-year-old Golden who had lived a tough life. He was twenty pounds overweight. He had fleas, ticks and heartworm, and had spent most of his life tied to a tree in a backyard in rural Georgia, chewing rocks and digging holes to entertain himself and pass the time. But we knew the minute we saw him he would be ours.

To keep Huck company, it wasn't long before we also rescued Abby—a nine-year-old female Golden Retriever who had an equally sad life story, being passed from one shelter and foster family to another because of her special needs. She was on Prozac due to separation anxiety and her inability to get along with other female dogs. She also suffered from arthritis and painful bone spurs in her vertebrae. The rescue told us that when she was turned in, she was severely malnourished and near death.

After the struggles and the pain we had suffered ourselves, Jennair and I both knew we needed them as much as they needed us. Without hesitation we welcomed Huck and Abby into our lives and spoiled them both rotten, taking them everywhere we went. We felt like we were a family again, and we couldn't have been happier.

We decided to hold off buying a home in South Carolina and instead paid off a substantial amount of personal debt with the equity from the sale of our house. Within a few months, Jennair landed a marketing manager job with a large parts manufacturer in Greenville. Greenville was home to a number of automotive and parts plants that supported a substantial part of the local work-force. It wasn't the ideal job or working environment for her, but due to the recession, she was happy to just be working and con-tributing, and she assured me she would make the most of it until something else better came along.

For the next five years we scraped hard to try to pay off the rest of our personal and business debt and somehow found time to enjoy each other. On weekends we tried new restaurants and breweries, hiked mountains and trails, made annual treks to visit Charleston and rented beach houses on Kiawah Island. For our anniversary, we spent the day on an exhilarating zip-lining tour to take in the breathtaking fall foliage in the gorge of North Carolina's Blueridge Mountains. And for my birthday, Jennair surprised me with a visit to the BMW Performance Center to race each other around the track in some of the fastest and most exotic perfor-mance cars ever made.

"Don't ever tell me how to drive again," she joked, having beat my slalom course lap by more than two seconds, "cause we both know I just smoked your ass."

And she had. And I loved her all the more for it.

The five years between 2012 and 2016 were some of the happiest days I can remember being with Jennair. We had fallen back in love with each other, and I delighted in her company once again. The spontaneous, confident girl I'd met when I was barely out of my teens had returned to my life. Then one email changed everything.

CHAPTER 6

TOTAL ECLIPSE

When I hung up with Jennair's parents, my hand still clenching the phone receiver, I stared blankly at the wall, waiting for my breath and heartbeat to return to normal. They had just learned their daughter was a murderer and now they knew she too was gone. Their lives would never be the same. Nor would the lives of anyone who had known and loved either of these two women. I had loved them both. I just wanted to lay my head down on the table and cry. But I couldn't. After more than six hours of questioning and waiting, the tears would no longer come, and I knew I had to keep it together to tell others before they saw it for themselves on the morning news.

When Chaplin Manuel had gotten permission for me to make calls, he also asked for a handful of phone numbers from the list of contacts on my phone and wrote them down on a sheet of scrap paper that sat in front of me. The next on the list was my friend Mike, who had been my best friend for more than thirty-five years. He lived on a boat in Key West and while we usually stayed in touch with calls, emails and text messages each month, we hadn't seen each other in person for more than six years. I dialed his number, and as it began to ring, I looked down at the phone to see the time. It was 1:09 a.m. No way is he going to answer a call this late from the Radnor Township Police Department, I thought. But on the third ring, I was surprised to hear someone pick up.

"Hello?" he said, still fumbling for the phone.

"Mike. It's Mark." I said anxiously.

"H...e...y...... m...a...n." He mumbled mid yawn. "What's up?"

"You... You're...You're not going to believe this. Jennair shot and killed Meredith and then killed herself."

Mike was one of a handful of people who actually knew about Meredith and me, including a select few who Jennair had also told.

"Holy shit," Mike said, still recovering from the fog of sleep. "What do you need?"

"Dude, I'm freaking out," I blurted.

"Okay. I'll be there," he assured me. "Let me check flights and I'll let you know. Philly, right?"

"Yes. Thanks, man." I said and then hung up.

Once archrivals as high school freshman, competing for girls and always trying to prove who knew more about any given topic, Mike and I eventually managed to become best friends, and more miraculously we managed to stay close for more than three decades. One of the unspoken rules we both understood was that if the shit ever hit the proverbial fan, we knew we would be there for each other, without hesitation. I had never thought I would have to cash in that promise, but I was in crisis and I felt like I was in way over my head.

With the list of numbers in hand, I began calling Meredith's best friends and former coworkers at the University of Delaware. After six months I too considered them my good friends, and while I dreaded it, I felt it was my duty to tell them the awful news as soon as possible, no matter what time it was. After leaving cryptic, somber voicemails for three of our mutual friends to call me back, I finally reached Keith, who had known and loved Meredith for the eight years they had worked together. Understandably shaken, he graciously agreed to call the other half of our friends and let them know, but not before making sure I was okay.

"How are you doing?" he asked sincerely. "Are you going to be alright?"

"I'm numb. Just numb, Keith," I told him. "It's been an awful night, and I can't even process it all yet."

Just as I hung up, Detectives Santoliquito and Metzler came into the room.

"Mark," Santoliquito said. "You're free to go." And then he handed me my phone.

"What about the gunpowder residue test? I asked. "I mean, I'll take it."

"That won't be necessary, Mark." Santoliquito said. "Between the letter, the GPS device and the texts on your phone, we were able to piece enough together—"

"GPS? What letter?" I cut him off.

"Your wife sent a letter to her family," he said. "And when we found GPS software on her computer, we looked and found a device on Ms. Chapman's car. We also searched your vehicle but didn't find anything."

"Holy shit," I said, putting my hands over my face in disbelief. "Can I read the letter?"

"No," Santoliquito said bluntly, shaking his head.

As we walked down the hallway, past the room the detectives and others had been hunkered into all night, I asked naively, "Can I have her phone?"

"No. We're still working on it. Trying to unlock it." Santoliquito said.

Walking out through a set of double doors and into the lobby of the station, we were met by three other men, two of them dressed in suits and the other in a crisp white and black police captain's uniform.

"This is Detective Schreiber and Detective Thomas," Santoliquito said. "They were at the crime scene tonight."

"Sorry for what you've been through tonight," Schreiber said to me, reaching out to shake my hand. "Are you going to be alright? Is there someone you can call? Someone who can be there with you tonight?"

"I've called people," I told him. "I have a friend coming up from Florida tomorrow."

"Look," Santoliquito said soberly, looking me directly in the eye, his voice taking on a noticeable tone of concern. "Do you feel like you want to harm yourself tonight?"

"Am I going to kill myself? Is that what you're asking?" I said, then paused to seriously consider the question. I mean, how do you know? What does that feel like? I hadn't even considered it. But would I later? Now I was worried. But I knew if I didn't give them the right answer, they wouldn't let me leave. "No," I finally said. "I think there's been enough death tonight."

Satisfied I wasn't a threat to myself, the detectives and captain said their goodbyes and Santoliquito pushed opened a steel door that led to the back parking lot and pointed to my car, which had been impounded for inspection. "Take care of yourself," he said, handing me my keys. Then the door closed behind him. It was 1:41 a.m. I was finally free to go. It would have been a wonderful liberating moment if I wasn't so in shock, still feeling like I had stepped into some strange alternative reality.

Sitting in my car with no real clue where I actually was, I entered the address of our apartment into Google Maps, the apartment I shared with my wife, where I had said goodbye less than eighteen hours before. But she wouldn't be there when I got home. That's when I realized I had forgotten to ask the detectives about our cat Gypsy and of course our Golden Retriever Huck. I had forgotten to ask if the police had searched our place and if they had found anything. I looked back at the door I had just walked out of. But I sure as hell wasn't going back in there to ask.

For forty-five minutes I drove back to Delaware in silence, surprised by just how loud my own breath was in my ears. The sky was pitch black and adding to my feeling of isolation, I felt like I was the only one on the road in the wee hours of a Tuesday morning. Then before I knew it, I was home, parked in my usual spot, but not remembering the drive or how I got there.

I walked into our building, through the lobby and down the hallway to our apartment and paused before I inserted the key. I had no idea what to expect when I opened the door. I prepared myself for the worst—our boy Huck and our baby Gypsy dead in a pool of blood. And I prepared myself to die if I were to open a boobytrapped kitchen cabinet or refrigerator. Because after what I had just witnessed and experienced, anything was possible. Anything.

I opened the door to the apartment. Dead calm. I walked in slowly and found Huck. He was lying on the couch, motionless. As I approached, he stirred and looked up at me with his big brown eyes as if to say, "Thank God." And that's all I could think to say to him as I grabbed him in the biggest bear hug I could muster. Then

Gypsy came slinking out of the master bedroom toward me and Huck in the living room. I scooped her up and held her close. They were both okay.

As I smothered them both in affection, I wondered about the tearful scene that must have played out just before Jennair walked out the door for the last time. She loved Huck every bit as much as I did. Together we had found him. Rescued him. Nursed him to health. And spoiled him rotten for six years. We also rescued Gypsy together, but she was really just Jennair's cat and Jennair was her human. They were inseparable. How did she leave them? How could she?

When I walked into the kitchen, it was spotless. Not a dish, a crumb or a water spot in the sink. Jennair had meticulously cleaned and neatly arranged things before she left. Laid out on the counter was a folder from the bank where she had opened her own account at the urging of a divorce attorney. She had neatly written the account number on one pocket of the folder and the online banking login credentials on the other. Across the room, on the opposite kitchen counter, sat an unopened bag of cat food with a Post-it note that read, "You'll have to exchange this. I got the wrong one. You can get it from Petco."

That was it. No letter. No bomb. Nothing. The kitchen counter looked strangely bare, especially the spot where her brand new laptop usually sat. It was gone, and so was our iPad and her iPhone. All, I suspected, in police custody. Exhausted and light-headed, I slumped onto the couch next to Huck and stared silently into the darkness of a blank TV screen, my mind wandering back to November 2016.

It was that email that had started everything in motion—the one about a mandatory meeting Jennair was required to attend.

She knew what was coming. For months the manufacturing company she worked for had been systematically reducing its workforce every quarter. As each round of layoffs came, she couldn't take the not knowing anymore. So, at 5:30 p.m., after everyone else had left the building, she would sneak into the president's office to look through papers and emails for the latest list of new employee cuts. As the marketing manager, she knew it was only a matter of time before her value to a company that manufactured valve fittings for the oil and gas industry had withered away to nothing. Jennair hated that job and kicked herself for not leaving sooner. She was overqualified and underappreciated for her position there and felt stifled in her efforts to create and implement a strategic marketing plan. "If they would just let me do the job I'm capable of, what they hired me for," she told me, "I could have accomplished so many great things for them." She knew she had so much to offer someone else who would appreciate her skills. But even she would admit that she had just gotten too comfortable there.

She never found her name on any list for layoffs, but the email, requesting her presence at a mandatory meeting, was all the evidence she needed. Not surprisingly, when she showed up the next day, purposely forty-five minutes late to the meeting to thumb her nose at the senior management team, she was immediately and unceremoniously escorted to HR to receive her walking papers and severance package. It was a blow to her pride, but it also fit perfectly into the dream we had to start a new life in Denver.

Three years prior, at the height of our happiness in South Carolina, Jennair had finally convinced me to take a vacation to explore Denver, Colorado. During a previous job, she had made several business trips there and absolutely loved it and wanted to share it with me. So for ten days, we climbed the Flatirons of

Boulder, watched the Rockies beat the Brewers, sat in the front
row of a Sting concert at Red Rocks amphitheater, and ate and
drank like the foodies we wished we could have afforded to be.

While we were enjoying our new life in the South, it was never
meant to be a long-term plan. Denver seemed to speak to us both
and we felt it was the place we needed to be. We spent the next
three years looking and interviewing to find the perfect opportunity to get there.

For weeks, while Jennair had waited to learn her own fate at
her job, I had been interviewing with an advertising agency in
Boulder and we were both just waiting for the formality of the offer letter. For our entire life together, I had always been the main
breadwinner, and Jennair was perfectly okay with that. She was a
talented marketer, but she saw herself as playing a supporting role
to my career. She didn't have the self-confidence to pursue the career she really wanted. Our future plans and happiness were hing-
ing on me getting this offer. But one email brought that dream to a
screeching halt. I didn't get the job. It was the second big blow for
us in a week.

For more than half of the six years I had worked for the agency
in South Carolina, we had our eyes and hearts on Denver. With
the opportunity in Boulder, my heart and at least one foot were
already out the door. And once you're that far gone, I learned,
coming back to work and keeping your head in the game is next to
impossible. In the days and weeks that followed, it was hard to
hide my discontent at work, and it didn't go unnoticed.

I had made it clear to everyone I worked with that I wasn't
sticking around. Nobody knew the details of specific interviews,
but our plans to move to Denver were common knowledge. After
three years of hearing about it, it became a distraction to the

agency team. Before long the owner of the company and I agreed it was time for me to move on. I had ninety days to find new work—and a new home.

To minimize the stress on our lives, I briefly considered temporarily making a go of being a freelance creative director to local agencies until I landed something more permanent. So, over the next few months Jennair applied for jobs and interviewed in South Carolina. But nothing seemed to fit. She wasn't unqualified for the jobs for which she was interviewing; she was actually extremely overqualified. Her résumé was packed with the impressive accomplishments of her twenty-five-year career. But marketing firms and agencies were looking for young, inexperienced, raw talent they could shape and pay next to nothing. Managerial and director level positions were few and far between, if they existed at all. At age forty-seven, Jennair felt past her prime and unwanted.

Marketing was just something Jennair had fallen into. In college she was a communications major, but her real passion was film and editing. For years I had encouraged her to explore what she really wanted to do and pursue it, even if that meant going back to school. "Do what you want and the money will come," I always told her, "I will support you." But she didn't have the fire in her belly to change course so far into her career. And I quietly resented her for that.

When I had first met Jennair, she seemed unstoppable. She was going to have an amazing career and accomplish amazing things. And while many of us never quite measure up to the careers and the lives to which we aspire, I had always believed in an ongoing commitment to learn new things, take chances and evolve who and what we thought we were capable of professionally. While I tried hard to get Jennair to subscribe to the same philosophy, she always played it safe, taking jobs that came to her, getting too comfortable and not asking, "What am I going to do for my next act?"

Her parents offered little consolation. They were sympathetic but told her she should just take any job she could find. For many in their generation, that's how it was done. You didn't have a career. You got a job, brought home a paycheck and stuck it out for twenty or thirty years until you were ready to retire. Jennair loved her parents, but from childhood, she told me she felt like she had never received the guidance or support she was looking for from them—or from anyone, for that matter. Her high school guidance counselor gave her bad career advice. Professors in college didn't give her the personal attention she wanted. Her bosses were all terrible managers. Our financial planner didn't give her the right financial advice. It was always someone's else's fault. Jennair claimed she just "wanted someone to tell her what to do." But when they did, she either ignored their guidance or complained about it if it didn't work out perfectly. The reality was—if you knew Jennair, you knew she wouldn't be told what to do.

Still, she was incredibly tenacious. She continued applying to marketing jobs for which she knew she was overqualified. She interviewed with an architectural firm, a real estate agency, and a recruiting firm, but she got nowhere. By mid-summer, the repeated rejection started to take its toll. Jennair's pride had taken a beating and a cloud of hopelessness and depression began to engulf her. By late summer she resorted to taking a job as a checkout clerk in a grocery store, so at least she felt like she was contributing to pay our bills. But taking a low-paying service job was demeaning to her, and that only added to her low self-esteem and depression. I truly appreciated her effort, but it was painful to see her like this. And as so often happens when living with someone else's depression, as the months wore on without a change in course, her depression became our depression, and our marriage imperceptibly sunk into a normalized despair.

While I finished out projects I was working on at the agency, we cut living costs to the bone. We moved from a very upscale home in a gated community to a substantially smaller home in a much less desirable neighborhood. We stopped dining out and started shopping at discount grocery stores. We cut cable TV and had dinner at home every night. We binged all five seasons of *House of Cards* in a matter of weeks.

Binge-watching that show was our escape from the drudgery of looking for jobs and not knowing where our lives were headed. But in a way it actually deepened our despair. The show's plot was built on a foundation of betrayal, infidelity, suicide and murder. That show and the bewildering presidential election had not only removed us from reality, I honestly think it also numbed our morality and likely had an unconscious effect on how our life played out in the months that followed.

During the last couple months of my job, I was also prospecting for new career opportunities. Unlike Jennair, who was waiting to see where I landed a job, I had the luxury of looking everywhere and anywhere in the country. And I did. From large corporations out west to small ad agencies in the northeast, I left no stone unturned. But I was also very selective of the positions I applied for. Having worked the previous six years at an agency that specializes in higher education marketing, I kept an eye out for opportunities with colleges and universities. Then I saw a position on LinkedIn, "Creative Director, University of Delaware."

I had never even been to Delaware but the more I read the job description, the more it seemed like a perfect opportunity. At the agency, we would drop into a campus for a week, ask a lot of questions, find out who they were and present their brand to them. Then we'd do it all again for another university. Delaware offered a long-term opportunity to really explore and build a university brand from the inside out.

Something about this opportunity spoke to me. The minute I saw the job posting, I applied, including a cover letter like none I had ever written. But I knew an application and a cover letter wouldn't cut it. So, I reached out to the person I would report to, sending an ancillary email to Meredith Chapman, director of marketing.

Subject: Creative Director position
8/05/17 - 2:02 PM

Hi Meredith.

I just applied to the Creative Director position at The University of Delaware. I'm sure that you and your team have been inundated with resumes, so I thought I would reach out to introduce myself to you directly.

After 6 years as a creative director for an agency specializing in higher education, I am looking for a new challenge. I think the description of the creative director position aligns very well with my background and what I am looking for.

Please review my credentials and my work. I look forward to the opportunity to speak with you.

Sincerely,

Mark Gerardot

————

I was thrilled when she promptly replied.

————

Subject: Re: Creative Director position
8/05/17 - 3:27 PM

Thanks, Mark! I've seen your agency's work before and look forward to reviewing your materials. This position reports directly to me on a marketing team of about 20 with about 6-8 of those people being on the creative team. I'm hoping to move ahead with resume reviews later this month to move along quickly and get someone here early in the fall, ideally by October. Thank you so much for your interest and hopefully you'll hear from someone on our search committee in the coming weeks.

The weeks that followed seemed like years. I had interviews in Columbus, Denver, Salt Lake, Philly, and even back in Indy. But to me, the job in Delaware surprisingly seemed to offer the best opportunity for creative challenges and my own growth.

In late August, Jennair and I took time out to enjoy a unique, welcome distraction. The Great American Eclipse (as they called it) was about to happen and Greenville, South Carolina, was ground zero to experience the total solar eclipse. The city was abuzz with a lively, festive atmosphere. We picked our spot early and spent the afternoon eating and drinking at our favorite downtown rooftop bar. Despite the months of pressure we had endured, we had so much fun talking and enjoying each other's company just like old times. We drank like we didn't have a care in the world, lounging on oversized lawn furniture, enjoying the unique perspective of the downtown skyline. When the moment of total darkness neared, we couldn't stop smiling at each other. We had no idea what life had in store for us, but we were sharing something special and unique with each other. That sixty-second period instantly became one of my most treasured memories.

Shortly following the eclipse came my bittersweet last day at the agency. At that same rooftop bar, Jennair joined me and my coworkers for drinks and a final farewell. I was glad to be moving on, but I was also sad to leave friends and unsure of where we were headed. Many drinks later, after everyone else had gone, Jennair and I were left standing at the bar. Knowing we were leaving people and a place we'd come to care about and starting a new and uncertain future ahead, our emotions got the best of us. We embraced and both began to cry.

Still staring into the blank TV screen, I was suddenly jolted out of my trance by the piercing ping of my phone. It was April, a friend and coworker from the University of Delaware who I had called and left a voicemail for earlier. Meredith had been especially close with her, just as she was with all the people she managed. It was 3:30 a.m. by then, but April sounded oddly awake and chipper.

"Hi, April," I answered nervously.

"Hey. What's up? Everything okay?" she asked.

"No, April. No, it's not," I said solemnly. "I don't know how to tell you this."

"Okay…?"

"Tonight, my wife killed Meredith and then she took her own life," I said it simply and directly, so she could understand.

"What?"

"I know. I—"

"So wait, you're telling me Meredith is… gone?"

"Yes. I'm sorry, April. I'm—"

"Oh, my God! Oh, my God!" she kept saying. "I think I'm going to be sick."

"I'll let you go," I told her and then we ended the call and I turned back to stare at the blank TV screen.

CHAPTER 7

THAT'S BANANAS

I didn't see her coming. Before I met her face to face in October, all I knew of Meredith was she was just the person who would be my boss. She was also my greatest concern about becoming the new creative director at the University of Delaware. After a quick look into her career highlights, I could see she was a UD alumna and after a brief time as a reporter and producer at the local PBS affiliate, and working on a couple of political campaigns, she had quickly risen through the ranks at UD's Office of Communications and Marketing (OCM). But I wondered, what could someone with so much less experience than me, who had only worked at one place for most of her entire career, teach me about higher ed marketing?

After a brief phone interview with Meredith and members of the search committee, I was invited for dinner with the vice president of marketing and a formal full-day interview with the entire OCM team.

As I walked up to her third-floor office for the first interview of the day with Meredith, I told myself, "Just be open and see where this goes." But within five minutes of sitting across from her I was thinking, "My God, who is this person? I want to work for her."

I could tell right away she was something special, a superstar without limits. She had a unique way of speaking that reflected her confidence, but she was anything but arrogant. Meredith was obviously brilliant, but she also acknowledged the things she didn't know, things that weren't in her area of expertise. I could see she was a dynamic, successful woman who could have worked anywhere she chose. And she chose UD. She explained her passion to do cutting edge work and launch full-blown national campaigns for UD like other major research universities were doing. I immediately loved her sense of pride and duty for her alma mater. And while I thought I already knew her career highlights, when she told me she had been an adjunct professor, and a consultant for one of the top higher ed agencies in the country, professionally I was awestruck.

But I was even more surprised when she told me how much she respected me for my own years of creative marketing expertise and career accomplishments, and how much she hoped I would consider joining the OCM team. For years, Meredith had carefully and purposefully assembled her own all-star team of digital marketers, and as the newly appointed senior director of marketing, she oversaw a team of designers and photographers as well. Meredith told me she was looking for more than a creative director to manage them; she needed a creative partner—someone who could help her build a strong creative team to do nationally recognized creative work.

As we wrapped the interview, she added, "Oh, I have your one word."

Weeks prior, during the phone interview with the search committee, I had asked them all for one word that described the creative director they were looking for. Two of them responded right away.

"Dynamic."

"Natural leader."

But Meredith had paused. She said she wanted to really think about it and get back to me. At the time, I thought she was dodging the question, so I brushed it off and assumed it wouldn't come up again. But for three weeks, she took my question to heart and searched for just the right response.

"Intrepid!" she said confidently and proudly.

I processed the word, took a beat, and responded, "Wow! Okay. Wow! I can be that. What a great word."

Meredith wanted a fearless partner who would be undaunted by the challenges to come. And there would be many. She didn't sugarcoat it. Despite these challenges, and her being fifteen years my junior, I wanted to work for this inspiring person. As experienced as I was, I could tell I had much I could learn from her.

After a full day of interviews and meeting with some of the team during lunch, the opportunity at UD quickly rose to the top of my list. I still had other irons in the fire, including at least one interview elsewhere, but without question, Delaware was where I wanted to be.

From the airport the next morning, I sent Meredith a thank you email.

————

Subject: Intrepid
10/06/17

Thanks Meredith. I can't get that word out of my head now.

Seriously though…. I am still processing the day, but I really enjoyed meeting you and the entire team. You are fortunate to work with a group of dedicated, hardworking people and I would be proud to help lead the team and collaborate with you.

Thank you once again for your candor. There are challenges, but you give me great confidence that we can help improve the processes, the brand and the level of work that comes out of OCM.

Thanks again. I look forward to continuing the conversation next week.

Sincerely,
Mark Gerardot

————————-

Re: Intrepid
10/06/17

Mark,

It was great to meet in person. I agree, I would enjoy collaborating with you and working to find innovative ways to elevate UD's creative, from print collateral to virtual experiences. We've got a talented group, and I need an intrepid creative leader to be my partner.

Meredith Chapman

————————

When I got back to South Carolina, I began a painstaking campaign to reach out and thank everyone with whom I had interviewed at UD, thoroughly researching each of their backgrounds, looking for shared interests and areas of expertise to mention. As I dug deeper into Meredith's background, I was even more impressed with what she had accomplished in just a little more than a decade.

In 2016, at the age of thirty-one, she mounted an impressive run for a seat in the Delaware State Senate, narrowly losing to the long-sitting incumbent by just 747 votes. She was a former NCAA Division I cheerleader and an accomplished athlete, having run several 5k races and marathons to raise thousands of dollars for charitable organizations. Meredith was also a model for young professional women, mentoring dozens of female college students. She was like Wonder Woman with a superhero heart to match. It was clear she'd be a formidable colleague and one I'd love to work with.

A week later, celebrating my birthday with Jennair at our favorite brewery in North Carolina, I received an offer letter and accepted without hesitation. It wasn't Denver, but Jennair and I would finally be able to put the past year behind us and look forward to a new life in Delaware.

"You sure?" she asked. "You've never managed a team this size before. I don't think you can handle it. You don't want to wait for something better? What about Denver?"

"Maybe someday. But for now, this just feels right. This is the challenge I've been looking for," I assured her. For a brief second, I considered addressing her lack of confidence in my abilities, but after so many years, I had grown accustomed to it. I also knew there was nothing I could say to change her mind. I'd have to show her.

"Okay," she said, raising her hands as if washing them of the decision. Then she added, "Obviously, this is happening to us for a reason." And that was enough assurance for me to know that regardless of any reservations, she was on board with the decision.

Despite her initial concerns, Jennair soon came around and began to get excited about another fresh start, a whole new job market and being so close to D.C. and New York, a place we had never expected to live. She immediately quit her job at the grocery store and began planning the move and searching for homes.

We agreed that Jennair would stay behind in South Carolina to lease our house while I moved ahead to Delaware to start the new job. We had lived apart briefly when I started the job in South Carolina, so we knew forty-five days would be nothing by comparison. In fact, while neither of us said it out loud, after the year we had just had, I think we both thought it might be good for us.

A month later I hugged my dogs, kissed Jennair goodbye and set out on the six-hundred-mile trek north to Delaware. It all felt eerily familiar to the move to South Carolina, almost exactly six years earlier to the date: a new job, a new city, an unknown future. As good as the South had been to us, it had never felt like home. Consequently, we didn't want to put down roots. As I left South Carolina in my rearview mirror, I replayed the past year and just knew this new opportunity would put us on the road to a better future.

After more than twelve grueling hours on the road, I finally arrived at the house where Jennair had found a basement apartment for rent. I immediately called her from the driveway and asked her to give me the keypad combination to get in the back door. But instead of a pleasant, helpful voice on the other end, I got a ten-minute lecture at the top of her lungs about how she had already forwarded me the email days ago and how I needed to learn to be more responsible. It wasn't exactly the welcome I was hoping for. Instead, it was a reminder that despite the new path before us, it probably wouldn't be an easy one. Regardless of her new-found optimism, Jennair still doubted me, and I resented it all the more. Despite the endless possibilities ahead, we were still us, battle scars and all.

My first week at UD was not unlike any new job: meet new people, attend meetings you have little or no context for, and hope you are taking enough notes to remember what you need to know. I had a brief lunch with a few of the managers, including Meredith, but otherwise our two paths barely crossed for the first three days.

On my fourth day I was invited to an important meeting with our agency partner and a dozen or so important internal stake-holders. After shaking hands with everyone, I found an open seat. Next to Meredith. It wasn't her meeting, but it was soon clear to me that everyone in the room looked to her for her opinion and listened intently while she shared her insights. From deans to de-partment VPs, she had clearly earned the respect of everyone, and it was obvious I wasn't the only one in awe of her intelligence.

At a couple of critical moments in the meeting, Meredith asked me to weigh in. As I made my points, she nodded approv-ingly and gave her signature phrase of agreement, "One-hundred percent." Soon thereafter it seemed like we were finishing each other's sentences. Everyone in the room must have thought we had practiced our answers together. We hadn't, but I could tell we were going to make a great team.

As the meeting wrapped up two hours later, Meredith asked me if I wanted to get a quick drink to debrief about the week. I gladly accepted.

Night had fallen on the brisk November evening as we walked down the street to a little Italian restaurant. We sat down at the bar for what I assumed would be a quick thirty-minute meeting. When I later looked at my phone, I was surprised to discover more than three hours had gone by. Funny thing is, I don't think the topic of the work week even came up. I remember telling her things about my personal life that I hadn't really discussed with anyone, let alone my boss. She was just so easy to talk to and seemed genuinely interested in what I had to say.

I told her about my parents' and brother's recent passing. I shared details of the difficult year Jennair and I had experienced. We talked sports, dogs, high school, and our mutual love of pizza and red wine. And she shared her hopes and dreams with me.

"Growing up I always wanted to be an interior decorator," she confided in me. "I love it. I loved decorating my little house, sketching it all out."

"Wow," I said, not expecting that, since she was so focused on her profession. This domestic side to her was a pleasant surprise. "I'd love to see it some time. The house I mean. Actually, both. The sketches, too." I was thrilled that we both shared a love of design and intrigued by the many layers she was revealing.

We talked about our families and she was floored to learn I had ten brothers and sisters, revealing to me that she had a brother and a sister. "We're inseparable. We call ourselves the Sullivan Siblings and get together for dinner in Philly as much as possible." I envied her closeness with her family and found myself wondering about who they were and whether they were any bit as engaging and charismatic as she was proving to be.

It was great to get to know each other outside of work, but above it all, we both expressed our tremendous respect for each other's abilities and how we couldn't wait to work together. We could have talked all night, but I told her I should probably get going. I didn't have any place to be, but I felt the need to collect my thoughts and gut-check my feelings. Who was this person I had known for all of four days and just spent the last three hours pouring my heart and soul out to? I didn't see her coming.

As we parted for the evening, Meredith suggested that if I was interested in getting dinner on Saturday night, she would be available.

"My husband is on a hunting trip with his family until next week," she offered begrudgingly. "I love him. He's a good guy, but I hate hunting. It's so disgusting."

Though I shared her distaste for hunting, I felt it was an interesting choice of words, but I didn't read much into it at the time. Maybe it was the way she said it that left me wondering how happy she was in her marriage, but I dismissed the thought and welcomed the company and the opportunity to continue our conversation.

On the phone later, I told Jennair about having drinks and appetizers with Meredith earlier.

"Yeah, I saw that transaction on your credit card tonight," she said. She had long ago set up our account so that she'd receive an email alert whenever I used my card. "Sixty dollars, Mark? Why did you pay if it was a work thing with your boss?" she asked.

"It's not like that here, Jennair," I explained to her. "I was with Meredith, but it was social, not official business. So, she couldn't expense it. I offered to pay. Actually, I insisted."

I stopped short of telling her about the plans for Saturday evening. I had no expectations for the evening, but given Jennair's reaction and our history, it seemed like the best decision to not mention it.

As Saturday evening approached, I started to question what this event really was. Was I having dinner with my boss or my new friend Meredith? Or did she just feel bad for me being all alone in a new city? Whatever it was, I found myself anxiously anticipating and worrying about the night as if it were a date with a new crush. By the time she picked me up I was a nervous wreck. But my nerves disappeared the minute I got into her car—one of my dream cars actually, a sexy little Audi A3 convertible—and we immediately began talking.

Meredith was so excited to share her favorite local pizza joint with me. A glass of wine into dinner, I had a moment of clarity. I told her about how strangely comfortable I felt with her and how much I was in awe of how she conducted herself professionally. She smiled and acknowledged our mutual admiration. Then, without even thinking, I blurted it out.

"I have a professional crush on you," I said.

"Hundred percent," she laughed in relief. "That's exactly how I feel."

Phew. That was that. It was just a professional thing. The rest of the evening was full of amazing conversation and much-needed camaraderie. From an outsider's perspective, the two of us probably looked like we had been friends for years. She at four-feet eleven-inches and thirty-three years old, and I at five-feet eleven-inches and fifteen years her senior, we couldn't have looked more different. But as the conversation unfolded, we were both amazed by the number of things we had in common. Besides our mutual love of pizza, we were both fiscal conservatives, pro-life, anti-gun, and so much more.

Then we hit an obstacle. She expressed a love of WaWa convenience stores. She swore by their coffee and loved eating lunch there two to three times a week. She wasn't alone. WaWa had a rabidly loyal following of fans in the Mid-Atlantic. I couldn't wrap my head around eating lunch at a convenience store and refused to jump on the bandwagon.

The following Monday, on the way back to campus from a meeting, I noticed I needed to get gas. It was nearing lunch time and I knew Meredith was scheduled in back-to-back meetings all day. As I walked into a WaWa just outside of campus, I sent her a text message:

Mark: *What can I get you from WaWa?*

Meredith: *What? Seriously? What are you doing at WaWa?*

Mark: *I needed to get gas. What can I get you for lunch?*

Meredith: *That's so nice of you. I'd love some fruit.*

Mark: *Okay. Can you be more specific?*

Meredith: *Anything but bananas. I can't stand bananas!!!*

Mark: *Are you messing with me? I must have already told you?*

Meredith: *Told me what?*

Mark: *Seriously? I absolutely hate bananas. They are my kryptonite!*

Meredith: *That's bananas!!!*

Bananas! That became our catchphrase every time we discovered something new we had in common. The list of things we had in common was growing so fast, eventually we thought it would be cute to start a spreadsheet. Column A) Agree: Pro-life, anti-gun, running, weak swimmer, red wine, bananas are evil. Column B) Disagree: Country music, eating meat, cats. I liked cats.

During Thanksgiving week, I had originally planned to go back home to South Carolina, but Jennair talked me out of it. With just the two of us at home, we never made much of a fuss over Thanksgiving, and we had no intention of traveling back to Indiana to see family. She had her hands full trying to get our house ready to lease, so I agreed. My new plan was to spend the day alone and try one of the area trails to run on and then get a pizza and beer at Whole Foods. To me, that sounded like an ideal Thanksgiving.

Meredith and I hadn't talked much for a couple of days, so on Wednesday we decided to catch up at lunch. I hadn't noticed it before, but when she was in "work mode," Meredith was like a speeding train, her words firing at a hundred miles an hour. She channeled much of her energy into a passion for working out almost every day of the week with a personal trainer and running seven-minute miles, one after the other like it was nothing. But her true passion was her work. She had so much she wanted to get done and so many thoughts in her head she wanted to express. Her excitement and her fire for the job were both mesmerizing and contagious. I marveled at her and found myself smiling as I watched her in her element and hung onto her every word.

Walking back to our office after lunch, we were deep in conversation when Meredith suddenly looked startled and confused. Just twenty feet ahead, a man stepped out of his black Chevy Tahoe and stood on the sidewalk as we approached. He was a tall, dark-haired guy, mid-thirties, sharply dressed in a crisp white shirt and tie.

"Whoa!" she said, laughing nervously. "I didn't even see you there. What are you doing here? This is Mark, my new creative director. Mark, this is my husband."

I was just as surprised as she was, and maybe a little disappointed, though he seemed like a nice enough guy. He wasn't at all the gun-toting huntsman I had pictured in my head, instead exuding a slick confidence and business-like acumen.

We shook hands and shared some quick small talk, establishing that we had a Hoosier connection. He expressed that Meredith had told him a lot about me.

"You mean she's complaining about me already?" I joked. We all laughed.

In that moment and back at the office the rest of the afternoon, the dynamic between Meredith and me changed. I think that's when we both became cognizant of just how personal and magnetic our connection had already become. Her office was just up the stairs from mine. And while we could have emailed, sent a text or an instant message when we needed to communicate, for the rest of the day we managed to find a reason to walk into each other's office and talk face to face.

"Can you please look at this proof?" she asked, placing it on my desk.

"Yes, ma'am," I said half-jokingly.

"You're so formal and polite, especially when you first meet people," she said with a smile. "Must be that Southern charm."

"Southern charm? I'm not from the South. I just lived there."

"Okay then, it must be that Midwest charm," she quipped, and walked out of my office.

I smiled and shook my head. "It's just a professional crush. It's just a professional crush," I kept telling myself.

It was the day before a holiday, so the UD tradition was to let staff wear casual clothes to the office. I'd been so distracted at lunch that I hadn't noticed Meredith's outfit. But now, back in the office after our lunch—and after being reminded she had a husband—I noticed. She was wearing jeans, a green sweater and leather riding boots. Seeing her out of her business suit and heels changed my whole perspective of her. It was truly the first time I recognized how physically attractive she was. *Oh, my God,* I thought. *This isn't going to be easy.* But I was determined there had to be a line, a line we wouldn't cross.

After work that evening, I decided to go to the mall to buy a winter coat and gloves. Living in the South for the past six years, I had forgotten just how cold November could be, and I was completely unprepared for the impending Mid-Atlantic winter. After a short shopping spree, I grabbed dinner at an Italian restaurant attached to the mall. I sat at the bar with a fork in one hand and my phone in the other, catching up on email. One email caught my attention. The subject line was simply "A Note of Gratitude," personally addressed to me from my old friend Joe Biden. Okay, we aren't actually friends. I was just one of millions of fans on a mailing list who received the same email. But Meredith did know Joe personally. So, in an attempt to be funny (and possibly cute), I forwarded it to her to say that she wasn't the only one who knew him.

My email prompted an immediate text response:

Meredith: *Where are you?*
Mark: *I'm at dinner.*
Meredith: *With whom?*
Mark: *Myself.*

Meredith: *#SoInviteMe*

My heart skipped a beat. I put my phone down for a second to think through my next move. What had just happened? Maybe it was nothing. I didn't want to read too much into it. I shot back:

Mark: *#YoureInvited*

Meredith: *Love to, but I just got out of the gym and I'm a hot mess.*

Mark: *Doubt that.*

The rest of that night is a blur. We exchanged text messages nonstop for the next seven hours, breaking only long enough for me to drive home. We were miles apart, yet it felt as if the two of us were huddled together just inches apart. I had never experienced anything like it before.

At some point during the evening I decided the name Meredith was just too long to type, so I shortened it to just "M." And that's what I called her in private the rest of our time together. Nobody ever knew that.

Meredith: *So apparently you've decided to call me "M."*

Mark: *Is that okay?*

Meredith: *I love it.*

Mark: *You know what else you might like? I have your one word.*

Meredith: *So what is it?*

Mark: *Spitfire.*

As I explained to Meredith, I didn't mean "spitfire" in the context of its official definition. She was hardly an "ill-tempered woman easily provoked to outbursts." To me, she was a spitfire because she was a bundle of energy, a real go-getter who refused to take no for an answer. That was the "M" I knew.

I told her about a green Triumph Spitfire Matchbox car I loved while growing up. I also told her I loved the full-size, real-life convertible version—especially in British racing green. Meredith loved the color green and her go-to personal hashtag was #alwaysthegirlingreen. Because she was, and she had the green eyes to match.

Early Thanksgiving morning I was awakened by another text message. It was from M—a photo of a coffee cup with large capital "M" on it.

M: *Drinking coffee out of my favorite cup. Made me smile.*
Mark: *Greenheart :)*

While M spent Thanksgiving Day entertaining her family, I spent the day trying not to think about her. I worked. I ran eight miles in the state park. I bought a pizza and beer at Whole Foods. Nothing seemed to work. Later that evening, I was so relieved when finally I heard the "bing" of a text message on my phone.

M: *Dinner at Harvest Saturday night after the move?*
Mark: *Okay. But I didn't know you were helping move too.*
M: *Yeah, we're both going to be there.*

Earlier in the week, I had agreed to help a group of my new colleagues move one of my more senior direct reports into his new townhouse on Saturday morning. It seemed like the right thing to do and a good way to get to know the people I worked with. But while Keith was one of Meredith's closest friends, I didn't realize she and her husband would also be there. I was excited and deflated at the same time. I told Jennair, during our daily FaceTime video chats, that I was going out to dinner with the group of friends who helped with the move. But the truth was, it would be my first official dinner date with Meredith. Or was it? Again, I started to second guess myself, wondering if I was reading too much into it. "She's married. You're married," I told myself. Why was I doing this? Why was I so confused and nervous? What was *she* thinking? Why was *she* the only thing I could think about? Yet after our first breakup in college, I had made a promise to never hurt Jennair again, and nearly three decades later, I still had no intention of doing so. But I was so inexplicably drawn to Meredith in a way I hadn't been attracted to anyone in more than twenty-eight years with Jennair. In Meredith's presence, I was somebody different. Invigorated. New. It wasn't just the way she looked or because she was younger. She stirred something inside me I just couldn't explain. And I didn't want to lose that feeling, whatever it was.

After a day of moving boxes and furniture, Meredith and I discreetly slipped off to dinner. We had been out just a week before, but it was different this time. As we sat across the table from each other, our gaze was more direct and our tone more personal than it had ever been. At some point during dinner our feet accidentally touched under the table. Neither of us moved a muscle.

Afterward, in the warmth of my house, I poured her a glass of Cabernet. Our eyes met again and we instinctively kissed. In that moment, we both knew we had crossed a line; we talked deep into the night, committed not to cross another.

After Meredith left my place that evening, I spent the entire night on the couch, agonizing in guilt over the kiss that shouldn't have happened and for the feelings I knew I shouldn't have been feeling. I had to draw a firmer line.

The next morning, Meredith and I met on the running trail behind her house for a brisk morning run. We didn't say a word about the night before; we might as well have been running in different states. After fifteen minutes of silence, I just stopped running. I had to say something. She stopped and turned to look back at me.

"What's wrong?" she asked, concerned.

"I can't do this," I said, straining to catch my breath. "I just can't do this to Jennair. I don't even know what this is, but it needs to stop."

Meredith's reaction took me by complete surprise. I could tell she was fighting back tears. "I knew I should have kissed you the moment you got here," she said, angry at herself. "If I did, you wouldn't be saying this."

I could tell she felt hurt and rejected. If she *had* kissed me, maybe it would have affected my decision that morning, though I'm not sure for how long. I felt like a jerk to have let it happen at all and an even bigger jerk for hurting her. After walking back to my car, I dropped her off at the entrance to her neighborhood and drove away, questioning my decision. But it was done. I'd drawn the line.

Just five months later, I woke to the sober reality that Meredith was dead. She was gone. And so was my wife.

And so was the line.

CHAPTER 8

GATHERING STORM

The sun had just started to rise, giving the morning sky that hazy yellow glow I would have normally welcomed. Somehow, I had made it through the worst day of my life. And I had little appetite for what would inevitably be the second worst.

I was still sitting on the couch, wearing the same wrinkled work shirt and pants I had worn all night at the police station. Instinctively, I looked down at my phone. "6:01. Shit," I said out loud. "I still have to call people."

Nestled on the floor next to my feet, Huck started to rouse with a loud rumbling yawn and his morning stretches. Then per his normal routine, he walked into the master bedroom to wake up his mommy to feed him his breakfast. Seconds later, he returned to my side, and put his head in my lap with a pitiful look on his face.

"She isn't here, buddy," I told him softly, then stumbled into the kitchen to peer into the refrigerator. Stacked neatly on the top shelf were seven Tupperware containers with perfectly portioned servings of the homemade dog food Jennair painstakingly made for him every week. It was a nutritious mix of boiled chicken hearts and intestines, turmeric, wild rice and brussel sprouts, with an odor that never failed to make me gag. I emptied a container into his bowl and gave him a pat on the butt, "You better enjoy that," I told him. "Cause you're going back to canned."

After a brief morning walk, I poured a cup of coffee and set up camp with my laptop at the kitchen counter. I scanned my brain for the names of Jennair's close friends I needed to call. But there just weren't any. She always said she didn't have time for friends. Sadly, in her darkest hour, it had been friends that she needed most.

I shifted my mind to Meredith. "Amy. I have to find Amy," I said to myself. I had never met her, but I knew she was a journalist in Wilmington and another one of Meredith's good friends. Amy was one of only a handful of people who knew about me and Meredith. This was news I didn't want her to find out about through the AP wire service at her office. Once I tracked her down through Instagram, I called her office and left a message to call me back right away. Within minutes she returned my call. The journalist in her knew. She had already seen something about a murder-suicide in Bryn Mawr, and my call was rare enough that she had started to piece it together in her head.

"It's Mer, isn't it?" she asked.

"Oh, God, Amy, I'm so sorry," I replied.

She was obviously devastated, but then Amy and I bonded over the fact that she knew about us, and about the precious time she had spent with Meredith in Miami just three weeks prior when Meredith sent me a Snapchat message with a photo of the two of them enjoying tropical drinks in their sunglasses.

Meredith: *Amy says I'm obviously in love with you.*
Mark: *I hope Amy is right.*
Meredith: *Amy's right. I'm madly in love with you.*

It was one of several photos and messages she had sent me from the beach, the pool and from the swanky clubs in Miami Beach where they had gone out dancing. Meredith had wanted so badly to take a vacation before she started her new job at Villanova. For years she and her husband made it an annual tradition to vacation with friends in the Caribbean to escape the bitter MidAtlantic winter. But this year would be different. Their nine-year marriage was just days from being officially over, though Meredith had told me shortly after we first met that her marriage had effectively been over for a while. For more than three years, she said, they were more like roommates, living in different parts of the house, but keeping up their public image as the perfect happy couple with "grip and grin" photo opportunities at work functions, public fundraising events, and plastered across social media. He was a sitting city councilman and she an aspiring politician, having narrowly lost her bid for a seat in the Delaware State Legislature in 2016. Making public their dissolving marriage was not an option. Supporting each other was what mattered. Even I was completely fooled by the façade they presented as being perfectly happy and in love.

But when they were not together, she presented a different image. More than once when we went out for drinks or dinner, she said to me, "I told him where I was going, but he couldn't care less where I am." It wasn't my place to judge, just listen. I knew what it felt like to be going through the motions of a marriage, wondering if things would ever be better again. As time went on, it was clear that whatever the truth was about their marriage, she was no longer happy in it.

We both knew our attraction for each other was not supposed to be. We both cared about our partners and didn't want to hurt them. And we both knew that in the cracks of both our marriages we had found each other and a chance to feel the kind of love and support we had each been missing for years.

I had already been scheduled to take the day off the morning after the tragedy, along with the following two days to take care of Jennair, due to her pending surgery. But I had agreed to call in to the office for a weekly senior management meeting that morning at 11 a.m. It was just hours away, but the apartment was so silent and time was moving so slowly. I couldn't stand it anymore. I had to talk to someone.

I picked up my phone and called a former colleague, Christian, an art director I had managed at the University of Delaware. He was close to Meredith, and I considered him a friend and trusted confidant. When I told him the awful thing Jennair had done, his immediate concern was my well-being. "I'll be right there," he told me. "I'll call into work sick."

When we hung up I happened to glance in the mirror, but the person looking back at me bore little resemblance to the person I was just a day before. I hadn't slept in more than twenty-four hours and it was starting to take its toll. I wanted and needed so badly to take a shower. Walking through the master bedroom, I was again struck by how neat and tidy Jennair had made everything in the apartment before she left it. The bed perfectly made. The laundry folded and put away into drawers. Her personal items arranged neatly on the dresser. I walked into the bathroom we had shared and it, too, was immaculate. Not a drop of water on the sink, and fresh towels were neatly folded and set out as if she was expecting guests.

I stripped down, stepped into the spotless glass shower and turned the dial. As I felt the warmth of the water washing over me and slowly breathed the steam into my lungs, I began to feel some of my tension washing down the drain. Then out of nowhere I felt a jolt of lightning shoot through my body and a vivid image flashed in my mind. Two days prior, I had just walked in the door from a morning run when I heard crying coming from the bathroom. When I went to investigate, I found Jennair curled up on the shower floor, the hot water beating down on her naked body, while she sobbed uncontrollably. I opened the shower door and handed her a towel. "Come on," I said gently, offering my hand. Still crying as she stood and then stepped out, I wrapped the towel around her and held her tight. I didn't know what else to say. It felt awful to see her hurt so much. Now that same pain was coursing through my body and piercing my heart. Closing my eyes and putting my hands over my face, I tried to will the image to go away. "I'm sorry, baby," I cried out desperately over and over again. "I'm so sorry." When I finally opened my eyes, the image had faded and the hot water had turned cool. I had no idea how long I had been in there.

After I stepped out of the shower and got dressed, I heard a knock at my door. It was Christian. Through his rectangular wire-rim glasses I could see his eyes were red and puffy. He too had been crying. He was thirty-three, the same as Meredith and the youngest on the creative team. But I always thought he looked like he could still pass for a college student. I never would have pegged him for a father of two. But he was. It was so good to finally see a friendly face. Without saying a word, we grabbed each other in a hug, and I just lost it. In an instant, tears came streaming down my face while I sobbed uncontrollably into his shoulder.

"Mer is gone!" I yelled over my tears. "She killed her."

"I know," he consoled me. "I know. But I'm here for *you* now. Let's make sure *you're* okay."

After a few minutes I finally managed to compose myself and Christian and I decided to walk to a coffee shop down the street. In stark contrast to the dark cloud I felt hanging over me, it was shaping up to be a beautiful, sunny spring day, the trees bursting with white blossoms and bright green buds, and new life sprung from the ground in the form of bright pink tulips and bold yellow crocuses. While we walked the few blocks, I divulged to him everything that had happened the night before, being careful not to disclose the nature of my relationship with Meredith. She wouldn't have wanted any of her friends to find out this way and I felt duty-bound to keep our secret forever.

"Don't believe what you hear on the news, man," I told him. "It's not true."

"Of course. I know, brother," he said elbowing my arm on the counter, and then taking a sip of coffee.

It was an uncomfortable lie, I knew, but a convincing one. After all, he had reason to have concern about Jennair. Just weeks earlier, she had hacked into my university calendar, and the whole department had been alerted.

On the way back to the apartment I called into the weekly meeting. Immediately I told my boss Erica that my wife had passed and I wouldn't be in the rest of the week. Not knowing the media storm that was about to be unleashed, I hoped she would just assume Jennair had died from complications due to the hysterectomy surgery, no questions asked. End of discussion. Erica was understandably shocked by my announcement, but she graciously extended her condolences and told me to take as much time as I needed. When the call ended, I breathed a much-needed sigh of relief.

An hour later, around noon, Amy called me back at the apartment.

"The police are holding a live press conference at 3:30," she said. "You need to get out of there now. The media will find you."

Talking to the media was the last thing I needed. I could barely function and hold my emotions together well enough to talk to friends. Within minutes I had booked a suite in the one hotel in downtown Wilmington that allowed dogs, packed a bag, left lots of cat food and litter for Gypsy, and fled the apartment with Huck.

When I arrived at the hotel, I checked in at the front desk and then took Huck and my overnight bag up to our room. It was a luxurious extended-stay suite with a full kitchen, two bedrooms and a long wood dining table that looked like it belonged in a corporate conference room. It seemed an ideal enclave to hunker down for a week and hide from the media. Behind a couch were floor to ceiling windows offering a sweeping panoramic view of downtown Wilmington. It was a familiar sight.

Just three weeks prior I had stood looking at the same skyline from the fifteenth floor of my prospective divorce attorney's office. I hadn't really wanted to be there. Jennair and I hadn't even made the formal decision to separate, yet she had already spoken to four or five divorce attorneys and she was insistent that I needed to speak to an attorney to at least get up to speed on the laws that govern divorce in the state of Delaware. Because what in the hell did I know about it? Why would I?

Searching for a divorce attorney was not something I had ever done before. I didn't even know where to begin, and she had been weeks and miles ahead of me. Reluctantly, I made an appointment with an attorney who came highly recommended by one of Meredith's friends, who described her as "tough as nails." I reviewed her profile online and she seemed to check all the right boxes, so I scheduled a meeting.

How did I get here? I wondered. Just a year before, I had been in South Carolina conducting competitive research about the University of Delaware for a client in Maryland, with no thoughts of divorce even close to my mind. Yet just months later I sat waiting to speak to an attorney about dissolving my marriage, thinking how it was all somehow strangely connected, as is every decision we make in the story of our lives.

The attorney walked in, sharply dressed in a blue suit and white pearls. I was nervous (and a little intimidated), but that changed the instant Jill spoke. She hardly seemed "tough as nails." She was real and personable and she really put me at ease. She wanted to hear my story.

I told her everything. I described how Jennair and I had first met, our careers, the details of our financials and our tumultuous twenty-four-year marriage. I told her about meeting Meredith, and about struggling with the idea that our marriage might be over and how difficult it had been for Jennair to deal with. I told her about the agreement I made to stay with Jennair while we had gone to counseling. I also told her that at the urging of one of the many attorneys with whom Jennair had had initial consultations, she had taken half of our liquid assets and opened a separate bank account I didn't have access to. Then it dawned on me. I was wearing a sport coat I hadn't worn in some time. I paused and held my finger up as if to call a timeout. I reached into my pockets, felt along my lapel and gave myself a pat-down.

"What are you—" she started to ask, puzzled.

"Checking for bugs," I said.

"What do you…What?" Jill chuckled, thinking I was kidding or crazy.

But I was neither.

Over the course of the past few months, I had come to make some unnerving discoveries about what Jennair had been doing to track my every movement.

As I shared the full story of the past few months, Jill just sat there, shaking her head in disbelief. And then she very firmly interrupted me. "—Mark! You have to get her out of there. She's stalking you. You need to file a P-F-A."

"It's not a big deal," I had assured her, confident I didn't need a Protection From Abuse order. "She's harmless."

Standing there in the hotel suite, I could see dark clouds forming on the horizon, an ominous sign that perhaps a storm was in the making. I closed the drapes and turned on the television. It was time for the local news.

"At the top of the hour, murder-suicide on the Main Line," the announcer teased, and then cut to a police captain standing at a podium with a mic.

"You had a man that was married, that was having an affair with this other woman, the wife knew about it and this was a calculated, planned attack," the police captain said in a monotone voice without even a hint of emotion, as if he were describing the plot to a TV show. "She broke into the house, was lying in wait and she shot her as soon as she walked in. Then she shot herself. There were emails and text messages indicating what she planned to do. And the detectives are still sorting that out. The husband was in the area, under the belief that he was meeting the other woman for dinner. And when she didn't show up, that's when he got concerned and showed up at the house. But again, that's unconfirmed. That's what we're working on now. There is no danger to the community. The fact that it's a murder-suicide is a tragedy, but it's cleared as far as we're concerned." Then the announcer cut away to promote the next story.

"What?" I yelled at the screen. "No. I was meeting Jennair for dinner! What the hell do you mean there were emails and texts that indicated what she would do?" I grabbed the remote and turned it off. "Come on, Huck," I told him. "Let's go get Mike at the airport. We'll fix this later."

But the damage had already been done.

CHAPTER 9

THREE THINGS

I'd drawn the line with Meredith. I had made a commitment to my marriage, a commitment I'd kept for decades. Yet it wasn't even five minutes after I had dropped her off at the entrance of her neighborhood after our morning run that I began second guessing myself. Sitting at a stoplight less than a mile away, my phone pinged. It was a text from Meredith.

M: *I feel like such a fool. So rejected.*
Mark: *Please don't.*

She didn't reply. By the time I got home, it took everything in my power not to call her. I had gotten so caught up in the hopefulness and possibility I felt when I was around her. It was intoxicating. Nothing else seemed to matter. She made me want so much more from life. She made me see myself differently. The last thing I ever intended or I ever thought would possibly happen had happened, and my efforts to stop it from going any further was hurting her. But I had a wife back in South Carolina and she would be coming to Delaware on December sixteen, just two weeks away. And I needed to focus on the job I was hired to do. I wanted to build the creative team and accomplish the things Meredith and I had talked about doing. I just hoped I hadn't screwed that up by falling for my boss.

The next morning at the office could have been awful. But that thought should have never entered my mind; Meredith was, as always, an absolute professional. In a morning meeting with her, she was her usual self, full of energy, laughing as if nothing was bothering her and laser-focused on the work her team was doing. After the meeting we walked across the hall to my office.

"Are you ready for your trip?" she asked. "Do you need me to take you to the airport?"

"No, it's okay. I'll just park in the garage or take an Uber," I replied, glad we were still talking.

"I still can't believe you're flying to D.C. and not taking the train," she giggled, poking fun at my decision.

Weeks before starting at UD, I had negotiated a day off to travel to D.C. for a meeting as part of a contract commitment with the South Carolina agency for whom I had previously worked. As that day approached, Glenn, the VP of marketing at UD, to whom Meredith reported, started to waver on his decision to let me honor my commitment. But behind closed doors, Meredith told me she had stood up for me and fought to honor my request. What she didn't know, and what I didn't have the courage to tell her at the time, was that the meeting I had committed to attend in D.C. had been postponed until March. Instead, I planned to use the day off for another commitment I had made weeks before—a job interview with the University of Denver.

That afternoon, before I left for the airport, Meredith walked into my office, clearly upset and holding back tears. "Glenn wants you to come into the conference room. He doesn't believe what you and I agreed to."

Meredith and I both knew Glenn was determined to restructure the team now that I had come on board. He wanted the video team to report to me directly, changing the structure Meredith had established with another one of her direct reports, the digital media manager, Holly, who was managing them. In the long term, I thought it made sense to consider restructuring, but I had just started and I was still learning how the team operated. I didn't want to rock the boat and break something that was obviously working.

When I walked across the hall into the conference room, the tension in the air was palpable.

"Mark," Glenn started candidly, "do you think the video team should report up through you?"

"Maybe eventually, Glenn, as I know we've discussed," I said with confidence. "But as I told Meredith just yesterday, let's keep looking at ways to improve processes and change the structure to support it. Let's not make a hasty decision based on the structure we *think* should be in place, and then not have a process in place that works."

Meredith's whole demeanor immediately changed, and so did Glenn's. She couldn't resist the smile that was painted across her face. And he couldn't help but pucker like a sourpuss. To him our lock-step alliance was a potential force within the office that concerned him greatly. To Meredith and me, we had proven once again why we had wanted to work together in the first place.

"Okay then," he acquiesced, "but we're going to revisit this in a few months." Then he stood and left the room.

"Thank you," she said, offering me a high five. I looked deep into her eyes, smiled uncontrollably and then slapped her hand. We were going to be an unstoppable team.

An hour later after I wrapped up some emails, I walked up to Meredith's office to say goodbye. We looked at each other without saying a word. I walked over to her as she stood behind her desk and kissed her on the top of her head. She smiled back at me with those big green eyes as we paused for a short embrace.

"See you on Wednesday, boss" I joked.

I didn't know it then, but as I made my way to Denver, Meredith stayed late that evening to apply for the assistant VP of marketing position at Villanova University. She too was weighing her career options, planning for a new future, one where she wouldn't be my boss anymore.

The next morning when I arrived at the beautiful, snow-covered campus of the University of Denver, I felt a confidence I had never experienced before an interview. Mostly because, for the first time in a long while, I didn't need this job. Being in Denver is what Jennair and I had dreamed about for four years, but during my flight there I questioned whether I even wanted this job. In the few weeks I had spent at UD, I realized how much I had already come to like my new job and the people I worked with—especially Meredith. It was a unique position to be in. I had nothing to lose.

On the phone the night before the interview Jennair warned me not to blow it. "Don't screw this up on purpose because you don't want it. This is where we want to be," she pleaded.

During the next four hours of back-to-back interviews, I answered questions and presented relevant higher education marketing case studies to deans, department heads, marketing associates and the creative team that would report to me. It was a presentation I had become accustomed to and grown quite proficient at giving over the previous few months, but this time I actually enjoyed giving it. For the first time in months, I felt no pressure. I could take this job or leave it. And that felt so liberating.

As I got into the back of the Uber car bound for the Denver airport, all I could think about was how Meredith had stood up and fought for me and the great team we would make. More than ever I wanted to work for her and with her. And despite having drawn a line only two days earlier, I still wanted to explore my feelings for her. There was something between us that wasn't just a crush, professional or otherwise, and walking away from that connection might be a decision I'd forever regret. Taking in the city skyline and the majestic snow-covered Rockies behind me, my thoughts grew firmly planted in a single direction—a direction I knew was risky and wrong on so many levels. But at the same time, it seemed the only right direction, the only direction that was true to my heart. I wanted Meredith.

Sitting in an airport restaurant, a sense of great clarity began to set in. I couldn't wait to send her a text message.

Three things I know:

1. You are my hero.

2. I would take a bullet for you.

3. No more lines.

I couldn't have known just how prophetic and life changing that text message would be.

In less than forty-eight hours I had completely changed my position about us and about my marriage. In less than a month, I had reached a point where I couldn't imagine Meredith not being in my life. She had a way of supporting me and lifting me up like no one I had ever met. She was a stark contrast to my wife who continually doubted my abilities and sought to control and constrict my growth. More than ever I was convinced Meredith and I were meant to be a team.

When I landed in Philly that evening, I drove straight to the office. It was after hours and nobody was there. But I had an idea to surprise Meredith with a selfie of me sitting behind her desk. Instead, the surprise was on me. Employees had started decorating their offices for the holidays. OCM's offices occupied the Academy Building. It had been the first original structure on campus and its red brick, white pillars and four-story staircase oozed of history. I practically ran up the creaky wooden staircase to my second-floor office, where it had been rumored Edgar Alan Poe himself had once stood to give a reading of his poem *The Raven*. I opened the door to my office, which had once been part of a classroom, but nevermore. Now it was one of the largest individual offices on the second floor that made up the creative department.

To my surprise, hanging from the painted white mantle above the fireplace behind my desk was a single red stocking with my name written in gold glitter. And below it, on my desk, I saw a sad but adorable Charlie Brown Christmas tree adorned with a single ornament. Under the tree was a white porcelain coffee mug with a black handle and a handwritten inscription: #soinviteme.

I texted her immediately: *#heartstrings*

Three days later I was headed to the airport for the second time in a week, this time flying back to South Carolina. Jennair had called me with bad news. Our eleven-year-old Golden Retriever Abby was not doing well. For nine months she had bravely fought an aggressive cancer that had started in her leg and then metastasized into her lungs. But sadly, her battle had come to an end.

I prepared myself for the emotional wrecking ball that comes with having to put down a beloved pet. Since we had rescued her four years prior, Abby had endured a number of health issues. And after nine months of radiology and a daily cocktail of cancer meds, it was finally time to put an end to her suffering.

As I walked into the house, I expected to see Abby curled up lifeless on her bed. Instead she greeted me at the door, wagging her tail like I hadn't seen in months. My visit gave her the shot of adrenaline she needed. Instead of putting her down while I was home, Jennair and I decided to give her a great last weekend with the family. We spent the next two days at the park and napping in the backyard under the unseasonably warm December sun with our two goldens.

That weekend was my first time home in three weeks. Over dinner, as the conversation naturally turned to the new job, I just couldn't hold back expressing my respect and admiration for Meredith. I had a lot of nice things to say about many on the team, but my focus always came back to M. She was my boss. I was her partner. But Jennair must have sensed something else in me. Later that night, as she climbed into bed and reached over to shut off the light, she instinctively warned me, "Just don't fall in love with her."

"Of course not," I assured her. "It's not like that." But even as the words left my mouth I thought, *I think it's too late.*

Meredith knew I had grown up a huge Notre Dame fan, so she had bought us tickets when the Fighting Irish basketball team came to town to play the Blue Hens. To return the favor, I asked her to dinner before the game at the Italian restaurant where we first shared our stories. We knew it was a risk. How would it look for the senior marketing director and her creative director to be seen together on campus at such a public venue? We were usually very careful to meet at places far away from campus. But that night, we let our guard down.

Simply sitting and talking at a bar over a glass of wine had already become our favorite thing to do. It's how we shared some of our most intimate moments together. That night in particular felt special. Our friends didn't know about us, and there was something liberating about not hiding. We carefully avoided any PDA, but when our hands or legs would inadvertently touch, sparks flew, and we just smiled at each other.

Not surprisingly, the Blue Hens were blown out by the Irish, 92 to 68, but we didn't care. It was just fun to be out with her in public. After the game, we sat in the car with the heat blaring, waiting our turn to leave the crowded, snow covered parking lot. Our eyes locked. Our cold hands entwined. We both knew what we wanted to say, but we were fighting the urge. It was eating us both alive.

And then I couldn't fight it anymore. "I love you, M," I said in relief.

She buried her face in my shoulder and said softly, "I love you too, Mark."

Neither of us could believe this had happened. In less than a month we had fallen in love. We felt like teenagers and joked that our relationship should be measured in dog years. What felt like six months had only been four weeks.

But what did it mean? Was it realistic? And was it worth wrecking the lives of two other people to find out? Over the course of the month we had shared the many challenges of our marriages with each other. But despite our mutual feelings, we both loved our spouses and didn't want to hurt them.

Jennair and I had been married for twenty-four years. We loved each other, but many times we were simply tolerating each other. Our dysfunctions had become normal and comfortable. She continually belittled me. I consistently blew up. And then occasionally we would have a great date night and write each other heartfelt sentiments in cards. Not that we didn't mean them, but our actions spoke louder than our written words.

Meredith told me many times that I was an amazing and thoughtful man. And whether it was true or not, she thought so—and told me so. Not once in twenty-four years had Jennair said anything close to that. I didn't know how it felt to hear someone say that to me. Jennair chose to control me by putting me down. Meredith chose to inspire me by lifting me up. Once you get a glimpse of how great life can be with someone, it's hard to unsee it.

Regardless of the tone of our marriage, however, I did not want to hurt Jennair. She was moving to Delaware on December sixteen and I needed to decide what we were going to do. I wasn't about to throw away twenty-four years based on four weeks—no matter how amazing Meredith was. I needed time. And Jennair deserved it. And while she wasn't happy in her own marriage, Meredith expressed to me many times that she didn't want to hurt her husband. "He's a good guy," she'd said. "I love him, but we're just not *in* love anymore."

Having been married for decades, I knew the "in love" stage inevitably faded or evolved, but that it didn't mean the end of an even richer love. But I was so smitten and had grown so unhappy in my own marriage throughout the years that I read into Meredith's statement a shared unhappiness and desire for something greater, an intimacy that went beyond the physical. And Meredith and I seemed to have it—on all levels.

119

For the next week, Meredith and I spent as much time together as possible. Sitting at our favorite bar for drinks. Making dinner at my place. And making out like teenagers behind closed office doors. But with Jennair's pending arrival, reality was about to hit us square in the face and seeing each other during office hours would soon be our only time together. Making matters worse, the university would be closed for two weeks for the holiday, and we wouldn't see each other at all. Instead of anticipating Christmas, I was dreading it.

Before we knew it, December sixteen had arrived. I had to fly back to South Carolina to meet Jennair and the movers and do my best to appear enthusiastic. But the Mid-Atlantic's first winter storm of the season hit that day. The route to the airport was arduous, heavy with snow and slow traffic. From the passenger seat of Meredith's car as she drove me to the airport, I pulled out my phone to check my flight. The alert flashed across the screen. FLIGHT CANCELLED.

It didn't make any sense to head back to Wilmington when downtown Philly was just minutes away, so we pressed on. I booked a room for the night and rescheduled my flight for the morning. Meredith made arrangements to stay with her sister who lived just five minutes from my hotel. We stopped for a quick drink and then kissed good night. As I walked through the snow to my hotel and watched her turn the corner to her sister's apartment, I wanted to run after her. I wanted to spend the night together. I wanted to stop time. Instead, I held her in my dreams.

In the morning, before I took an Uber to the airport, I met Meredith for coffee and one last goodbye. Standing on the fresh snow-covered corner of 16th and Walnut, we looked at each other with wonderment as I held her and said softly, "I love you, Emmy."

"Uh, I love it when you call me that," she swooned, and we kissed deeply, magically, a kiss like no other. I had to go, but there was no way I could walk away from that love. I was all in.

CHAPTER 10

RIP IT OFF

It was going to be a new start for us. Moving to Delaware, starting new jobs and exploring an area of the country that was new to us both was just the change we were convinced we needed. Delaware and the nearby area had so much to offer—beaches, state parks and running trails—not to mention the ability to jump on a train and be in D.C. or New York in a couple of hours.

We had come to explore the area and look for houses two months before in October, starting a short list of places where we wanted to stay, from row houses in downtown Wilmington to a log cabin in Maryland's horse country just five minutes from the UD campus. But we hadn't made any decisions and opted instead to sign a short-term lease on a furnished apartment in Greenville, an affluent Wilmington neighborhood and home to Delaware's most famous resident, Joe Biden. Our long-term plan was to rent a home for a year or at least until Jennair landed a job and then, once settled, we'd buy another house.

But that plan, for me at least, had been effectively shot to hell. The connection Meredith and I had made had completely changed the equation. Neither of us had gone looking for a relationship, but we had found something in each other that was too strong and too real to deny. We had fallen in love. Now what?

When I landed in South Carolina, a day late due to the snowstorm in Philly, Jennair and Huck were waiting for me at the airport. I gave her a hug. She gave me a sigh. Understandably, she was exhausted. For days she had been coordinating movers to take most of our belongings to a storage unit while she packed a small moving truck and her Hyundai Tucson with the essentials we would need for a month or two. Not surprising to me, she insisted on driving the moving truck, because she didn't trust that I would be careful and not break the precious cargo she had packed so carefully. Packing was both a science and artform for Jennair and she was proud of her skill and proficiency at it. "Just let me do it," she had told me many times. "I hate the way you pack, and I want it the way I want it." It was a battle I knew better than to wage.

I loaded Huck into Jennair's car and led the way out of the neighborhood one last time as Jennair followed behind. A couple of hours later, from the highway somewhere north of Charlotte, I couldn't stop thinking about the past few weeks with Meredith and what we were going to do about the love we both felt. As exciting and intoxicating as the feeling was, we both understood we had to put it in perspective and ask ourselves if we really wanted to pursue a relationship, knowing the potential cost and collateral damage it would cause. I tried to sort out my feelings and make sense of it all. I had to talk to someone about Meredith, but there was only one person I trusted enough to tell. I picked up my phone and dialed.

"Hey, sir," Mike offered his usual greeting. "How are you?"

"Kind of freaking out, actually," I blurted.

"Why? What's going on?" he asked, concerned.

"Kind of fell in love. Well, more than kind of. I *am* in love. With my boss."

"Holy shit!" he exclaimed, then he took me off speakerphone. "What?"

"I know. I know," I said. "I sure in the hell didn't plan on it. But she... Meredith... she's amazing."

"Does she feel the same way?" he asked.

"Yeah. She says she does," I said. "I don't know what I'm going to do. You're the first person I've told. So, I guess I'm asking you for advice."

"You really want me to tell you what I think?" he asked, making sure he could be frank.

"Of course. That's why I called."

"I think this is amazing," he said.

Since I had introduced Jennair to Mike twenty-six years before, the two of them claimed, for my sake, to like each other. But the truth is they merely put up with each other. He hadn't wanted me to marry her in the first place. Then after a falling out in 2004, the two of them hadn't seen nor spoken to each other in thirteen years. He and I had gone to Berlin on a business trip to promote a sustainable eco-resort he had developed in the Bahamas. While having more than a few drinks at a bar, my inhibitions hit an all-time low, and before I knew it, I was in an apartment in East Berlin with an Austrian woman. When I woke up beside her the next morning, I knew I had made a huge mistake. Standing on the corner trying to hail a cab outside her building, I looked up, surprised by the colorful, foreign-looking onion domes of the Soviet-era architecture.

Where in the hell am I? I wondered. ***Who in the hell am I?*** This wasn't me. I felt so ashamed. From the back of the cab, I sat in silence, taking in the surreal landscape. It was 2004, almost sixty years since the end of the war, and yet many buildings were still riddled with bullet holes, and ruins of churches still stood like corpses, a far cry from the life I had become so accustomed to living comfortably back home. What was I trying to escape? Why would I risk losing it all, I wondered.

When I arrived back at the hotel, Mike knew what had happened. He had watched the whole thing playing out and later told me I had never looked happier, so he wasn't about to stop me. Worst of all, when I had returned home, it wasn't long before Jennair knew about it too. And it was the first time I had truly experienced what Jennair was capable of.

When we returned from Berlin, I had sent Mike an email about the mistake I had made that evening. Little did I know Jennair had been hacking my email accounts *for years*, reading every email I had ever written to anyone. When she saw the email conversation between Mike and me, she knew something had happened over there. And in an attempt to find out more, she baited Mike by sending him a leading email message from my account, pretending to be me. Suspicious, instead of replying, he called me.

"Hey man, I wanted to follow up on that email you sent me this morning," he said to me.

"Email?" I asked, perplexed. "I didn't send you an email this morning."

"Yeah you did. Berlin?" he chuckled.

"No, man." I paused. "Shit," I sighed with dread. "But I know who did."

That's when I realized Jennair knew about my one-night stand. At the time, I was more upset about hurting her than the fact that she'd hacked into my account. I had no choice but to come clean.

After a tearful conversation, I offered a sincere apology and asked for her forgiveness. She was crushed. She said it would take time to trust me again. Eventually we went to marriage counseling to work through it. And eventually she forgave me. But she would never forgive Mike. I think putting the blame squarely on his shoulders was the only way she knew how to forgive me. "He's such a bad influence on you," she would tell me often in a motherly voice after that.

Berlin had been a mistake, an indiscretion based solely on physical beauty, alcohol and sex. But with Meredith it was different. As I often told her, "First, I love your brain. Then your heart. Then, well, look at you." I went on to explain to Mike the whirlwind romance that had taken both Meredith and me by surprise. We were both married and now wondering what in the hell the next step was going to be. If anything.

"Look," he said. "If you don't do anything, will you regret it for the rest of your life?"

"Wow," I said, stalling to answer the question. "Yeah. I think so."

"And if you pursue this and in a year it doesn't work out, will it have been worth destroying your marriage? Is it worth it for a chance for true happiness? And would she say the same?"

"Shit…." I said, exasperated. "I don't know."

"Look, Hoosier," he said poking at my otherwise conservative life. "You haven't been truly happy in years. You need to be. This may be that chance."

As we drove north through the night, the warmth of the South got farther and farther away, and so did the past. Was I truly unhappy? Or was I mad at myself for not taking control of my life earlier, for not changing the dynamic between me and Jennair so I could be more happy in the marriage? Was I going to stay stuck in the past or look forward to a completely different future—one where I could be truly happy again? I didn't know. The cost to Jennair would be great, and if it didn't work out, what then? It was an answer to a question that deserved time.

During Jennair's first week in Delaware, we fell into the routine we had always known. I walked the dog in the morning and went to work. After work, we walked the dog together and explored our new neighborhood. Thick snow blanketed once lush green courtyards flanked by aging brick brownstones while giant oak trees stood bare and leafless, flanking our silent walks. Our words were as cautiously placed as our steps on the sidewalks slick with ice. On the weekends, we would bundle up to brave the cold and walk to local coffee shops, bars and restaurants, find a nearby neighborhood to walk into. Some days we'd drive to a nearby park to explore trails and meandering creeks. We'd done the same in the many neighborhoods we'd lived in, and exploring our new communities was something we'd always enjoyed doing together.

A week after she had arrived, we celebrated Jennair's forty-seventh birthday at the Delaware Museum of Art. Art was always something we could truly appreciate together and we had a tradition of going to the local art museum whenever we visited a new city, and always on Jennair's birthday.

That evening, we enjoyed dinner, drinks and pleasant conversation at a Mexican restaurant she had chosen near our apartment. Halfway into her third top-shelf margarita, Jennair began to let her guard down.

"I don't even want to work anymore," she admitted to me. "I just want to win the lottery and say fuck it."

If that had been the first and only time I'd heard her say that, I would have brushed it off. But winning the lottery and not working anymore had been a consistent dream of hers for quite some time. The deeper she sank into depression, the more lottery tickets she would bring home with each trip to the store. My opinion about gambling and playing the lottery is admittedly extreme and probably in the minority. I don't do it. I don't like it. And I hated that she played it, even occasionally. She knew I hated it and probably played more often than I knew. Jennair didn't have a gambling problem, but in my opinion, banking on a lottery win gave her unrealistic hope and an unhealthy outlook for something that was never going to happen.

But after more than a year of job searching and clerking at a grocery store, Jennair was emotionally drained. Where she'd once been a catch for any employer, now pushing fifty and out of work, her résumés went straight to the bottom of the slush piles. Hope was hard to come by. I get that now. But I didn't get it then. Even though she was celebrating her birthday and letting off steam that night, I was still disappointed in her. She had once been such a driven woman with unstoppable energy and aspirations. She had been let go from jobs in the past and had gotten back up to fight another day. But this time it was different. Despite encouragement from me and others to pivot her career and do something else— something she had always wanted to do, something that she loved —she wouldn't listen. She had the talent and skills to do almost anything she put her mind to. Her sister and I agreed and told Jennair she would have made quite a successful realtor, but she didn't want to have to learn the industry, get her license and start at the bottom. She didn't want to go back to school because when we got married and she moved to Indianapolis she went to school part time, taking her a total of seven years to complete her bachelor's degree. Her career life, she felt, was over. At forty-seven she was ready to retire—but without the pension to support it.

That wasn't the plan we had agreed to nor would it support the lifestyle we had once enjoyed and were hoping to enjoy again someday. She was pinning her hopes of our success on my success—and hence, on my shoulders. And I resented her for that pressure.

Christmas came two days later. Jennair had bought tickets for us to see a Christmas tree exhibit at Longwood Gardens, a nearby horticultural nature preserve. Seeing the acres of trees all decked in seasonal lights was a local tradition. I agreed to go, but I was a million miles away.

Walking through the Christmas tree exhibit, my mind wasn't on the many Christmases Jennair and I had shared. That's because nothing I had ever given her seemed to please her. Every Christmas became filled not with joy but with dread. We never put up a tree. We didn't decorate. And we had long since stopped trying to exchange gifts. When we did visit her family, it would inevitably end in a senseless shouting match between Jennair and her father or sister. I hadn't really enjoyed Christmas since I was a child.

That evening I did my best to smile and play along, but my mind kept wandering, thinking of a Christmas scene from three days earlier. Meredith and I had only known each other 112 days (yes, we were counting!), so it wasn't a given that we would exchange gifts. We had never even discussed it, and I'd assumed that the surprise she'd left me at my office the week before had been her loving gift to me. But on the last day before the long holiday break, I walked up to her third-floor office to surprise her with a gift, something I had purchased online the night before Thanksgiving while we were exchanging that flurry of text messages that had started it all. She wasn't in her office, so on her desk I left a scale model of a green convertible Triumph Spitfire wrapped with a big red bow.

Before the end of the day, Meredith came into my office and closed my door. She was smiling bigger than I had ever seen as she fought back tears. "I love it. I love you." she said softly. "It's the best present I've ever gotten."

Then she handed me a gift bag with a reticent look of pride. As I pulled out the tissue, I found a copy of Joe Biden's book he had debuted at UD just weeks before.

"It isn't signed. Not yet anyway. But we'll get it signed together," she promised.

I don't know if the Spitfire actually was the best present Meredith had ever received. It doesn't matter. I think it was unexpected and she appreciated the thoughtfulness behind its meaning. Even if she thought it was the worst gift she had ever received, I think she would have had the same reaction. Like me, she wasn't as concerned about the value of the gift or how it served her, but the sentiment behind it. And her response to my gift, real or not, had made me feel great, which was a sharp contrast to how I had felt on Christmas in 1991—and for the twenty-six Christmases that had followed.

After Christmas came New Year's Eve, another holiday that in most years had been a big disappointment. As much as we had both wanted it, we had never experienced the "When Harry Met Sally" style New Year's party, where everyone got all dressed up, went out on the roof and kissed at the stroke of midnight. It's not like we had friends, and the people we knew casually weren't inviting us to those kinds of parties. More years than not we would fall asleep by 10:30 or 11:00 after a few glasses of champagne and a toast to have a better year than the one before. Except for one memorable year, that is. It was 2005, and we were still the new kids on the block, living in that cavernous six-thousand square foot house. Still a work in progress, the sounds of Dick Clark's countdown echoed up to the second story catwalk and throughout every empty room. I don't know what had gotten into her, but suddenly Jennair came to life. She wanted to celebrate. She wanted to be spontaneous.

"Let's go outside and run around the house naked and screaming," she dared me as her face lit up with a huge beaming smile like I hadn't seen in such a long time.

"No, no, no," I balked. "Are you crazy? It's like five degrees out."

"Well, I'm doing it," she challenged.

"Okay, fine. You're on," I returned.

And for the next three glorious minutes our neighbors probably thought we were nuts as we ran screaming and running around our giant house through the hard, frozen snow without a stitch of clothes on. We vowed to make it a tradition.

But we never did that again.

Now, as 2017 came to an end and we had hopes and aspirations for a better year in 2018, it wasn't going to be much of a New Year's celebration. After hiding my feelings and putting up a façade for two weeks, I felt emotionally exhausted and completely out of sorts. And Jennair sensed it. As midnight drew closer and she began preparing to go to bed, she couldn't take it anymore.

"What's going on?" she asked, buttoning her red plaid flannel pajamas.

"Nothing. Why?" I replied.

"You're acting different. Just tell me," she pleaded, pulling back the covers of the bed then climbing under them.

"I don't know what you're talking about," I lied, sipping the last of the champagne from my glass and setting the empty glass on the nightstand.

I thought once I'd crawled into bed the conversation would end and we'd both fall asleep. But it didn't. It went on for close to an hour. She repeatedly asked what was bothering me. I repeatedly denied the truth. But she knew me too well. She knew how to get under my skin and pry information out of me.

"Just rip off the band-aid and tell me, you fucking pussy."

It was more than I could bear. So I did as I was told. I ripped the band-aid off.

"I want my independence," I confessed. "I want out."

CHAPTER 11

THE RAINBOW BRIDGE

Holed up in a downtown hotel suite for days following the tragedy, I experienced crippling waves of shock and a sense of suspended reality that tested my own sanity—and sometimes the basic instinct of just wanting to be alive. Like unpredictable random bolts of lightning, the flashbacks kept coming mercilessly. Sometimes minutes apart. Sometimes hours would go by, giving me a barely perceptible sense of calm, and then, out of nowhere, a hailstorm of horror, grief and uncontrollable pain pelted my very being. Instinctively, I closed my eyes, covered my face with my hands, and sheltered in place.

Relief came in the form of distractions during conversations with friends and family who I continued to call just so I could feel some connection to the real world. At times, I could talk about what had happened like any rational, detached observer, discussing the most horrifying or astounding details of Meredith and Jennair's deaths, and pondering how it had all come about, as if I was some accidental witness to events broadcast on the news. These talks seemed to ground me, insulating me from the abyss of my own dark thoughts. I recognize now that the moments when I was able to function normally were produced by my own body's self-defense mechanism hard at work. My mind would send me signals, cleverly disguised to convince me none of this had actually happened. Normally, people think of shock as a bad thing, but if I could bottle it as a wonder drug and sell it, I would. Shock enabled me to get up in the morning. Shock enabled me to brush my teeth. Shock enabled me to get dressed. To drive. To eat. Even to speak. For days and weeks, shock kept me alive. And albeit to a lesser degree today, it still does.

In the immediate days following the tragedy, I knew my grief and altered state of mind were putting a heavy burden on those around me, but I dreaded the notion of being alone with my own thoughts. I always thought I was an independent person who enjoyed my alone time to think and reflect. But the world had changed, and now being alone with my thoughts was the last thing I wanted. I had never before experienced the desperate neediness I was feeling in the aftermath of their deaths. But I didn't care. I was scared out of my mind to be alone, and I wasn't afraid to admit it.

Fortunately, my divorce attorney, Jill, was kind enough to arrange an emergency appointment with a psychologist colleague of hers, Sam, the first of many much-needed visits. And while each session brought some consolation, allowing me to lift my head a little higher, that relief usually dissipated within hours, leaving me mired in the same dark malaise of grief, disoriented from the rollercoaster of uncontrollable emotions that flooded my soul.

My oldest and best friend Mike never left my side during the first week as he tried desperately to keep me from seeing the news by distracting me. Just the two of us were sitting at one end of the long solid wood dining table in the suite when Mike opened our third bottle of wine of the night. Just then, my phone pinged. It was my friend Josh in Indianapolis.

Josh: *Thinking of you. Let me know if there is anything you need.*

Mark: *Thanks Josh. That means a lot. Mind if I ask how you heard?*

Josh: *Sartori (a mutual friend) saw it on Fox News.*

I put my phone down and shook my head in disbelief.

"Shit," I told Mike. "It just went national."

And within forty-eight hours, the story had reached around the globe. Fox News, *Newsweek*, *The Washington Post*, *The Guardian*, all couldn't get enough of the story of the cheating husband who drove his wife to murderous madness, and the murdered woman who had it coming. The coverage was unrelenting, and the comments that flooded the internet ranged from compassion to (more commonly) condemnation, declaring each of us had deserved it. Our social media accounts were scrutinized for the slightest indication of how monstrous we all were. Some pounced on the fact that Jennair and I were Democrats to blame our moral failings on the left, while others pounced on the fact that Meredith was a Republican to blame her moral failings on the right. It had all become a nightmare of epic proportions. Surreal. But surprisingly, thanks to my state of shock, the coverage had little effect on me. At the time I was more concerned with what damage the salacious half-truths and misinformation of the stories they were telling would do to Meredith's friends, her family and her reputation. My wife had killed her. And my love for her had brought her to that final deadly moment. I couldn't undo the past, but I could do everything in my power to control any further damage to her memory and family.

While I had only known Meredith's colleagues and friends at the University of Delaware for just half a year since I'd started working there, I considered a handful of them my good friends. Just weeks before, a group of them had joined Meredith and me for drinks to wish us luck with our new jobs. And just days prior to the tragedy, I had exchanged friendly, light-hearted jabs with a few of them. The truth was, I loved those people. I didn't want them to believe the things the media was saying about Meredith, as they made her out to be a homewrecker who deserved no sympathy. Instinctively, as the reports started mounting, I began sending each of her friends text messages to mitigate the damage.

"Please don't believe the crap the media is saying," I pleaded. "It's not true. Meredith deserves better than this."

One of our mutual friends replied almost instantly. "I know. It's terrible. She does deserve better. How are you holding up?"

"Okay, I guess." I replied, "My sister and her husband are here and my good friend is on his way."

The others simply didn't reply, but I didn't take any offense. We were all still reeling and dealing with our grief in different ways. Then, while at lunch with Mike, I received an unexpected phone call. The screen on my phone read "University of Delaware."

"Is this Mark?" the voice on the other end asked.

"Yeah?" I said with some hesitation.

"This is the University of Delaware police. We've been getting some complaints about you making harassing phone calls to university employees. I'm calling to ask you to stop."

"What?" I said in disbelief. "No, I didn't. I didn't call anyone." "You didn't?"

"No. I did send text messages to six of my friends there, but…"

"Well, I'm asking you to stop or we will serve you with a restraining order. Is that understood?"

I paused, letting his words sink in.

136

"Is that understood?" he asked again.

"Yeah," I said, momentarily stunned. I pushed the "end call" button. My friends and former colleagues had reported me to the police? For texting them?

Why would they do that? Meredith was my friend, too. I loved her, too. I shared their pain and shock. I was also a victim of this horrific crime. Did they think I was a threat? I couldn't find the words. I was being shunned by the people I'd reached out to, people I considered my friends. And it hurt profoundly.

That afternoon, Mike and I decided to cautiously venture back to the Wilmington apartment to check on Gypsy and collect more clothes and a few items I didn't have time to pack the previous day. We expected to find news vans and reporters waiting to pounce, but as we pulled into the parking lot, we instead spotted two parked Delaware State Police cruisers, the troopers sitting inside. At the risk of drawing attention to ourselves, we parked in the spot next to Jennair's SUV. It was a leased vehicle and the lease was maturing in a matter of days.

Despite having a thousand other things on my mind, I knew this would be the best opportunity to return the vehicle. And quite frankly, it was painful to look out the window and see it sitting in the drive. I asked Mike to follow me to the dealer in my car.

On the way out the door, after grabbing my clothes and a few things, I took Jennair's car keys and returned, pointing the fob toward the vehicle. Just as I was ready to press the button, a sudden fear gripped me and I stopped in my tracks—picturing the car bursting into flames, exploding and throwing shrapnel everywhere.

"Wait! Holy shit!" I shouted at Mike, "what if there's a bomb in the car?"

We just looked at each other and didn't say a word. I grabbed the driver's side door handle and closed my eyes. A quick jerk of the handle and I flung the door open. A feeling of relief washed over me. But we weren't out of the woods just yet. I got in. Mike opened the door and climbed into the passenger seat.

"Are you crazy? Get out of here!" I implored.

"No, man. If you go, I'm going with you," he said. He was dead serious.

We looked at each other. The air was thick with tension. I felt like I was living someone else's life. Then, out of nowhere, we both began to laugh nervously. I couldn't help but think how Jennair's plan to blow me up in her car would be even more perfect with Mike sitting next to me. In her mind, Mike had engineered the indiscretion in Berlin, or he was at least complicit. And Jennair just knew in her gut that Mike would be supportive of my relationship with Meredith. "How sweet!" I could almost hear her say. "The two men I hate most, GONE with the push of a button."

"This is so messed up," I said, then closed my eyes and pushed the ignition button on Jennair's car. Relief.

With Mike following behind me in my car, I led the way to the dealership forty minutes away, across the border in Pennsylvania. As we drove the twisting back roads, I couldn't help but take in the beauty of the countryside on such a warm sunny day. Spring was now in full bloom. The rolling green hills. Wildflowers alongside the road. And a chorus of every species of bird seemed to sing in perfect harmony. I just wished Jennair could have held on a little longer to see it. To hear it. To feel the sun on her face. To feel hope and joy again. Could one beautiful day have been enough to change the course of time, I wondered. Would she have realized that no divorce is worth dying—or killing—for?

The next morning, Mike and I tried to shake off the effects of another three bottles of wine. I had to prepare myself for the sad and unenviable duty of identifying Jennair's body at the funeral home. It seemed that during those days in the hotel room, those efforts to reach out to my friends and colleagues, the endless loop of news reports about the shooting and my desperate attempts at human contact, time had been suspended. Yet it had been just days before that I had discovered Jennair, her body lying no more than ten feet from Meredith's, face down on a hardwood floor surrounded by a pool of her own blood. The bullet entry wound just behind her right ear was surprisingly small. Clean. There was no blood at all in the hole that had drained her of her blood, and of all her life.

My reaction to seeing Jennair lying there when I'd first found her had been cauterized by my shock as I took in what I was seeing. But now seeing her lifeless body again, this time in the context of a funeral home setting, would be different. Clinical. Morbid. Final. I was nervous, uncertain of what my reaction might be.

Mike insisted on joining me at the funeral home to provide moral support, which I gladly accepted. The funeral director, Nick, a middle-aged, third-generation mortician was, unsurprisingly, an odd fellow. Like all funeral directors, he was sharply dressed and bore a kind yet somber expression. It was his disposition, however, that struck me as particularly peculiar, as he shifted between the formality of the forms I needed to sign and his awkwardly insensitive and inappropriately descriptive comments and questions.

"Now about the clothes your wife was wearing," he said, then hesitated. "They are quite soiled with a lot of blood. Do you want those back?"

I looked down at the floor and closed my eyes, trying hard to keep my composure. I slowly raised my head, and then opened my eyes, looking directly at him. "No. Absolutely no," I answered without emotion.

"Well," he began, as if my answer hadn't satisfied him, "given the amount of trauma her head endured, I strongly suggest you opt to identify her by viewing a photo of her face. I've strategically taken it to avoid the graphic view of the bullet's exit wound. But ultimately, it's your choice."

I really wanted to see her in person. Didn't I owe her that much? I wanted to touch her one more time. Grieve for her by her side before her body was reduced to ashes. As I wrestled with the decision, I remembered something Jennair had said to me many times. "If I die, do what you want with my body and ashes. At that point, it'll be just an empty shell that I won't be using anymore."

If she thought of her own lifeless body as an empty shell, then, I reasoned, it made little sense to honor it. I would have to honor my wife in other ways. I took another deep breath and slowly let it out through pierced lips. "Okay," I said. "Just show me the photo."

Seeming particularly proud of his photography skills, Nick placed the photo of Jennair's lifeless face on his desk and pushed it in front of me to see, then stared at me, waiting anxiously for my reaction.

As I studied the photo, I could feel myself welling up. I couldn't stop the memories from flooding in. Her face. It wasn't the face of a killer. This was the face of the girl in the ponytail and Taco Bell visor who had caught my eye and captured my heart thirty-two years before. The face was older, but to me no less beautiful and entirely too young to be gone. She had so much potential. So much life still to live. Behind her closed eyelids that I used to love to kiss, feeling the wonderfully strange tickle of her long lashes on my lips, were the same iridescent blue eyes that had once stared back at me on our wedding day, streaming tears as we pledged our vows to each other. Her tiny, perfect nose that she would wrinkle up to make me laugh was now still, as were her soft lips and huge bright smile. Gone. Never to be seen or touched again.

What have I done? I wondered. *What have I done?*

Instinctively, uncontrollably, I blurted out, "That's my girl," as I passed the photo back to the funeral director. He nodded, then checked a box and scribbled something on the form in front of him, content that the identification was complete, and I left, knowing my life never again would be.

On Friday, two days later, Nick called to let me know Jennair's ashes were ready to be picked up. The cremation process was something Jennair and I had sadly both become quite familiar with, having put down and cremated three of our beloved Golden Retrievers, the last one, Abby, just five months prior when we were living in South Carolina. Each time was slightly less painful. Each time left us a little more at peace. But when it is your spouse you are saying goodbye to, you can't really prepare for how it will impact you. Jennair had always been the matriarch of our untraditional little family. The de facto leader. Her torch, now extinguished, was mine to carry.

Inside the funeral home, Nick showed me the purple velvet bag in which he had placed Jennair's ashes.

"She always loved the color purple," I told him.

He gave a slightly awkward smile and then placed the bag into a box. As I carried it to the car I couldn't help but feel its weight, or the lack thereof. For most of her life, Jennair's slender five-foot, four-inch frame weighed in at 111 pounds. But after the past four months of distress, since that fateful New Year's confession, that small frame had been lessened to just ninety-five pounds, where it remained at the time of her death. Now, at most, the body of this beautiful woman had been reduced to a mere five pounds.

I opened the back door and placed her gently on the back seat next to Huck. "I'm trusting you to look after Mommy, Huck," I told him and kissed the soft white fur of his head. Huck lay down next to her and sighed, as if to let me know he took his duty seriously.

Mike had told me he needed to leave that afternoon. My sister and her husband had already left after a brief visit to see me and make sure I was okay. I wasn't. Soon I would be alone and I wasn't prepared for that. As if an answer to my prayers, my phone rang. It was my younger brother Barry.

"How are you hanging in there?" he asked.

"I've been better," I told him frankly.

"Dude, if there's anything I can do," he started.

"There is." I said. "Come to Philly. I can't stand to be alone. Not yet anyway. Plus, I need to get out of that apartment. I can't live there another day."

"I'll be there. And I'll help you move."

That afternoon, as Mike flew back to Key West, I picked up my brother at the airport.

The next morning, Barry and I rented a moving truck and began hastily loading everything of mine from the apartment. An hour later, Jennair's Aunt Rose and her son met us at the apartment to collect Jennair's belongings, as well as her ashes. I would not be welcomed at the memorial. I'd been effectively erased as Jennair's husband.

"What about the cat?" she asked. "Am I taking the cat?"

Three days earlier, Jennair's mother had sent me a text message. It was an excerpt from Jennair's final letter, asking that she be put down.

"...*if nothing else, get Gypsy. And I know you will be appalled at my request, but please as lovingly and peacefully as possible, please put her to sleep. This request is an act of love. I am Gypsy's human. Her only human. We are utterly bonded like no other creatures and she will be beside herself without me. I cannot tolerate the thought of her being with any strangers and without me. I can't fathom her fear and loneliness missing me. She calls out for me every day when we are separated. Please don't put her through this emotional torture. Let her go to the rainbow bridge to be with me.*"

"No, Rose," I said firmly. "You know Jennair was not of sound mind when she wrote that. She already decided the fate of two lives. She doesn't get to decide a third."

Packed and ready to go, Barry and I drove the truck to my new apartment in a Philly suburb. I knew of it because it was among a few contenders Meredith and I had looked at. I didn't have the luxury of time to consider others. When we arrived, I signed a lease and they handed me the keys to my new apartment.

By Sunday night it was still all over the news. "Radnor Murder-Suicide a Calculated Attack." "Man's Affair Leads to Ambush Killing of Lover." "Gun Enthusiast Shoots Her Husband's Lover, Then Herself." I wasn't sure I would even have a job the next day. I wouldn't blame my employer for not wanting to be a part of the media circus that had only just begun. There was no escaping it. This story and my name were plastered all over the TV news, newspapers and the internet. There was absolutely no chance Erica and my new colleagues wouldn't see it—and realize that Jennair had not died from a hysterectomy as I'd let them assume.

After a beer and an awkward brotherly hug, I dropped Barry off at the airport. Whether I liked it or not, I was now completely alone. For my own sanity and self-preservation, I told my new employer I would be back to work on Monday. Having only been working there for five days, I really didn't know anyone yet, but I just needed to be around people, especially given the unexpectedly cold response I'd received from my former colleagues at UD.

When I walked into the office that Monday morning, exactly one week since the killings, Erica waved me into her office and genuinely welcomed me back with open arms. She was so great and quick to put me at ease. We even managed to laugh at a joke together, as she thanked me for not updating my LinkedIn profile. As a result, except for a handful of friends, nobody knew where I worked. Here I had found refuge from the media, which continued its relentless pursuit of an interview, calling me, emailing me and reaching out through nearly every one of my social media channels. I couldn't imagine I would have anything coherent to say, so I gladly welcomed the opportunity to hunker down at work and completely fall off the grid.

Erica assured me it was my story to tell whenever and to whomever I felt it was right. There had been an announcement to the entire division not to approach me or discuss it. While that seemed like the wise thing to do at the time, the edict not to discuss it didn't come without complication. On my first day on the job I had been paraded around to meet all 150 members of the team, but now two weeks later, I didn't really know any of them and hadn't yet had the opportunity to make an impression. Unfortunately, a week of news coverage had done that for me. To many of them, I'm sure I was just a poor sap, or that creepy guy who cheated on his wife and drove her to commit an unspeakable crime. As I walked through the office to my desk, I could feel an unsettling energy as team members averted their eyes. There were no pats on the back, no condolences, no "how are you doings" or "hang in theres." There was just awkward silence and an even more awkward attempt to conduct business as usual.

I didn't blame them. I was just as uncomfortable and at a loss for words. Sharing my feelings and the thoughts going through my head would have been completely inappropriate. It was a strangely surreal experience for us all.

On that first day, I was in a late morning meeting when I realized that somehow my brain and my mouth were holding their own in a conversation, yet I had no idea what I was saying. I'd heard of "out of body experiences" but never put much stock into the phenomena. Yet here I was, floating above myself, watching this meeting play out, both a participant and voyeuristic spectator.

The meeting wrapped up around lunchtime and I drove myself home. I needed to collect myself and try to find reality again. I stood in my kitchen and had the overwhelming feeling that I couldn't go on, that the pain was greater than I could bear, and that life wasn't worth it. I felt as if Jennair was communicating with me from afar, sharing the depths of her despair and hopelessness that I'd been unable to grasp when she tried so hard to express it during life. From my knees on the kitchen floor, I called out to her.

"*Okay! I get it! I'm so sorry, Jennair!* I feel what you must have felt. My God, please forgive me!" I said aloud as I felt the salty warmth of the tears streaming down my face. "I don't want to live either!"

And just like that, it was over. I had survived yet another storm. But I knew deep in my soul this was just the beginning. What I didn't realize was that it wasn't just more grief I would face in the months ahead. I was about to come face to face with the wife I barely knew.

CHAPTER 12

FOLLOW THE MONEY

I could still smell the paint on the walls. Everything about this apartment was new, from the unused kitchen cabinets to the sparkling clean appliances. A new apartment. A new city. A new life. But as I stumbled through the kitchen, dodging the obstacle course of corrugated moving boxes, haphazardly placed plants and a slew of file folders, I started to feel overwhelmed. As much as I feared my own thoughts, I just needed to sit and think. I emptied the clutter from one of the distressed Italian leather bar stools Jennair and I had picked out together years before and sat down. I looked around at our belongings, scattered in disarray around the apartment, and a feeling of isolation and loneliness I had never known hung in the air. Silence. This wasn't just my new apartment. This silence was my new reality.

My old colleagues at UD had turned on me. My new colleagues were keeping a safe distance. Jennair's parents had stopped answering my calls and texts altogether. And my family and best friend had gone back to their own lives. Except for the company of Huck and Gypsy, I was completely and utterly alone. How in God's name had I ended up here? What in God's name had driven Jennair to such madness?

A little more than twenty-four hours before she'd killed herself and Meredith, we had enjoyed a leisurely Sunday hike at the state park with Huck. The next morning, we had exchanged mundane text messages about setting up the auto-deposit for payroll and whether Huck had done his business on his morning walk. Had she known all along that that would be the day? Or had she just wanted to see where Meredith lived and it spiraled out of control? And most baffling, where in the hell had she gotten a gun? She hated guns. We both did. It was the last thing she'd own.

I had to know. I had to get inside her head and understand what she could have possibly been thinking. It had been over a week since she'd died and the Radnor police detectives weren't sharing what they learned, so if I wanted to know anything, it was going to be up to me to roll up my sleeves and launch a full scale investigation of my own. And the first clues were right in front of me.

There on the cold concrete kitchen bar sat the neatly organized pocket folder she had left for me and I had carefully carried in by hand. Inside were the details for Jennair's private checking account information, including her online login credentials. I still hadn't gotten up the nerve to log in. I knew almost instinctively that she hadn't just left it for me so I could access the money and pay the bills. I suspected that the folder, so perfectly organized, contained clues—clues I'm sure she wished she could have been there to see my reaction to when I discovered them. And I knew once I looked, I couldn't unlook. Once I knew, I couldn't unknow.

For most of our marriage I had been, at best, passively involved in our day-to-day household finances. Money was a constant source of tension between Jennair and me. She insisted on having complete control over our money and leaving me in the dark. Asking her for the password to our accounts was just asking for a fight. So I didn't. She accused me of not trusting her. In hindsight, it seems ridiculous—even weak—but to me it just wasn't worth the battle. If she wanted to take care of the finances, it was one less thing I had to worry about, and besides, she seemed to enjoy it.

But that had all changed on March 3, the day she told me she took half our liquid assets and opened her own private checking account. An attorney had advised her to do it, she said, just in case the divorce turned ugly and I tried to take all our money. When she told me this, I knew it was time to stop being so passive and I demanded immediate access to our joint account.

But I wasn't upset about her moving the assets. In fact, I thought her logic made a lot of sense. But I was sad she mistrusted me; it hurt that she thought I would leave her with nothing. It never crossed my mind that I couldn't trust her. Yet, just as I never could have imagined she would murder someone, I never could have imagined she would use the account in the ways I was about to discover.

Sitting there staring at her online banking login screen, my hands trembled on the keyboard. I could feel my heart beating in my chest. I grew nauseous and thought I might throw up. I sat there, my eyes closed, wondering if I might be better off just not ever knowing. But like it or not, I reasoned, these were my finances now. It was time I take responsibility for them, no matter what they'd reveal.

When I had finally composed myself, I entered the username and password written inside the folder. Then I took a deep breath, closed my eyes and pushed ENTER.

When I opened my eyes, the screen read, *"We did not recognize the information you entered. Please check the information and try again."*

Okay. So I tried again, carefully, deliberately typing each character and saying it out loud. Same error message. Damn! I tried a third time. This time the system locked me out. It was a bust. I called the local branch to see if they could help me gain access, but they said I had to come in and bring along a copy of Jennair's death certificate, a document I had already come to hate, a morbid, sober reminder that Jennair was dead. Its sole purpose was to prove I wasn't falsifying my wife's death for my own gain. But as I'd already discovered in the short time since her death, each time I was asked to produce this certificate, I had to endure the awkward moment of presenting yet another stranger with the painful, intimate details of my wife's official cause of death. Line 26 a: "Single Perforating Gunshot Wound of the Head."

The next morning, I waited nervously in the bank's parking lot before it opened, looking at everyone with suspicion as they passed by. I'm not usually one to self-aggrandize my position or importance in the world. If anything, I struggle more with self-confidence and accepting compliments and praise. But just days before, my name and face had been plastered across television and computer screens around the world, branding me as the cheating husband whose extramarital affair had caused two women's deaths. Especially in the Philadelphia market, I felt like I was public enemy number one. Admittedly paranoid, constantly looking over my shoulder, I was convinced someone would recognize me, publicly accost me, or worse.

As I entered the bank I was keenly aware of the cameras that were pointed at me. Nervous as a novice bank robber, I did what I could to act normal, but that probably just made me stick out even more. Within seconds of entering the lobby, a young woman approached me. She introduced herself as the branch manager and asked if she could help me. I told her I was there to access my late wife's account.

"Her name?" she asked.

I paused and scanned the room to see who might be listening. Without saying a word, I gestured with my head toward her office, as if to say, "Let's talk in there."

"Thank you," I said, as we stepped into her office, "this is kind of sensitive." I gave her Jennair's name and account number and handed her a copy of the death certificate. "I just need a statement of her activity since she opened it back in March," I pleaded, unable to shake the feeling that I was somehow doing something wrong.

"Of course," she said, entering the account information into the computer. I wasn't sure if she recognized Jennair's name or not. God, I hoped not. I just wanted to get what I needed and get out of there. After a few keystrokes, I heard the soft mechanical whir of the printer behind her warming up and in less than a minute, she handed me a still warm two-page statement, which I slipped into my bag, and then thanked her and walked out the door.

Back in the car, I wanted so much to comb through the statement, but I had to be at work in less than ten minutes. As was the usual routine, I had back-to-back meetings throughout the day and wouldn't be able to look at it until I got home. But no matter how hard I tried to focus on the work before me, I couldn't keep my mind off what was in the bag I'd placed under my desk. While I had a brief opportunity after lunch to peek at it, I resisted the temptation. I didn't want to risk someone walking over to my desk while I was obviously distracted by a highly sensitive personal matter, particularly given how chilling the atmosphere at work had become. My coworkers continued to avoid me, speaking to me only when necessary and quickly departing. If I entered a room where people were engaged in conversation, it quickly turned to silence and they scattered, each one eager to return to their offices or cubicles or wherever it was they felt safer or less awkward.

I swear it was the longest workday of my life, and when it finally came to an end, I grabbed the bag from under my desk and rushed home, opened a bottle of wine and settled in to read a simple bank statement, something that in any other context would be as uneventful as reviewing the water bill. Yet I knew intuitively that what I was about to read in that statement would be more than just an interesting reminder of all the things Jennair had spent money on over the past month and a half. But nothing could have prepared me for what I was about to discover. Jennair's bank statement, so seemingly benign, told a truly chilling tale—revealing a secret, dark side of my wife I could never have guessed existed. It would also leave me with the unmistakable conclusion that the murder and suicide that had been Jennair's final acts on earth were no mere acts of sudden rage. The madness that had lived inside my wife had left a long and frightening trail I would relentlessly pursue for months, as day by day I uncovered another dark and diabolical twist and turn in her obsession to destroy me.

It was all there in descending order and startling detail. Coffee, donuts, a salad, and a full tank of gas just minutes before Jennair had broken into Meredith's home and lay in wait. And just two hours before, an hour of target practice at a firing range in nearby Chadd's Ford, Pennsylvania, just minutes over the Delaware state line. Target practice. While I was at work and dreaming of a new future with Meredith, Jennair was rehearsing her murder.

Nervously, as my hands shook and I felt the heat in my heart rise, I continued to quickly scan the list of transactions back in time, first through April and then beginning at the end of March. And then, there it was. It jumped right off the page.

"Fuck!" I said out loud. On March 20, a Tuesday morning at 10 a.m., Jennair, an outspoken anti-gun advocate for as long as I had known her, had gone to a gun shop, bought a gun, walked out and drove home with it. This had actually happened. Until then, I had been in denial. Somehow it was easier to just accept she'd shot the gun than to consider she had actually purchased it—and done so not on some mad impulse earlier that fateful day, but nearly one month before taking Meredith's life and then her own.

Stunned and now angry, I scanned forward in time to look for other major purchases. March 27 for a two-hour handgun class. March 29, twenty-three dollars for target practice at the firing range. And then again on April 20. My God, she'd been practicing her skill for weeks. With each shot fired, I imagined her fantasizing about the ruinous pain she would inflict, and the final justice she would ultimately serve.

April 9, thirty-one dollars at Discount Beauty Store in downtown Wilmington for what I assumed was the purchase of that wig. An ominous disguise, as she mercilessly pursued her insatiable thirst for revenge. My anger soon gave way to a sick feeling and a dull ache in my head and neck. I pushed the papers away on the kitchen counter and refilled my empty wine glass.

The next morning, I awoke on the couch, startled, abruptly sitting up. "March 27. March 27? Why does that seem so familiar?" I wondered out loud, thinking of the day she'd spent two hours in a handgun training class. I opened my laptop and pulled up the Google calendar Meredith and I had shared to make personal appointments. March 25. March 26. March 27. There it was. While I was driving back from the job interview with my soon-to-be new employer, Jennair was sitting in a gun store, being trained to kill. She had asked me to call her from the road to let her know how the interview had gone.

"Hey," I said when I heard her pick up[1].

"Hey," she returned. "Are you on the other phone and am I on speaker phone, so Meredith can hear me?"

"No," I said, irritated. "How would she be able to hear you?" It had been two months since Jennair had discovered the truth about me and Meredith, and in just that short time she'd seemed to come to accept that Meredith was now a part of my life as we steadily eased into divorcing on civil, if not strained, terms. Still, I bristled each time she slipped Meredith's name into our conversation, always spoken of coldly, if not triumphantly.

"Okay," she replied, still with a tinge of mistrust. "So why didn't you answer your phone when I called?"

"I was at Starbucks, trying to send a thank you letter," I said defensively.

"Oh, so you just got out?" she asked, surprised.

"Yeah, it was—" I started, before she cut me off.

"So how do you feel about it?" Her tone had softened, becoming sweet and supportive. I began to relax.

"I don't want to be overconfident," I said. "I tried to be as positive and upbeat as possible, because—"

---

[1] Recorded conversation dated March 27, 2018.

"What about the marketing person, overlapping to the creative director, like we talked about?" Now she was excited, diving right into the details of the position. She was actually interested. "And what about learning Spanish? Do you have to learn Spanish?"

"I don't have to," I said. "But they strongly encourage it." Because the company managed properties throughout Latin America and most of senior management and many of its clients were from Latin America, learning to speak Spanish made a lot of sense.

"Spanish or Portuguese?" she asked, again, so inquisitive about the details of the job despite our pending divorce.

"Spanish. Just Spanish," I clarified.

"How did you feel about the people and the culture?"

"Well, I mean," I explained, "they said everyone gets along great."

"So how did you feel about the drive and the town?"

"It's so close to Wilmington," I said. "Just sixteen—"

"Yeah," she cut in. "It's not very far at all, to be honest. But what about the town, I mean, did it feel janky or nice and developed?"

"It's nice," I said. "And it's not that far from Philly, so—"

"So when do they want you?" she asked. "The second week of April, did you say?"

"Yeah. I told them I could start on April 16," I confirmed. "I might hear something yet this week. So I guess we'll see. I'm going to give my two weeks at UD, and I have two weeks of vacation coming, so," I paused, "I'll just quit and start work the next day."

"Yeah, but didn't Meredith get paid for that when she did that?" she asked, sending chills down my spine. Meredith did get paid for her vacation days when she resigned, but how did Jennair even know that? But before I could ask, Jennair continued. "They just cut her a check for what they owed her, right?"

"Well, look," I said uncomfortably, my mind still swirling around the fact that Jennair knew such a random fact about Meredith's pay. But I knew this was neither the time nor the way to confront her. "I'm not going to get my hopes up just yet, so—"

"Okay," she shifted gears. "Well, you might want to stop and get a bite to eat on the way back in."

"Yeah," I replied, surprised how quickly she had so effortlessly shifted into her role as the doting wife.

"But don't leave that food in your car though," she added.

"Mm-hmm," I said dutifully, knowing I couldn't get off the phone without instructions on something as simple as how to feed myself.

Then, out of nowhere, she added, "So, not to beat a dead horse," her voice down-shifting into an octave of utter disdain. "I suppose you already talked to Meredith and told her about the job, didn't you?"

I paused. I smelled a trap. Standing in the parking lot before I had even gotten back into my car, I had just gotten off the phone with Meredith before I called Jennair. But instinctively I knew telling Jennair the truth in that moment would serve no purpose other than to escalate an otherwise civil conversation into a war of words. "No," I lied, then said nothing, hoping she would change the subject.

"Are you wearing your suit back to the office?" she asked, oddly.

"No. Changing on the way back," I replied.

"Well, you better wait until you get to the parking lot," she said with a chuckle. "You don't want to die on the way to work."

"Yep," I said, cutting her off. Then, shifting the conversation from me to her, I asked, "What are you doing?"

"Umm, I'm…." she hesitated. "I'm eating lunch. I'm hungry. And then I'm going back home to finish up taxes." It was just the answer she knew I was looking to hear.

"Okay," I said, wrapping up the conversation. "Have a good day. I love you."

"Okay. Love you. Bye," she said, and then hung up.

I assumed that on the other end of the line she was at home, sitting at her computer as she always was when I got home from work. But she wasn't. She was calling from the gun store, where she was taking a two-hour class on how to use a handgun. But on whom? Herself? Meredith? Me? All of us? What had been her plan the day she'd bought that gun?

Later that same day I received a formal job offer over the phone, just ten minutes before Meredith had received her offer from Villanova. At the time it had felt like such an auspicious sign we were meant to be together. Now it felt like a deathly omen.

"Goddammit!" I shouted and threw the bank statement across the kitchen, where it landed between the stacks of corrugated boxes her parents had helped me carry in from the moving truck. "These damn boxes! What the hell is even in them?" I wondered out loud, not caring if the neighbors heard. Somehow all the material crap that surrounded me now seemed so meaningless, so absurd, now that so much life had been destroyed. I looked at the boxes as if they were my adversary, not our once cherished belongings.

I grabbed a box cutter from the counter and recklessly sliced through the tape on the top box and ripped open the flaps. "Candles! Candles?" I said loudly in disgust. Inside the box were dozens of multi-colored scented candles and ornate glass votives, each wrapped meticulously in bubble wrap and newspaper. Sitting on the floor and sliding the box out of the way with my foot, I cut open the next one. "Canning jars!" I said in disbelief, freeing one from its neatly wound plastic and paper cocoon. "When did we ever *can* anything?" Again, I slid the box to the side. Then another. And another. Animal figurines. Ornate plaster cast cornices. Wine corks. Dozens of boxes full of knickknacks and reminders of our years together, schlepped from one house to another for ten, twenty years. Our ever-growing stockpile of things hardly worth the intrinsic sentimental value she told me they held for her. I hadn't dared touch them during our marriage, nor ask her to part with any of it, not since that first time early in our marriage when I'd thrown out her magazines. But she wasn't here anymore. She had made a choice. A choice about the value of life. Now it was up to me to make a choice. A choice about the value of things.

My breath began to quicken, my heart raced and my eyes swelled with tears. Without saying a word I grabbed a box, flung open the door and walked down the hall, past the elevator and to the trash chute. I paused for a moment, looking down at the box, and then force-fed it into the square metal receptacle in the wall and then gave it a final shove. After three seconds of eerie silence, the time it took to get from the fourth floor to the compactor in the basement, I heard the most exquisitely violent metallic clatter.

Exhilarated, I practically ran back down the hall to my apartment, grabbed another box and pushed it too down the chute to the same calamitous end. One after the other. *Crash!* My face now red and swollen from tears, I went back to my kitchen for the last box, which had already been opened. As I picked it up, I noticed among a few other odds and ends inside, a glossy black box emblazoned with a bold abstract graphic of a bull, and white letters that spelled out TAURUS. I let out an exhausted sigh.

It was the box the gun had come in.

"I told them not to leave it here!" I said out loud in frustration. "I don't want this fucking thing near me!" I reached down, plucked it out of the box, walked down the hall and pushed it against the chute. My heart, flooded with adrenaline, was now pounding loudly against my ribcage. All I could hear was my own breath and a voice that kept telling me, "Do it." But I couldn't. I couldn't. For some reason, I couldn't bring myself to get rid of the damn thing. Deflated, I carried it back to my apartment, sat it on the kitchen counter and walked away.

After pouring my coffee and picking up the statement from the floor, my mind exhausted from my tantrum, I sat back down to resume my work from the night before. As I again began scouring every debit purchase on her bank statement, I again saw the name of the gun shop where she had purchased the murder weapon.

Where is that? I wondered, and then, curious, I Googled it.

No way, I thought in disbelief. *This has to be a coincidence.*

I clicked on Google maps, and there it was. Startled, I clicked on my mouse and used it to turn the street view 180 degrees, and sure enough, directly across the street was the coffee shop where Meredith and I had met so many times to discuss our plans for our new life together. Jennair could have chosen any number of places to buy a gun. This choice was no accident. Again, that sick, uneasy feeling returned to my stomach. She'd been sitting outside, watching us. And watching the gun shop.

For the next few days, as I continued to unload my life of all the boxes of old memories that filled my new home, I grew obsessed with what I had just learned. I couldn't stop imagining the scenario. Late one Tuesday morning, while I was interviewing for a new job, Jennair had strolled into a gun store, bought a gun and called me to chat about my future job like any loving wife would do. I couldn't wrap my head around it. I had to see it for myself for it to be real. I had to get to that gun shop.

CHAPTER 13

BUY, SELL, TRADE

That box. That damn gun box still sat on my kitchen counter, taunting me, just daring me to do something with it. Where did she keep the gun? In the box? In her closet? Under a pile of clothes in the laundry basket where her aunt had found the box? I walked over to the counter and picked it up, held it up to my ear and shook it. Something was inside. I sat it back down on the counter and opened the lid. There looking back at me was Jennair's signature on a credit card receipt for $554.95, and right next to the salesman's name a notation, "Register failed and took whole amount in cash." Jennair and I almost never carried cash, just one more thing that made the whole thing not seem real. Late on a Tuesday morning, Jennair strolls into a gun store and buys a gun, with cash. Impossible. I had to go there and see this place for myself for it to be real. If I saw the gun shop for myself, maybe I could somehow understand the truth—that Jennair really had walked into one. But why stop there? Why not ask to see the same gun and feel the weight of it in my hands? Why not buy it and go to the same firing range Jennair went to? Why not pull the trigger and feel the kickback and hear the sound reverberate in my own ears? Why not? Why not put myself in Jennair's place to somehow try to understand what she'd felt and done in the last few weeks of her life?

On a hot Sunday afternoon, I left the parking lot of the church where I had started attending every week with friends who had reached out after that life changing day. Turning left on 202 would take me back home. I turned right.

As I pulled into the parking lot, my hands were wringing with sweat on the black leather steering wheel. Overhead, I saw the giant red and white sign. GUNS - BUY • SELL • TRADE. I pulled into a shady spot on the north side of the building and sat there for more than ten minutes with the air conditioner blaring. *Well*, I thought, *at least I made it this far*, fully expecting to lose my nerve and pull away. But out of the corner of my eye, I caught sight of a security camera mounted to the side of the building, pointing straight at my car. It was official. I was there.

I got out of my car and walked up to the door, carrying the black box, which was almost too hot to hold from sitting in the sun on the back seat of my car. I took one last deep breath and opened the door.

"Hi. Help you?" a portly man asked with a slightly backwoodsy drawl.

"Is Jason here by chance?" I asked in return.

"Nope. He's off on Sundays. Somethin' I can help you with?"

Holding out the now open box, I couldn't believe what came out of my mouth next. "I want to buy this exact gun. The same one my wife bought."

Peering into the box, he scratched his head, confused. "Lose it?"

"No," I replied. "It's in police custody."

Nodding, he seemed surprised, but not that surprised—like he heard that a lot. "Oh. Well... I hope everything worked out okay, that she's safe and all. Yeah, it sucks. Once a gun is fired as part of an incident, they don't usually give it back."

"Hmm," I said simply, not wanting to give him the full story. I was actually surprised and thankful he didn't recognize me. My face had been splashed across the news for two weeks.

Handing him the purchase receipt, I asked, "Can I get this exact gun?"

He studied the receipt intently and started to walk toward a locked display case on the back wall, motioning me to follow. The glass case was stocked floor to ceiling with guns of various brands, sizes and calibers. Pointing to the spot in the display where that particular gun should be, he said, "Well, it looks like we got the two-inch barrel and we got the six-inch barrel, but what your wife got there was the four-inch. Basically the same gun, just a different length barrel. If you want, I can order it for you."

"Just like that?" I asked.

"Well, I'd need to do the background check on you. Doesn't take long. And then take a deposit. But yeah, I can get you that gun," he replied confidently.

What I really wanted to ask was, "Is that what my wife did? She just did a background check and walked out of here with a gun?" But I couldn't find the cojones to ask. I later checked online and I was shocked to learn that Delaware has no waiting period to buy a gun, as long as you're a resident. According to the law, the gun shop did everything by the book. They did a standard background check. But Jennair didn't have a felony conviction. Nor had she committed a misdemeanor of a violent nature. So she checked out.

Just as I would have. For all that salesman standing in front of me knew, my wife had bought that gun to use on me and I was now buying the same one to use on her. He showed no curiosity—just a willingness to replace the weapon the police had seized with another one just like it.

Losing my nerve, I told the guy I'd have to think about it, and then walked out of the store into the stifling heat. I was shaking and sweating. I wanted to throw up.

Two days later I was sitting on my patio eating dinner by myself when my phone rang. It was the Delaware State Police. Hesitantly, I tapped the green ANSWER button.

"Hello?" I said suspiciously.

"Mister Gerardot?" a male voice said.

"What can I do for you?" I asked without acknowledging his question.

"This is Detective Smith from the Delaware State Police. We need to talk to you. We're sitting outside your apartment. Can you come out?"

"Where are you?" I asked.

"In your parking lot in Greenville," he replied.

"I don't live there anymore," I said frankly.

"Well, shit, he doesn't live here anymore," he said to someone else close by, slightly muffled as if covering the phone. The other person said something back to him, but it was inaudible.

"Where do you live now? We'll come there," the detective said.

I stared up at the sky without answering. My world had been turned completely upside down. For weeks I had been hounded by the press, ostracized by friends at UD, and I was living somewhat covertly in the suburbs of Philadelphia. I wasn't sure who knew my identity and who didn't. Just walking alone at night or in a parking garage was unnerving, constantly checking over my shoulder, waiting for someone to approach me, finish me off. Outside of a handful of friends, I didn't trust anyone.

"I'm not telling you where I am," I finally told him. "I don't know that you are who you say you are. You could be the press or who knows."

"Well, shit!" the detective said in frustration. "What if I send you a photo of my badge?"

"Alright," I agreed.

Within seconds I got a text message with a photo attached. Detective John W. Smith. Not even someone pretending to be a cop would choose that name, I thought.

"Okay, so you're a detective," I said to him. "What do you want to talk about? Why all of a sudden is DSP getting involved in this case? I told Radnor detectives everything I know."

"This ain't about that case," he said bluntly. "Can we come talk to you?"

"No," I said. "Were talking right now. What is this about?"

"Well, shit," the detective blurted. "I'm not allowed.. I have to talk to you in… Fuck it. Okay, look…" he sighed and then paused. "You tried to buy a gun and now I have to come talk to you."

"What? My wife buys a gun in Delaware and walks out with it that same day? No questions. No hassle. I *don't* buy a gun, and I get a call from the Delaware State Police?" I asked, outraged.

As it turns out, the portly backwoodsy gun salesman did feel uneasy about my inquiry and had reported my visit to the ATF. There had been just the one recent sale of a four-inch Taurus Tracker, so it wasn't hard for the store and ATF to put it all together. I wasn't sure if I should be pissed off or impressed. I opted for slightly disgruntled.

It was clear that Detective Smith wasn't going to give up. His orders were to follow up with me and have a face to face discussion to make sure I wasn't going to do anything stupid. Clearly, just by walking into the gun store, I had already crossed that line. We agreed to meet at a neutral halfway point, a grocery store parking lot in Chadds Ford, Pennsylvania, a twenty-minute drive for us both.

As I approached the parking lot, I saw a Pennsylvania State Trooper interceptor, parked, with blue lights flashing. Outside the car stood two neatly uniformed officers standing at attention next to their vehicle. Parked perpendicular to it, there was an un-marked red Ford Fusion with a man in street clothes, standing, arms propped against the open driver's side door. As I parked and exited my car, he walked forward to meet me halfway.

"Thanks for coming out here," he said, with his right hand ex-tended, offering to shake. "I know it's kind of bullshit, but I have my orders."

"Okay," I said, shaking his hand. "So now what?"

"I have to call our crisis prevention line and have you talk to a counselor. They just want to know you're not going to hurt your-self," he assured me. "Will that be okay?"

I nodded. Detective Smith then dialed a number, introduced himself to the person on the other end of the line, and then hand-ed me his phone.

"This is Mark." I said tentatively.

"Hi, Mark," a female voice greeted me. "Can you tell me why you were trying to buy a gun?"

I sighed, then answered, "Research."

"Research?" she asked. "For what?"

"I just wanted to know what my wife went through, what it felt like to be in a gun store and how it felt to buy a gun. That's it. It was stupid, I know," I admitted, now embarrassed. What was I "researching," after all? My wife's mind?

"I just need to know you're not going to hurt yourself. Have you...Do you feel like you're going to hurt yourself?" she asked. The concern in her voice seemed genuine.

"No." I said directly "I'll admit, I'm not good. But no, I'm not going to hurt myself. As bad as things are, I need to see how this life turns out."

The only problem was, my life wasn't turning out so well. It was getting darker every day.

CHAPTER 14

#TIMESUP

Jennair's bank statement told a disturbing story about a side of the woman I had loved for twenty-eight years, a side of her I didn't know was possible.. Troubling behavior she kept hidden, not just from me, but from everyone she knew well and those she had just met. A gun. A wig. Target practice. GPS tracking devices. Looking at her, talking to her, you would have never known. When she wanted to, she could present herself as normal—cooking, shopping and actively looking for employment. But the truth was all right there in black and white and excruciating detail. Every item, price and purchase date—a perfectly preserved timeline that underscored her gift for meticulous planning as much as her capacity for malicious intent. But it didn't tell the whole story. She had opened that account just two months prior to her killing and suicide, on February 21, but by that time, she had already been wreaking havoc on Meredith and me for weeks—recording conversations, cloning my phone, meeting with Meredith's husband, sending a letter to our employer. I knew it was going to take a lot more digging, documenting and remembering to understand the full extent of her elaborate plot. But I had plenty of time on my hands, so I got to work.

I began downloading every credit card statement, phone bill and email I could get my hands on, spreading them across my desk and plotting important dates on my calendar, painstakingly trying to connect all the dots. And while I couldn't find it on any piece of paper in front of me, I just knew in my gut that it had all started on New Year's Eve.

The minute the words had come out of my mouth that night, the words that had set everything in motion, I couldn't believe I'd said them, and wished so much that I hadn't. I didn't plan on telling her—at least not then and certainly not in that way. If I had, I would have told her before she'd moved to Delaware so she could have made a choice about her future. As much as I was lovestruck by Meredith, I didn't know where it would go. I'd made no decision about ending my marriage to Jennair. But she had provoked me, controlling me like only she knew how to do, ordering me to tell her, challenging me as a "fucking pussy." I'd grown so tired of her orders and her putdowns.

"I want my independence. I want out," I had told her, looking her square in the eyes.

As soon as I heard myself say those words, I knew I had to do damage control.

"Look, I don't know if I even mean that," I said, trying to recover. "I need time to think about this. Forget what I said."

She didn't say a word.

I explained that living alone for four weeks had given me a sense of freedom and independence that I had been missing for so long. I decided when to get up, what I was going to do, what I was going to eat and when I was going to be home.

She paused to process my explanation and then calmly asserted, "It's Meredith, isn't it? I told you not to fall in love with her."

"No. It's not Meredith. It has nothing to do with her," I lied. "Seriously, just forget I said anything. It's late. I didn't mean what I said. I shouldn't have said anything."

I was surprised that worked. The questions stopped and eventually she turned out her light and fell asleep. But in the morning, the barrage of questions started again. But I wouldn't give in. She pressed and pressed about Meredith, but I denied it like my life depended on it. The stakes were just too high. I was Meredith's direct report, and while I hadn't read the UD employee handbook cover to cover, I knew it wouldn't look good for either of us. More importantly, I hadn't actually made the decision to leave Jennair. In fact, I was still struggling with the thought of it. I needed time.

Hours became days. Days became weeks. Occasionally Jennair continued to press me about what I had said on New Year's Eve and I continued to minimize its significance. I tried to convince her I had made a mistake and wished I hadn't said it. Or perhaps I was trying to convince myself. But I knew her too well, and I could tell she wasn't buying it. We were quietly suspicious of each other but resumed our normal routine. We doted on Huck, who was struggling to adjust to winter. He was born and raised in the South and couldn't comprehend why we had dragged him to the frozen tundra of Delaware. Jennair bought him coats, a scarf and boots, which became great fodder for Instagram and a welcome distraction from the strain and discomfort between us.

By mid-month I thought we had really turned a corner when Jennair asked me to go with her to the second annual Women's March in Washington. I was surprised she asked. But I think she was more surprised I accepted. "Really?" she said. "You sure you know what you're signing up for? Lots of angry women…"

"Absolutely," I said. "I think it will be fun."

"Awesome," she replied cheerfully, smiling like I hadn't seen her do in weeks. "Cause I didn't want to take the train by myself." Then, in an instant, she pulled up the train schedule on her computer and began buying our train tickets.

"Let's go as early as possible," she said excitedly. "We'll get breakfast somewhere in D.C."

"Okay. You plan it," I told her. "I'll do whatever. This is your thing. I'm just going along for the ride."

The night before the march, Jennair stayed up late to create large posters for us to carry. CHANGE THE THINGS YOU CANNOT ACCEPT. #TIMESUP, she wrote in blue and hot pink marker.

"You wrote this?" I asked. "That's really good."

"Seriously? Thanks," she said, basking in the moment with pride. And in that moment, I saw a glimpse of the proud young woman I had married—and wondered where she'd gone.

Our signs in hand, on a brisk January morning we stood on the platform in Wilmington, watching the sun rise while waiting for the first train out to D.C. We wanted to get there early enough to get a great spot on the mall. While Jennair stood guarding her signs from being bent in the frigid wind, I sipped from a cup of coffee, letting the warmth of the wet steam waft onto my cold face. As the sound of the train approached, passengers edged closer, and I got into position to get the perfect sunrise shot of it for Instagram. Not long after we boarded, we smiled together for another Instagram moment and then both drifted off to sleep. Two hours later we were standing with 100,000 other men, women and children, listening to courageous, outspoken women whip the crowd into a frenzy of pride. It was a proud moment for us both to be a part of such an important historical event.

As Jennair stood there beaming with her sign hoisted high, I snapped another pic and posted it to Facebook "#Marchon JennairGerardot" the caption read. I felt immensely proud of her for wanting to be there and for putting the whole trip together. Later we marched to the White House, where she and her sign even made NBC Nightly News that evening, which she proudly shared on her Facebook page.

When we got back to Wilmington, New Year's Eve seemed like a distant memory. The stress seemed to lift and we began exploring the local food scene together, visiting museums and touring homes we were considering leasing. I was easing back into a comfortable routine with Jennair, but in the back of my mind I still silently wrestled with my feelings for Meredith. Our only time together had been limited to stolen moments at the office, coffee before work and an occasional drink after work. Privately Meredith and I talked about a possible future, the trips we might take and the many things we would do together. But as careful and discrete as we tried to be, it wasn't enough. And it must have showed. Eating dinner at home one night, Jennair dropped a bomb.

"So, you're in love and you're planning your future together," she said calmly.

"What are you talking about?" I said bewildered.

"You and Meredith are making plans to be together. Don't deny it. I fucking heard you!" she said sharply.

"Heard us? What did you…How? When?" I stammered.

"I have a whole team of people working with me," she said smugly. "People at the bookstore, at Starbucks, at the bar next door. Who knows, maybe even people you work with. I can hear everything you fucking say."

I didn't believe her, but I didn't know what to believe. Was she just guessing? No. She knew specifics. She started quoting things I had confided privately to Meredith in her office, in my office and even things that were discussed in team meetings. It was both un-settling and bewildering.

"I hired a private investigator with a parabolic microphone," she boasted with pride. But this time her pride was different. In-stead of basking in a compliment, she was proud of herself for hav-ing conjured up this story. "You know, like the ones they use on the sidelines of a football game. He can hear everything you and Meredith say from the street outside your office. So, I'd be careful what you say."

Again, I didn't believe her. I looked everywhere in my office for bugs. Nothing. I rifled through drawers, crawled under my desk. I found nothing. *How in the hell?* I wondered. I didn't know how she was doing it, but whatever it was she was up to, I could tell she was just getting started.

Now, scouring more than ten credit card statements spread out on my desk, I searched for purchases made in January. Noth-ing jumped out. Not until the very last day of the month, January 31, Meredith's thirty-third birthday, just barely a week after the Women's March. For twenty-nine dollars, Jennair had purchased a background check on Meredith, instantly downloading everything about her—every phone number she had ever had, the address of her current home, its assessed value, the names of her relatives, her employment history, right down to the items on her Amazon wish list. I later found the electronic file in her email and read all 112 pages of it. It was useless information, but it was a disturbingly remarkable document, nonetheless.

Five days later, on February 5, the day after the Eagles were crowned Super Bowl LII champions, Meredith and I had a meeting in downtown Philadelphia with our agency. It was a half-day planning meeting to discuss the rollout of UD's new brand, but then Meredith and I planned to spend the other half of the day downtown just relaxing and talking. I told Jennair I had a full day meeting in Philly with Meredith, which naturally made her very uncomfortable.

"Let me go with you. I'll drive you guys," she said with a straight face.

Of course, I wasn't going to let that happen. It was inappropriate to even suggest it. But it did make it crystal clear I needed to be careful.

Before sunrise on the morning of the meeting, I watched my rearview mirror closely as I drove to meet Meredith in Wilmington. I pulled into a gas station to see if Jennair was following me. But I didn't see her car. I was just being paranoid, I convinced myself.

After the meeting with the agency which lasted for more than three and a half hours, Meredith and I walked up the street to a coffee shop to escape the cold and to just talk. It had been weeks since we had been able to openly be ourselves but being away from campus and Wilmington gave us the opportunity to let down our guard. We walked hand in hand, ducking into shops and the lobby of the Benjamin Franklin Hotel to warm ourselves and watch people pass by on the sidewalk. Eventually we decided on a cozy Italian restaurant and spent the rest of the afternoon where we always felt most comfortable—at the bar, sipping Cabernet, staring at each other with wonder, deep in conversation that seemed to have no end.

Up until that day, I had so many doubts about a future with Meredith. Our first few months had been incredible, but in so many ways I felt she was way out of my league. She could have had anyone she wanted. She was that amazing. Why did she want to be with me, a man fifteen years older? I challenged her to be honest with herself and with me. But she was sure about what she wanted.

"I want *this*," she told me, pointing to herself and then me. "I want this."

I did too, but at what cost? Her confidence about us gave me confidence, but was I prepared to destroy someone else's life for my own happiness? There were no guarantees Meredith and I would work out. In fact, the odds were stacked against us. But as usual, being around this amazing person for even a short amount of time energized me and instilled in me the feeling that together we could do anything.

That afternoon at the bar she felt compelled to finally tell me that back in December she had applied to be the assistant vice president of marketing at Villanova, and she was on the short list of contenders. The thought of not working with her was a blow. It meant giving up on everything we had planned to accomplish together. But it also meant having a future together that far exceeded either of our expectations. Ultimately, however, the decision to leave UD was largely out of our control until and unless one or both of us found new jobs. Fate would ultimately decide our future.

We talked for hours, sipping wine, laughing and occasionally holding hands. Before we knew it, we realized we had been so wrapped up in the conversation that we hadn't even eaten dinner. It was getting late, so we ordered a pizza for the road. And on the forty-five-minute ride back to Wilmington, I fed her pizza as she

175

drove. We laughed. We kissed. We sang. We were us again, and it felt amazing.

When I got home, Jennair wasn't there. Thirty minutes later she walked in the door with Huck, but she wanted nothing to do with me. She went straight to bed, slamming the door behind her. She was furious, but I wasn't sure why, and I knew better than to ask. Instead I poured myself a glass of wine and settled in on the couch for the evening.

The next morning, I got up to make coffee and get ready for work. Suddenly the master bedroom door opened and Jennair came storming out, her hair tussled wildly, her hands on her hips. Everything in her demeanor told me to get ready for a fight. "You're a fucking asshole liar!" she blasted. "You guys had planned on spending the day together all along. Your meeting didn't last all day!"

"How do *you* know what I did yesterday?" I asked in defense. "Who says I didn't have meetings all day?"

"Because I fucking followed your ass," she yelled, her face turning a bright shade of pink. "I was one step behind you everywhere you went. And I heard everything you said."

I didn't put it past her. Certainly, she was capable of it. But after the many wild stories she had been telling me about her team of coconspirators, I didn't know what to believe. "Okay," I told her. "I wasn't in meetings all day, but Meredith and I talked about work and checked email constantly. We were basically working out of the office."

"You're so full of shit," she yelled in disgust. "I know what I saw. And I heard what I heard. You were holding hands all day and kissing the whole way home."

In that moment I felt hunted, trapped in my own lies and deceit. I was angry that Jennair had followed me. I was even angrier at myself for getting caught. I wanted so much to tell her the truth. But I just couldn't. I had to protect Meredith. I had to protect Jennair from the painful truth. I wasn't going to stop seeing Meredith, even if it meant the eventual end of my marriage. But at the same time, I wasn't ready to end my marriage. I couldn't let either of them go. I had to continue the lies. So I said nothing. I just looked at her, shook my head in denial and walked out the door.

Whatever she knew, however she knew it, Jennair knew more about my interactions with Meredith than I thought she could possibly know. Now, both of them gone forever, I thought back to the confrontation with Jennair that morning. I looked at my calendar. It had been on February 6. Nothing in the credit card statements came up for near that date. I turned to the phone bill. Maybe that would trigger some memories.

"Wait," I said out loud. "She made a call on February sixth." I scanned the phone bill, marked the date with a highlighter, and looked up the number. When I saw who she'd called, I was taken back. It was her first call to Meredith's husband. I'd forgotten about that. Now the memory of that call came rushing back.

I was at the office late on a Friday evening, trying to wrap up a few things before heading home, when I heard my phone buzz. It was a text from Meredith.

M: *Shit. I'm in the car with him. He's asking about Jennair.*
Mark: *What?*
M: *She called him. Told him we were having an affair.*
Mark: *Shit.*
M: *Hang on…. Can I call you and put you on speaker phone for him to hear?*

Mark: *Okay??!!*

Suddenly my phone rang. "Hello," I said as if I wasn't expecting the call.

"Hi Mark, it's Meredith," she opened. "I'm sorry to bother you on a Friday after work."

"That's okay," I played along. "What's up?"

"I'm with my husband, driving to an event," she said, setting the scene. "Can I put you on speaker phone?"

"Sure," I said nonchalantly.

"Jennair left a voicemail for my husband," she said seriously. "She told him that you and I are having an affair."

"What? That's crazy!" I said as convincingly as possible. "I'm so sorry to both of you."

"Well, I just wanted you to know..." she started.

"No, of course," I replied. "I'll have a conversation with her the minute I get home. She's obviously upset about me working so much. But calling you, she stepped over the line. I'll talk with her."

"Okay. thanks," she said. "Again, I'm sorry to bother."

"Not a bother," I interrupted. "I'm the one who should be sorry. Have a good night." I ended the call and took a deep breath, convinced we had just averted a crisis. When I got home, however, I didn't say a word to Jennair about it. I wanted to see what she would do next.

A few days later Meredith forwarded me an email from a woman neither of us knew. It was addressed to Meredith's husband, telling him once again that she and I were having an affair. Meredith and I met outside in an open area on campus to discuss it. We knew in our guts the letter had to have come from Jennair, using a fictitious name and email address. It was eerie and very unsettling to read. Meredith told her husband that Jennair had most likely sent the email because she was so convinced we were having an affair.

Later that night I confronted Jennair about the fictitious letter. She vehemently denied sending it, claiming instead that the woman who had written it was very real. But even more disturbing, Jennair seemed to know every detail of the conversation Meredith and I had just had earlier that same day, sitting out in the open on a campus quad. Again, she raised the specter of a team of people conspiring to watch our every move and hear our every word. "How else would I know?" she mused. Suddenly the use of a parabolic mic seemed more and more to be real. But the actual truth was about to get surreal.

On Friday of that week, two days after Valentine's Day, Jennair made dinner reservations for the two of us to celebrate the occasion as we would have done any other year. It was a rustic farm-to-table restaurant that had been converted from an old farmhouse, packed with couples sitting at small tables lined up one after another with just enough room for a server, and very little privacy for serious discussion. During dinner we kept our conversation to awkward small talk, avoiding any sensitive topics. But after dinner, the conversation took a dramatic turn the minute we walked through the door of our apartment. As though it had been eating at her for days and she couldn't hold it back anymore, Jennair took a deep breath and then unloaded.

"I cloned your phone and sent it away to get a copy of everything you have ever said. Every text. Every photo," she said, threatening me. "You've been lying to me from the start and now I'm going to get the truth."

For the first time, I truly began to understand what Jennair knew and the extremes to which she would go to find out what she didn't.

"Oh, I also sent your clothes away for DNA testing," she added. I stood there in the kitchen, stunned. Testing my clothes for DNA! She had taken her investigation to a whole other level. "If you've been fucking her, I'm going to find that out, too."

This time I believed her. Soon she would know everything. It was time to come clean.

"I'm in love with her," I said, thick with guilt.

"So, now you actually admit it?" she asked.

"Yes," I said unequivocally. Saying it out loud, I felt ashamed. I felt disloyal. But most of all, I felt liberated, no longer encumbered by lies and coverups. Three straight months is a long time to suppress the truth.

I told her how Meredith and I had just clicked shortly after I had started at UD. I explained that we hadn't planned it, but before we knew it, we had fallen in love. I apologized for not telling her earlier and told her that neither Meredith nor I knew what we wanted to do.

She paused, letting my words sink in, and then returned fire. "I met her husband. I told him everything."

"You what?" I said, closing my eyes and cringing to absorb the blow. She hadn't just called him, hadn't just emailed him—she had actually met him?

"I made an appointment under a fake name, saying I needed help with my investments," she boasted. "And when he came in the room, I told him I wasn't who I said I was and then played him a recording from you two in Philly." Then her whole demeanor changed, her pride fading to frustration. "But he didn't believe me.

He told me that he and his wife were happily married. And then he asked me to leave."

She began to cry. "This is such bullshit!" she screeched. "It's like you're all in this fucking thing together and I'm the only one getting hurt."

The conversation continued deep into the night. Before it was all said and done, we agreed to see a marriage counselor so someone could facilitate our conversation and determine our next steps. In my newfound freedom of truth, I felt it was the least I could do. I honestly welcomed the forum to share my side of the story and a moderator to help us untangle the mess our lives had become.

That night we had bared our souls to each other, a rare moment of complete honesty. But was it too little, too late? I had learned long before not to trust everything Jennair told me. For weeks she had been lying to me every bit as much as I had been lying to her. Our marriage had been reduced to a game of cat and mouse. She hunted me like a stealthy cat, and I hid from her like a timid but tricky mouse. It was no longer a marriage. It had become a performance.

Sitting at my paper-strewn table just three months later, all the lies we had told each other now seemed so pointless and perverted, as if each lie took us one step further toward our tragic fate. But credit card statements and phone bills don't lie. As I continued to align the credit card transactions with phone calls, the picture began to come into focus, confirming much of what she had told me about her interaction with Meredith's husband. But there was so much more that she had held back.

From Jennair's phone bill, I could see that she had called Meredith's husband's office at 10:31 a.m., two days before she said she met with him, most likely to set an appointment. But after she left the appointment, she made at least five more calls to him that afternoon, getting his voicemail each time. Early the next morning Jennair called him back once again, this time, actually speaking to him for thirty-five minutes. And again, four days later. All in all, there were over ninety-eight minutes of phone conversations between the two of them. *For what purpose? To what end?* I wondered, knowing I'd likely never know, since he wouldn't speak to me in light of Meredith's divorce from him—and her death at the hands of my wife.

Still, my curiosity about the calls only grew, especially given what else I knew Jennair had had up her sleeve that week. She had just gotten started.

CHAPTER 15

TIL HER DYING DAY

I could feel the hot sun on my face, the bright light burning through the lids of my eyes, relentlessly coaxing my mind toward consciousness. I slowly opened one eye, making out the blurry outline of an empty wine bottle and glass on the end table by my feet. I fumbled for my phone in the couch cushions, then the floor, finally finding the familiar shape of my digital appendage on the coffee table, and brought it to my one open eye. **8:37. Saturday, February 17.** I had to tell Meredith.

Mark: *He knows. She told him.*

M: *What?*

Mark: *Didn't believe her. Said you were happily married.*

M: *Okay…Interesting. Talk later?*

Mark: *Of course.*

Before I put my phone down, I saw that my email inbox was full of unread mail, but a message from Jennair stood out to me, titled, "Marriage Counselors." I clicked to open it. It was a list of local psychologists who specialized in family and marriage counseling. Lying in bed all night after I'd confessed my love for Meredith, it had seemed that Jennair had wasted no time in trying to save our marriage. I wasn't as committed to doing so, but I *was* committed to caring about Jennair and the history we'd shared together. A part of me did want our marriage to work. And a part of me, a big part of me, wanted to end it. If Jennair wanted us to see someone, I had no problem with that. After reviewing each of their credentials, I sent her a reply. "I'm happy with any of them. You choose."

I didn't know it then, but the list of counselors hadn't just come from hours of diligent overnight research on her part. According to media accounts that surfaced two days after her murder-suicide, Jennair had reached out for marriage counselor recommendations through social media and through NextDoor.com, two days before she had confronted me about being in love with Meredith.

"Please recommend an EXCELLENT marriage counselor for couple on brink of divorce," she wrote. "Does anyone recommend a marriage/couples counselor/therapist? We will need someone who is very educated and experienced dealing with couple issues including infidelity, depression, traumatic experiences, child/parent dynamics, being accountable for actions, etc......Hopefully there is someone with a good track record of helping couples communicate better and do the right work necessary to rebuild the relationship or even come to clarity about its probability of success."

People were so surprised she had made such a public plea for such a personal crisis. But not me. For years she had turned to social media for recommendations on doctors, local restaurants, or places to live. She hadn't known the area and now she was so desperate for help that she didn't care who knew. She had become an open book. But it hadn't always been that way.

In 2007, when I had finally caved to peer pressure and joined Facebook, Jennair thought I was crazy. "You want everyone to know what you're doing and where you are?" she'd ask. "Just keep me out of it." She was convinced someone was going to steal my identity or break into the house if anybody saw that we were on vacation or at dinner. To prove how risky my social media activities were, she would often log onto my account and lurk on my friends' activity and posts, then criticize them to me. "Why did he say that? Can you believe she posted that? Oh my God, her kids are so homely."

"If you want to be on Facebook," I told her, "you need to get your own account." But she refused, content to hide in the shadows behind mine. And I relented to having her there. More than a year later, when she finally succumbed to her own curiosity, she reluctantly joined Facebook to connect with family and eventually a few very select friends. More importantly, she soon came to realize the power of the Facebook platform. Within days she had joined animal rights groups and anti-gun groups, sounding off about hot topics and making comments on controversial posts. She absolutely loved the public venue and the stage it gave her to share her opinions and voice. And much like in person, Jennair had little filter, holding almost nothing back until, that is, Facebook closed her account, a claim to fame for which she was quite proud.

She couldn't help herself. Jennair saw a group of men who traveled to the Bahamas to hunt iguana and proudly posted photos of themselves cooking one over a roaring spit. "You're a fucking asshole for hunting defenseless animals," she wrote. That's all it took. The owner of the account complained to Facebook and, just like that, Jennair was banished. Within a week, she opened a new account and continued her newfound love of social media—a little wiser, but no less vocal or passionate about the causes and organizations that mattered most to her.

On Monday morning, I walked across the street from the campus bookstore to my office, two coffees in hand. Since sending her the text over the weekend about Jennair and Meredith's husband having met, I knew Meredith would be anxious to talk. But I didn't see her car in the lot, so I sent her a text.

Mark: *Your coffee is in my office. Come see me.*

M: *K. On the way.*

Five minutes later, Meredith walked into my office. "Hey," she said with a bright smile on her face.

"Hey," I said back. "Close the door, please." When she did, I stepped toward her and wrapped her in my arms and whispered in her ear, "I told her. I told her I'm in love with you," I confessed.

"What? Wow," she said in a mix of exuberance and fear, pulling away from my embrace. "How? What…"

"I had to," I said. "She cloned my phone. She sent it away and in a matter of days, she's going to know everything." I paused. "And she's going to *see* everything, if you know what I mean."

"Okay…." she said. "This just got very real." Then she shrugged. "Oh, well…"

"I know," I agreed. "Did he say anything to you yet?"

"No. I haven't even seen him," she said.

"He knows," I said. "So what is he up to?"

"Shut up and kiss me," she said with a beautiful smile, and pulled me back toward her.

Later that evening, Jennair was practically giddy watching me ironing my clothes, getting ready for work the next day. "So, you going into work tomorrow? Cause you're both about to get a big surprise."

"What?" I asked, setting the iron upright. "What in the hell have you done now?" An undefinable dread came over me as I imagined Jennair doing something to damage my and Meredith's lives—and careers.

Jennair just smiled, seeming to be enjoying the power she had over me.

"Oh, just wait," she chortled. "But it's not just me you have to look out for."

I stared at her. She was actually feeling something I hadn't seen in her in months—joy. But there was something else, something in her eyes, that I'd never seen before. Something frightening. Was it hatred? I didn't know. And I didn't dare ask. In that moment, standing there behind the ironing board, watching my wife delight in her ability to wound me, I didn't dare ask anything more. I didn't dare explode. I'd become a child about to be punished, somehow, some way. For doing something I knew was wrong. Whatever the punishment, it would be awaiting me at work, and it would be deserved. And my punishment would come again. And again. I wanted out. I wanted to be with Meredith. And I would take whatever punishment I had to in order to escape this madness and be with the woman I loved. I turned away from Jennair, picked up the iron, and finished pressing my pants.

That evening I got a call. Not recognizing the number, I let it go to voicemail. It was Glenn, the VP of marketing at UD. He wanted to meet first thing in the morning.

"Shit! You didn't. You wouldn't," I said under my breath. Of course she had. Of course she'd called him. Then almost immediately, Meredith sent a text message asking me to call her ASAP. I stepped out to walk Huck and called her.

"I just got out of a meeting with Glenn," she said tearfully. "He's separating us. You no longer report to me. You report to him."

"Goddammit!" I said loudly, catching the ear of a neighbor passing by. "She told him."

"Oh, and the video team reports to you now," she continued, her voice turning angry. "He's breaking up the team, basically demoting me. He said I can keep my title, but half my team is gone."

"To hell with him! You're going to get the Villanova job," I said to her. "You'll be fine. This means nothing to you. Your career won't even feel it."

"And what about you?" she asked.

"Me? I'm probably screwed."

"I don't think so," she said. "It didn't seem like he was going to do anything else. It's practically a promotion for you."

"I don't see it that way, babe," I told her, dismissing it. I knew I was the new guy. I was the one who was expendable. And Jennair had undoubtedly embellished her story in a way to make me out to be the most untrustworthy man this side of the Mississippi. At the age of forty-nine, I knew my career was going to take a hit that would be slow, if not impossible, to recover from.

But if what Meredith said was true, I reasoned, if in fact we still had jobs, then maybe this was actually good news. Our relationship would no longer be a conflict of interest. But there were no guarantees. At least I knew what Jennair's surprise would be, and it was a punishment I'd just have to take. I walked back to our apartment, removed Huck's leash, and said nothing. I didn't want to give Jennair the satisfaction that I knew, and that I was more than a little worried.

In the morning I met with Glenn, who confirmed what Meredith had told me, and then he announced it in an email to the team. Meredith and I knew exactly what the catalyst had been, but Glenn didn't give a reason for his sweeping decision, causing wild speculation and sending rumors throughout the team and half the university. It was just one more punch in the gut, one hitting closer and closer to Jennair's ultimate goal of destroying me.

Later that afternoon, driving to meet Jennair for our first marriage counseling session, I was seething. When I arrived at the counselor's office, in a converted house in a north Wilmington residential neighborhood, I immediately saw Jennair's car parked out front. I was five minutes late, and she had already gone inside. As I approached the door to the office entrance, I took a deep breath and collected myself, not knowing the buzz saw I was about to walk into. When I walked through the door, I saw Jennair sitting casually on one end of a sectional sofa, her arms wrapped around her legs, which were folded casually in front of her. Our therapist, a man in his fifties with a thick salt and pepper beard, sat behind his desk in a faded pair of Levis, his arms crossed comfortably behind his head. "Welcome," he said. "I'm Richard."

"Mark," I said, shaking his hand, quickly taking my place on the other end of the L-shaped sectional. Richard then opened with a seemingly simple question to us both.

"What do you hope to get out of our time together?" he asked. Jennair and I looked at each other and she gestured with her head for me to go first.

"I want clarity," I said bluntly. "I'm lost. When I moved here back in November, I fell in love with someone I work with—my boss. I want to understand how that's even possible, and ultimately make a decision. I know I've already hurt Jennair and I don't want to hurt her more. But I also don't think I can live without Meredith."

Jennair choked back tears as she began, "I want to reconcile. I want to save my marriage. I want Mark to stop seeing her and commit to working on us. We've been married for twenty-four years and now he wants to replace me."

"Do your coworkers know?" Richard asked me. "Do they know about you and uh…"

"Meredith," I finished his sentence. "No. Well, they didn't. Maybe now. Her boss certainly seems to. Apparently she called him, wrote him a letter or something," I said, looking directly at Jennair.

"Did you do that?" Richard asked Jennair, leaning in toward her.

"Maybe I did. Maybe I didn't," she said, not sure whether to be proud or ashamed. "But I'm not the one on trial here."

"Wow," he said. "Clearly there is a lot of hostility and pain between the two of you. But neither of you are on trial."

"She also told Meredith's husband," I told Richard. "She secretly recorded us and played it to him. She had my damn phone cloned."

"Look," he told Jennair. "I understand how you feel. Truly I do. But ending the relationship with Meredith is a decision Mark has to come to on his own. Love isn't something you can just turn off. If you force him, he will resent you for it. He won't forget her and he will always wonder if he gave up something wonderful. He may decide down the road that it isn't right, but you have to let his feelings run their course."

Jennair's whole demeanor changed as she listened to him speak, her arms now crossed tightly across her chest. Her face contorted with disdain, and her breath heaved in and out of her lungs like a seething bull, about to jump off the couch. "So basically you're giving him permission to have an affair," Jennair shouted. Then she began to cry. *"This is such bullshit!"* Clearly she had come hoping for a completely different answer, and now she was losing control.

In that moment, my heart ached for her. I wanted to slide over and just hold her. She hadn't expressed herself so vulnerably since I told her I wanted my independence on New Year's Eve. Practically everything she had said, everything she had done since New Year's Eve had been purely out of anger and spite—or so I had perceived. Now I could truly see how much she was hurting. But clearly there was a chasm between what each of us wanted, and more specifically, what we each hoped to get out of therapy. She had every right to be angry. To feel betrayed. To be hurt. And as Richard pointed out, she also had every right to leave, to file for divorce. But our marriage had become her identity, her reason for living, and she couldn't imagine starting over. I on the other hand couldn't imagine just giving up my feelings for Meredith. I still loved Jennair, but something was missing. Something for which I was willing to risk everything because I had found it in someone else.

"I think you both need to work on having empathy for the other's position. Right now, you are both rooted in your respective corners. And that's just not a constructive place to start."

It was a painful but helpful session and as we stood up and walked out and toward our cars, I grabbed Jennair's shoulder, turned her around and hugged her as hard as I could.

"What's that for?" she asked.

"Because I love you," I told her. "And I always will."

Frustrated and angry, she grumbled, "This is total bullshit. He's a male chauvinist quack." Again, she began to cry. Angrily, she wriggled her way out of my arms, hurried to her car and then drove away. When we got home, I told Jennair we could find someone else, another counselor. But she agreed and we decided to stick it out, to give him another chance.

The next morning, Meredith beat me to work. And as was customary, I climbed the stairs to her third-floor office to retrieve the coffee she had gotten for me at the bookstore across the street. When I walked into her office, she glanced up at me, didn't say a word, and then looked back down to her desk, shaking her head.

"You okay?" I asked.

"He's screwing me," she said angrily with tears in her eyes. "He's totally screwing me over. Look at this." She pushed a large bound document toward the front of her desk. "He wants me to admit to adultery, and then agree to an expedited divorce process."

"I'm so sorry," I said. "This happen last night?"

"*She* did this," she said, "And now he's punishing me. He said I could stay in the house, but I had to move out by April. I don't even know if I have a job yet."

"I know. I know," I consoled her. "You'll get it. It will all work out. Don't worry."

"Well, I'm not signing this," she said, "not until I talk to my lawyer tomorrow."

"Good," I said. "Yes. Talk to her first." I grabbed a tissue from the box on her desk and wiped her tears. "We'll get through this. I promise."

Later that afternoon, after a day of meetings, I walked toward my car a block away in the pouring rain. As I approached the parking lot, I was surprised to see Jennair walking Huck. "What are you..." I started to ask.

"I'm not here to argue with you," she contended. "I just want to talk."

"Get in," I said, unlocking my car and helping Huck into the back seat. Jennair got into the passenger seat and closed the door.

"Are you happy with yourself?" I started. "Did you get what you wanted? He's divorcing her. Is that what you wanted?"[2]

"I didn't do that directly," she said in defense. "The information I gave him convinced him to do what he did, and get some clarity for what he was already going to do. He heard something that convinced him of that. But I need to hear more. I need to hear details."

"No. I'm not giving you lurid details, Jennair."

"Why won't you tell me the truth?" she asked. "I have a recording that you guys did something. It all adds up to show that it's clearly more than professional."

"I told you it was more than professional. It's personal!" I yelled in frustration.

"I need to know details," she demanded. "I need it. I need it to move on. To make decisions."

"Give me your phone," I demanded. "I don't trust you." There could be only one reason she was asking me for "details" and that would be because she wanted me to say something incriminating—she was recording me.

"No," she said defiantly, pulling her phone away from my outstretched hand. "You're recording *me*. Are you recording me?"

"About what?" I asked, confused.

---

[2] Conversation from February 22, 2018 recording

"Go ahead. Feel me up!" And with that, Jennair started removing her clothes.

"I told you to give me your phone, not take your clothes off."

She stopped, then buried her head in her phone and began typing into it.

"What are you doing?" I asked. "Deleting the conversation you just recorded?"

"No," she answered. "I was deleting a text. Go ahead and look." She tried to hand me her phone.

"No," I raised my hands, refusing to take it. "I'm not going to look at your phone. That's your private information. I won't."

"No, it's not," she protested. "We're a couple. It's not private, really."

Sitting in my car in the campus parking lot, the rain started to pick up. Soon a downpour opened from the sky, pounding my car with a deafening rhythm.

"We can't go forward with our lives," she said. "I can't get closure unless I know the whole truth. It's obviously bad because you don't want to tell me."

I had told her I was in love with Meredith, and now she was pressing me for more truth. "The whole truth." What more could I tell her? What kind of details did she want and why and what kinds of details would it take to constitute the whole truth?

"I don't want you to hear details," I pushed back. "It does you more harm than good."

"I am not recording you," she said inexplicably, and loudly, straining to be heard over the rain.

But she was of course recording me, recording us. Her phone had become her weapon, and every word spoken was intended for an audience—an audience I couldn't imagine but Jennair certainly had in mind.

"You're just trying to protect her til her dying day," she said in disgust. "You're protecting her to the grave, even now."

"Yes," I said, simply. "I am."

"Bottom line is, you shouldn't have done what you did, and this is part of the consequences." Again, the promise of another punishment, this time feeling even more ominous. "Maybe if you were truthful with me from the very beginning, I wouldn't have had to dig around like that and get exasperated and angry. You kept putting me off. Lying to me. And then stringing me along. And that was emotional abuse. And I couldn't take it anymore."

"Emotional abuse? How?" I asked.

"By being nice to me," she said with a whimper. "Making me feel like we had a chance." And then like a switch, her sadness turned to anger, her voice raising, demanding an immediate answer. "Right here and now! Tell me that you have no intention of working on our marriage at all! You have no interest in going to counseling again. And you do want a divorce. If that is how you truly feel."

"I told you like I told Richard," I said in frustration. "I don't want to make a rash decision or a wrong decision. He said slow it down. Let it play out. Understand your feelings. And then come out on the other side of it with clarity. I mean, that's what I need, Jennair."

But she had no patience for my indecision. She kept pushing and pushing for intimate personal and sexual details about my relationship with Meredith. And she wanted an immediate decision about our plans for the future. Nothing else would satiate her.

"I'm not going to use what you say against you. I'm not going to go cause any more trouble. Knowing is for me," she insisted. "I need to know for my own personal health."

"You just want to hurt her," I said.

"I don't want to hurt her," she professed. "I just wanted to level the playing field. All I ever wanted to do."

I could tell in her voice that there was something more, something she wasn't telling me.

"There's more, isn't there?" I said. "You've done something else, haven't you?"

"Yes, I did something," she admitted. "But I'm not going to tell you anymore, until you talk to me. Until you tell me everything. What is your plan?"

But the truth was, there was no plan. I had choices to make. Choices which had consequences either way.

"This is what I'm wrestling with, Jennair," I told her. "Decisions have not been made."

"But if I'm not in your heart, and there is nothing there, be honest," she pleaded.

"I'm telling you that I'm struggling with this," I said. "And I don't want to give you false hope, but I'm not ready to shut the door."

"On us?" she asked.

"Yes," I confirmed. "You. Us."

"Again, answer my question," she begged. "Your heart, your soul, your desire is all for her, isn't it? If you want it so bad, then why not do it already?"

"Because I'm not sure I can do this to you," I told her.

"I need to hear that I'm still in your heart, that you still want me," she pleaded.

"You are in my heart," I confessed. "It's not going away."

"You didn't say you wanted me."

"I don't know," I said, now exhausted. The circular argument had gone on for well over an hour and I knew it would be an argument without end. "I just, need, time."

As the days passed, the pressure Jennair continued to put on me and that I put on myself became relentless. I wished I could make a decision, but there was so much riding on either choice. The more pressure she put on me to decide the future, the less I was able to make a decision. And then something pushed me over the edge.

I was leaving the office for our next marriage counseling appointment with Richard and grabbed my jacket from the hook on the back of my door. The weather was not quite winter and not yet spring, so I had worn a lightweight navy blue raincoat to combat the cool, wet weather. As I straightened my lapel, I felt something shift inside the jacket and fall toward my pocket. I reached into my pocket and felt something odd through the jacket lining. It felt like it could be one of those anti-theft devices that the store had forgotten to remove. But why was it sewn inside? I remembered that I kept an X-ACTO knife in the top drawer of my desk. Carefully cutting the stitches inside the pocket, I made a small hole and managed to slowly slip the device out from the lining. A chill shot through my body when I saw it—its small green light still blinking.

CHAPTER 16

IF IT'S MEANT TO BE

I climbed into the back of the Uber and shut the door.

"Where you headed?" my driver asked.

"Philly airport," I replied.

"I know that," he said, looking into the rearview mirror, slightly indignant. "Where you *flying* to?"

"Oh, Costa Rica," I told him. "It's a work thing."

"*Muy bien,*" he smiled and said, nodding his head and turning up the Latin groove station he'd been listening to.

"*Si. Si,*" I replied, trying my best to look upbeat. It was one of the perks I had been looking forward to with the new job. With resorts all over the Caribbean and Mexican Pacific, I'd be traveling every few weeks in an official capacity, but also enjoying two free vacations a year at any of our fifty-six resorts. Meredith had been beyond ecstatic, so excited for the vacation opportunities she too would get to enjoy. "Girlfriend perks," she called them.

She was the one who was supposed to be driving me to the airport that morning, writing on the May 14 slot on our shared Google calendar, "Happy to give you a ride from my place ♡." She was supposed to pick me up at the airport five days later and drive me to my new apartment in Bryn Mawr, less than a mile from her own. Her divorce would soon be finalized and my own petition papers would have been filed by then; it was supposed to have been the unofficial start of a new life together. But twenty-one days prior, it had all come to an end.

When I returned I was going to surprise her with a ring I had ordered. Nothing official. Nothing overly fancy. It actually wouldn't have been much of a surprise either. More a sign that I had taken her not so subtle hint seriously a few weeks back. As we sat in my car after dinner, she turned to me and gave me a coy look. "So, confession…. The other day when I was talking about putting something else on here," she said, rubbing the spot on her finger that her wedding ring once occupied, "there's part of me that doesn't want to do the whole getting married thing again. But I would absolutely melt if there was a day that came around that you offered a gesture like that."

"And what would that say?" I asked.

"It's a promise. That's all it is. A promise to love each other until we don't anymore. A promise to be real. To be honest. A promise to call it when it's time to call it. I hope we never have to call it, but, yeah. So…" She looked up at me and put her hands in mine. "I know this is real, and I don't doubt that at any moment. But if you did something like that, not necessarily in the next three months, or even the next year…" She looked down at our hands and then back to my eyes. "Is that okay to say?"[3]

Speechless and a bit taken back, I nodded. Just as I had given Jennair a promise ring twenty-five years before, now Meredith was hoping for one too. But what was it she was asking me to promise exactly? My devotion? My eternal love and commitment, as I'd

[3] Recorded conversation March 2018

once promised Jennair? Yes, I would promise her everything, maybe even one day marriage. Because if there's anything love promises us, it's the irrational and unexpected. And so, still married to Jennair, I went shopping for another ring, to promise my future to a woman I'd only known for half a year but couldn't imagine living without.

Twenty minutes later, at the airport, I got out of the car and the driver handed me my bag from the trunk. *"Ten un buen viaje,"* he said with a smile, wishing me a nice vacation.

"Gracias," I replied in turn and then walked through the revolving doors. The Philly airport had become a familiar scene since I had moved here in November. But this time, with Meredith and Jennair both gone, it was different. No one to drop me off. No one to check in with. No one to put down as an emergency contact. Standing there in the security line, I had never felt more alone.

For the next three days I sat in an auditorium with hundreds of fellow employees from around the world at the annual meeting, learning all about the company I had just joined. I had never worked for such a large organization. But to my surprise everyone seemed to know one another, greeting each other with hugs like family or long-lost friends, leaving me to feel even more conspicuous in my solitary state. On the last night of the five-day meeting, it was an annual company tradition to throw a big themed costume party. This year, everyone was encouraged to dress up as their favorite decade. For me, that was the seventies, the decade of my most formative years. I had packed a white leisure suit, white patent leather shoes and a pair of stick-on sideburns, but in my room, laying the outfit on the bed, I just couldn't bring myself to put it on. I had nothing to celebrate, and nothing but quiet, reflective solitude felt even remotely appropriate.

On the nightstand I spotted a bottle of red wine with a tag tied around the neck. "Enjoy with our compliments, Mr. Gerardot," it read. I grabbed the bottle and a glass and stepped outside my sliding glass door, down past the pool and headed toward the beach to watch the sun set. As I poured my first glass, I found a lounge chair and dug my feet deep into the still warm sand and stared blankly into the horizon, now blazing with bright orange and pink hues. Within minutes I poured a second and sank back into my seat and closed my eyes. Like flashes of light, thoughts and memories raced uncontrollably through my mind.

"When you get the job at Villanova," I had told Meredith, "I think we need to seriously consider taking a break."

"What? Are you serious?" she had asked with a look of horror.

"Just for a while. Ninety days tops," I told her. "You'll need the time to get settled at the new job anyway. And I need time to, well, end things right with Jennair. I need to do this. If I don't, I'll regret it later."

Meredith's eyes welled up with tears. "I can't believe you're considering this. She is just trying to drive a wedge between us."

"It was my idea," I told her. "But it's not definite. Let's talk about it later. Call me if you have too much to drink," I told her, kissing her gently on her cheek.

"Okay," she said wiping her tears away and laughing at the absurdity of my offer. "I won't. But thanks." Her husband vacationing in the Bahamas without her, Meredith was having drinks with an old friend on the riverfront in Wilmington that evening. I left her there at the coffee shop and walked toward my car.

I had just started my car and put it in gear when my phone rang. It was Meredith.

"Hey," she said with an upbeat lilt. "I just wanted to apologize for my reaction. You're a good guy. And you're just trying to do the right thing. I get it. I don't like it," she giggled sweetly. "But I get it."

"Thank you," I said. "Have fun tonight."

When I got home and walked into the apartment, Jennair was standing in the kitchen making dinner. "You know," she said. "If we're going to do this ninety-day trial thing, you can't just go meet her for coffee whenever you want."

"She doesn't even have the job yet, Jennair," I snapped. "And who says I was with her?"

"Obviously you were or you wouldn't be so defensive," she said, pouring a delicious smelling sauce of garlic and butter over some shrimp she was browning in the iron skillet. I sure would miss her cooking. But I hadn't married her for that. Sensing her desire to go a few rounds, I walked into my bedroom to change. Minutes later I could hear the flatware clinking against the plate as Jennair began eating dinner at the kitchen counter without me. I walked out into the kitchen, loaded my plate from the skillet and sat on the couch to watch the news. For forty-five minutes, we ate without saying a word until I walked into the kitchen to rinse my plate. "Thank you for dinner," I said to her and then poured myself a glass of red wine and retired to my bedroom.

Later that night as Jennair was getting ready for bed, my phone buzzed. It was Meredith.

M: *Does your offer still stand? I'm too drunk to drive home.*
Mark: *I'll be right there. Stay put.*

I looked toward Jennair's bedroom, the room that since New Year's Eve I had used only as a passageway to the master bathroom, and saw she was turning out her light. I knew if I told her I was leaving I would never hear the end of it, and I would be back in an hour tops, I reasoned. Confident she wouldn't hear me, and just as confident she'd know exactly what I was up to, I quietly found my keys and gingerly slipped out the door. When I stepped outside, the snow had just started to fall, sticking to the wet black asphalt parking lot the second it hit the ground. By the time I reached my car, the ground was completely covered, the flakes growing bigger and bigger by the second.

Ten minutes later I pulled up next to Meredith's car. The engine was running, the wipers flapping away at full speed, struggling to keep up with the wet snow falling from the black sky. Meredith was fast asleep behind the wheel. I tapped on the window to rouse her and then opened the passenger side door.

"My hero!" she said with outstretched arms. "I knew you would rescue me."

"Oh boy," I said, shaking my head. "Somebody's a little tipsy."

"A lot tipsy, actually," she admitted with a giggle.

"Come on, tipsy girl," I told her. "Let's get you home."

On a normal night, Newark, where Meredith still lived, was just twenty-five minutes away from the Wilmington riverfront. But the flakes had grown to the size of half dollars and were falling at a pace I had never seen before. It was like driving through a dizzying kaleidoscope, and I became mesmerized by the giant dancing flakes in my headlights, made even more treacherous by the growing accumulation of slick wet snow on the road.

"Do you love me as much as I love you?" Meredith asked with a slur. "Cause I really love you."

"I do," I assured her.

"And you want to be with me?" she asked.

"Yes," I said curtly. "Sorry, I'm trying to concentrate on the road."

She smiled, leaned her head on the passenger side window, and closed her eyes. Just then a song came on the radio. I didn't recognize it, but Meredith popped up in an instant and began dancing in her seat. "I love this song," she said, turning up the volume, and then began to sing out loud in a slightly out of tune country twang.

"...Who knows where this road is supposed to lead
We got nothing but time
As long as you're right here next to me, everything's gonna be alright
If it's meant to be, it'll be, it'll be
Baby, just let it be...

We were so certain that it was meant to be. And we were so certain we had time.

Suddenly I felt the sensation of cold water on my feet, and my hands were no longer on the steering wheel. When I opened my eyes, it was pitch black, except for the stars that lit up the Costa Rican sky like millions of LED lights. I heard the crash of waves and again felt the cold water of the Pacific cover my feet. The wine bottle, once half full and nestled in the sand next to me, now lay on its side, being coaxed into the ocean by the tide. I reached for it, picked up my glass and walked back toward my room.

Once in the room, I grabbed my laptop and sat up on the bed. After a few minutes of searching, I found the letter I had written to Meredith just after that night and began reading it out loud.

M,

On October 4, 2017, my life changed. I met one of the most intel-ligent, most driven and inspiring people I have ever known. Leading up to that fateful day, UD was one of six opportunities I was consid-ering. And to be honest, it wasn't at the top of my list. But I left that day thinking, "Wow, I want to work for her."

I still do. But sadly our professional partnership is coming to an end, and I find myself mourning the things we didn't get to do. The world we didn't get to change. Together. I've never met anyone like you, Meredith Sullivan. You have redefined the word "leader" to me. And you will forever be my professional crush.

What neither of us saw coming was that we would say "I love you" just 64 days after we met face to face. What we have, the con-nection we found, was inevitable. Our paths were supposed to cross. I was meant to love you and I couldn't stop it if I wanted to.

What will our lives look like in a month? In a year? Can we sus-tain and grow our personal relationship long term? Can I make you happy? Fulfill your hopes? Your needs? From here, a future with you looks so full of fun and love. So many experiences to share together. Doing everything. Doing absolutely nothing and being completely satisfied with it.

But to be honest, I'm scared that our love is fleeting. I need to know that we are built to last.

I owe it to you, to Jennair and to myself to know for certain that ending my marriage is the right thing to do. No looking back. This isn't a decision for the next few months, but hopefully for the rest of our lives.

It will be one of the hardest things I have ever had to do, but for the next 90 days, I think we need to put our personal relationship on hold. It will give you the time you need to get settled at Nova and reflect on the past few months and understand what you want for the future. On the other side of it, I hope we both have clarity and confidence to start the rest of our lives together.

Your professional future is boundless. I am so proud of you and excited for you. Thank you for trusting me to be a part of your journey to Villanova. I know you will make a huge impact there. You've had huge impact at UD, but you've paid a heavy price for it. And now it's time to move on. I get it. I am happy for you, but I am equally sad to see you go.

I love you.

Mark

I never sent the letter to her. In fact, it would be weeks before I ever brought up the subject of a break again. I closed my laptop, laid down on top of the covers and cried myself to sleep.

In the morning, I boarded the resort's shuttle bus for the ninety-minute ride to the airport in Liberia. The bus was abuzz with stories of the epic party that had gone late into the morning. I put my headphones in and drifted away into my own world, again letting the memories swirl uncontrollably in my head.

It was a Saturday morning when my phone rang. It was Meredith. I walked out of the apartment and took the elevator to the basement lobby for some privacy.

"Hey you," I answered.

"Hey," she said in a chipper voice. But then it quickly turned. "Are you sitting down?" she asked. "You might want to."

"Okay," I said and took a seat on a couch in the lobby.

"UD Human Resources has started an investigation," she said soberly. "A friend, whose name I promised not to disclose, was approached by HR. They interviewed this person about us, asking questions about our relationship. They asked them if they noticed any unprofessional behavior."

"Wow," I said. "What did they say?"

"They said they didn't notice anything. They came to me because they thought I should know," she explained. "And you know if they interviewed one person, they've spoken to multiple."

"Shit," I said, and heaved a deep sigh. "Now what?"

"Most likely we're going to lose our jobs," she said. "Or at least I am. They've started a pretty standard protocol investigation that most likely will lead to termination."

I stood up from the couch and began pacing around. "Guess I better start looking for a job," I said. "Thanks for the info. We can talk more about it later."

As I hung up, I walked toward the elevator and pushed the button to go up. To my surprise, I saw Jennair hiding around the corner. "Did you get all that?" I asked, looking straight at her and holding the elevator door open. "I'm going to lose my job. They've started an investigation. Are you happy?"

"Tell them she forced you," she said with a straight face. "Tell them your boss came onto you and you were afraid you would lose your job if you didn't submit."

"No," I said, shocked. "First of all, that sounds ridiculous. And it isn't true."

"So what," she said. "Take the skill you have perfected, lying your whole life, and just do it. You have to save yourself," she pleaded. "She's going to leave anyway. Do it for us. We need this job."

I stood there shaking my head in disbelief. "You should have thought of that before you told them," I said to her, and then got onto the elevator. Alone.

Back in our apartment later that afternoon, Jennair handed me a USB thumb drive. "Here. Read this," she said.

"Why, what is it?" I asked, suspicious.

"Just read it. Go in your room and read it."

Reluctantly, I took the drive into my room and stuck it into the USB port on my laptop, where I found a single file, titled "Mark.job.022518.doc." I opened it and began reading.

I know you don't believe this, but it is more likely that you will not lose your job. Especially, if you play the game right.

More than likely she will lose her job (or not), and that's ok because she has the new job anyway. This record will not follow her. There will be no fallback. She'll keep her 401K, and all will be fine with her. She has money to live off of while she waits this out and then to move to her new job. She has her home until it is listed in April/May. She has family and friends and lots of resources that WE don't have. She is still young and in the prime of her life and she can easily recover from this little bump in the road. This is not a little bump in the road for us.

Of course, you need to deny anything is more than professional with the two of you and that you really admire Meredith and think you make a great team in fulfilling UD's goals and doing good work for them.

But, you are in a probationary state of employment and if pressed, you need to respond to the university that you felt coerced in order to save your job. You need to express in some way that she's a strong and impressive woman. (Certainly a force majeure). You did not want to let Meredith down.

Throwing her under the bus will never get back to her unless you tell her. And ultimately, after all this is said and done, you two will be together. It is just a minor detour to get to the ultimate goal of being together. She can and will forgive you for this.

If you lose your job, I will have to move to my folks with Huck and have no clue what will be of our future while you look for another job. I have no idea where you plan to go to do this. (I doubt they will let you come, too). The logical thing is to move in with Meredith, especially if she moves to Philly.

I have a lifetime of love and passion and emotion and memories to say goodbye to and to somehow get rid of. This is a daunting task that I can't handle. I am so broken and drowning that I cannot see the light or the point. Despair and hopelessness is a very heavy and choking anchor, especially for a person already down and depressed, mentally.

I don't want a life or future with you if you cannot love me back. That's just pushing my head back down in the water I'm already treading. I don't want to be a backup plan or be the cause of your misery. Your health and happiness are important to me, Mark. Because I love you and want you to succeed and be happy. I will always have your back.

I walked out of my bedroom and handed her the USB drive. "I'm not doing that," I told her.

"You have to, Mark," she insisted. "You're an idiot if you don't."

I knew I had hurt Jennair profoundly, but I wanted nothing to do with the dark, deceitful corners of her mind. Make a false report of sexual harassment? Damage if not destroy Meredith's career to satisfy my wife? And then move in with Meredith and pretend I hadn't done it? I just looked at Jennair, trying to discern a flicker of that kind young girl I had married. But I didn't even recognize the woman staring back at me.

CHAPTER 17

NOTHING TO ME

I walked up to Meredith's third-floor office and, not saying a word, stepped through the door and held the device up, the light still blinking. The look on her face was a mix of astonishment and disgust, her mouth gaping open, her head shaking in disbelief. I flipped the switch to the off position and tossed it into the empty wastebasket next to her desk. "That explains a lot," I said.

"Where the hell was that?" she asked.

"Sewn inside my jacket," I told her, showing her the incision I had made along my pocket.

Instantly, her expression turned from disgust to anger. She stood up and slapped her hand down hard on her desk. "This is so illegal." Her breath began to quicken. "This is a state institution. She could go to jail for this."

"Whoa, whoa, whoa," I said, raising my hand in protest. "I don't want her to go to jail. Let's figure out a game plan. Use this to our advantage. I have to go to therapy right now. So please don't do anything just yet," I pleaded.

"I'm going to make a couple of calls," she said. "Find out our options."

"Okay," I conceded. "I'll call you when I get out."

As I walked the two blocks to my car, I grew increasingly enraged at being so violated. And I felt so stupid for not discovering earlier how Jennair had known so many details of my conversations with Meredith. How had I not seen it? She had played me. But she wasn't going to get away with it.

Twenty minutes later, driving to Richard's office in north Wilmington, my phone rang. It was Meredith.

"Hey," I greeted her.

"Hey," she replied. "I just wanted you to know I have it. I took it out of the trashcan. I'm giving it to my attorney for safe keeping. I know the state attorney general personally," she said. "And I'm this close to making a call."

"No, don't," I told her. "Let's just use the threat of legal action to get her to stop and make her turn over any others. I'll talk to her tonight."

As angry and indignant as I was, I knew in my heart that Jennair wasn't a violent criminal. She was just jealous and being a pain in the ass and needed to be scared a bit. She'd knock it off once she realized how serious the repercussions might be.

When I walked into Richard's office for our marriage counseling, Jennair had once again beat me there, taking her same spot on one end of the sectional couch. To my surprise, when I looked down, Huck was sitting there, wagging his tail at me.

"What are you doing here, buddy?" I asked and then knelt down to hug him.

"Richard said I could bring him if I wanted," Jennair said.

"Nice. Thank you," I told Richard and took a seat in my usual spot.

"So anything new?" he asked us. "Any new developments this week?"

Jennair looked at me blankly.

"Developments?" I asked flippantly, rubbing my face as if searching diligently for anything relevant to the discussion. "Developments? Well, let's see. You mean like my wife has been bugging me for weeks, sewing listening devices into my clothes?"

Dumbfounded and in utter disbelief, Richard looked at Jennair. "Did you..." he began.

Jennair rolled her eyes. "Whatever," she said, minimizing the importance of my discovery. "Fine. I'll stop."

"You're right. You will," I said. "Meredith has it and she's already called her attorney. This is illegal, Jennair."

"Now you guys are threatening me?" she asked in defiance. "I'm not giving them to you. I'm not giving you shit."

"Wait. Them? There are multiple recording devices?" Richard asked Jennair. "How many?"

"I don't know," Jennair replied. "Maybe a dozen."

I let out an audible gasp.

"Well, he's got like six different coats," she said in her defense. "He comes home from work. I cut it out. Download it. Sew it back in. Sometimes they don't even work. Most of the time, there's nothing."

Richard shook his head in disbelief. "This," he paused, "this just isn't good for you," he said, with obvious concern for Jennair. "And it certainly isn't good for building trust in the relationship. You've got to stop."

"I will," Jennair said. "I promise. No more. But I'm not giving them up. Not to him. And definitely not to her. I'll give them to my attorney."

"Okay, okay," Richard said, seeming satisfied with the progress of the discussion. The rest of our session, we stayed on the theme of trust. But our trust in each other was clearly damaged beyond repair. For months I had been lying to Jennair, covering up my relationship with Meredith, constantly dodging her inquisitions about the intimate details she insisted on knowing. For months, she had become obsessed with knowing every intimate detail, following me, eavesdropping on my private conversations. I couldn't imagine how we could repair all the damage we had done to each other and to our marriage of more than twenty-four years.

While Jennair held out hope that our sessions with Richard could somehow miraculously save our marriage, the more our sessions went on, any glimmer of hope I'd had became smaller and smaller. I began to think of our sessions more as grief counseling, trying to make sure Jennair had support and that she could make it on her own.

When Jennair and I got home that evening I insisted on seeing all the devices. "Stay here," she demanded and then went to her bedroom and closed the door. A few minutes later, she reappeared, walking out with a shoe box, and dumped the contents onto the kitchen counter.

"There," she said. "That's all of them. But you can't have them. Tomorrow I'm giving them to my attorney to keep."

"Jesus, Jennair," I said to her, looking at a whole pile of recording devices of different sizes and brands. "What a waste of time and money! Where are the audio files?"

"On the cloud," she said smugly. "And don't think I'm getting rid of those. She thinks she can threaten me with the one recorder you have? Pfft. I can release anything I want, whenever I want. Tell her to give it back and I'll delete everything."

"She's not giving it back, Jennair." I told her. "So I guess we're at a stalemate. Just get rid of those and stop hiding this shit in my clothes!"

"I'll stop," she promised. "No more." Without saying anything else, she gave me her sad, apologetic look with those big blue eyes looking up at me. And I believed her.

I know in that moment I should have been angry. I should have been livid. I should have packed my things and moved out or forced Jennair to leave. But at the time, those thoughts and feelings barely entered my mind. My privacy, I reasoned, was a small price to pay for what hell I knew I had been putting Jennair through. But the more erratic her behavior, the more she pressed me, the more she made malicious choices and struck out in anger, the more I came to realize I needed to distance myself from her. I needed to make a decision and move on, once and for all. But I had more immediate challenges to worry about, every day worrying that the next day at work might be my last.

On the bright side, if the worst would happen, I still had consulting opportunities to fall back on. In early March, a little more than a week after Jennair had come clean with the recording devices, I took the train to D.C. to meet my former colleague, Brandee, from the agency I had worked with in South Carolina, for a presentation we had developed for an educational institution.

Jennair was convinced I would use the opportunity to rendezvous with Meredith in D.C., which I could understand as our trust in each other had been eroded. "It's just a quick forty-eight-hour work trip," I told her. "There and back. I don't have time to do anything social."

"Let me take you to the station then," she insisted.

"Okay. Yes. Great," I told her.

Early the next morning, Jennair drove me to the Wilmington train station to catch the same train she and I had taken to the Women's March just weeks before. She didn't say a word on the drive, but I could sense her growing concern. At the curb, I got out of the car and turned to her. "There and back," I said, and then waved to her and shut the door. She began to cry, then pulled away.

Within an hour, sitting on the train, Jennair sent me a text.

Jennair: *I'm not doing so great.*

Mark: *I'm sorry. Please trust me. I'll be back on Wednesday.*

Jennair: *How will I know for sure she's not there?*

Mark: *Because I told you.*

I was asking Jennair to trust me, based on nothing more than my word. But by this point, my word meant no more to her than her word meant to me. But I was being honest, which only made it undeniable that the trust between us had been shattered. And what kind of future could we have if neither of us felt we could trust the other?

When I got to my hotel, just blocks from the White House, I immediately began making final edits to the presentation and rehearsing. Within an hour, my phone rang. It was Jennair.

"What's up?" I said with an upbeat tone.

"What are you doing?" she asked.

"Rehearsing," I said.

"Alone?" she asked.

"Yes," I assured her. "But Brandee gets here tonight and we'll go through it together."

"Okay, I just sent you an email. Please look at it when you get a chance," she asked.

"I will," I promised.

When I sat back down at my computer, I saw the email Jennair had just sent me, titled "In Your Eyes."

"Oh shit," I said out loud, knowing that was the title of the Peter Gabriel song that had played in our wedding video. She had texted me the same song just two weeks before in a video of her crying to it. It crushed me to see her like that. When I opened the email, it contained a single link to download a library of photos. I knew it would be a distraction from the work I still needed to do, but I had promised I would look at what she had sent me. As the zipped file began downloading, the estimated file size and download time kept growing. First it was one gigabyte. Then six. Finally the sixteen gigabyte download was completed. "What *is* this?" I whispered, then double-clicked the file, expanding it to a folder, which I immediately opened.

"Hooooly shiiiiit!" I said out loud, slapping my hand over my mouth. There had to be dozens—dozens of photos and videos of Jennair spread out on the bed in various stages of undress and pleasuring herself. She looked beautiful. Stunning. Her skin, radiant and flawless. Her straight blonde hair falling onto her shoulders. And her smoothly shaven, toned legs outstretched toward the camera. Despite having lost more than twenty pounds from the stress she had been under for weeks, at age forty-seven she could have held her own with any woman of any age. She knew what this might do to me. It was, of course, her intention to arouse me, to force me to remember the physical chemistry we had once shared for nearly twenty-eight years. She wasn't going down without a fight, and she had just unveiled her newest weapon in an all-out war she was determined to wage.

But she was fighting the wrong fight. My draw to Meredith went far beyond any physical attraction or sexual chemistry. From the beginning her beauty had always been overshadowed by her intellect, her positive outlook and her inextinguishable zeal for life. But it was her respect for me, the kindness she showed me and her way of making me feel like I was capable of doing anything I set my mind to that I found so damn irresistible. And that was something Jennair would never think to do.

If only Jennair could have found the fire that had once burned inside her. If she could have found her true worth and her true self —for herself. And in so finding her own self love, we could have possibly been able to find our way together again, evolving and growing in mutual respect for each other. But she wanted the past. She thrived on dysfunction. And she refused to believe in me. Instead, she wanted to manipulate and control me just as she had done for so long.

Later that afternoon, Jennair sent me a text.

Jennair: *Did you get them?*

Mark: *Yes, Jennair*

Jennair: *You think I'm disgusting*

Mark: *God no. But I can't let myself go there*

Jennair: *Yes you can*

I couldn't bring myself to reply.

The next day, during a break from the full-day presentation with our client, Meredith sent me a text, asking me to call her. I did and the second she picked up I could sense the stress in her voice.

"HR is all over my LinkedIn profile," she said.

"What?" I asked in confusion.

"The head of HR," she said. "She's visited my LinkedIn page three times in two days. Why? Why would she do that?"

"Hang on," I told her. While Meredith was still on the phone, I checked my own visitor stats.

"Shit," I said. "Sure enough, she's been on my profile, too."

I didn't know exactly what it meant, but it seemed the noose was tightening. And so was the lump in my throat.

After the presentation, Brandee and I decided to get a drink to relieve a little stress from the day. We found a swank little wine bar where we enjoyed a couple glasses of wine and good memories of our time working together. Then suddenly I realized I was about to miss my train back to Wilmington. Frantically, I hailed an Uber from the corner outside, but it was too late. I sent Jennair a text that I was going to have to spend the night in D.C.

Immediately she tried to call me, but I didn't answer. I was too frustrated having missed the train. Jennair was the last person I wanted to talk to. I just knew I would never hear the end of it. She tried calling again and again, but I ignored her attempts. Eventually, however, she left me a voicemail. Despite everything we had been through in the previous two months, the tone of her message was surprisingly sweet and nurturing—characteristics I hadn't heard or felt from Jennair in such a long time.

"Mark... It's okay. I got you a later train," she said. "It's only seventy-four dollars for the total thing. If you can get a ride in time for an eight-thirty train, you'll be home by ten. Please call to let me know you got this. Everything is going to be fine. Please call me."

From the back of a cab, I sent Jennair a text message. *Got your VM. Thanks. On the way to Union Station. See you at 10:00.*

Sitting on the train back to Wilmington, I spent the entire two hours wide awake, just thinking. She was there for me. It had been a small gesture really, but clearly she was concerned and had selflessly gone above and beyond to see that I would get home safe and sound. Despite everything we had been through. Despite everything I had put her through, she still loved me. *What am I doing to her?* I wondered.

When I walked out of the station, Jennair was sitting in her car along the curb in the same spot I had left her. "Did you eat?" she asked me before I had even gotten into the car. "Are you hungry? Can we go somewhere?" she asked, in rapid succession.

"No, I'm not hungry," I said.

"I have to tell you something," she blurted out. "But you can't get mad."

"Okay…" I hesitated with dread. "What?"

"I wrote a letter to Villanova."

"What? When?" I squawked.

"Two weeks ago. The same day I wrote the letter to UD."

"What did you say?" I asked.

"That Meredith was a horrible person and they shouldn't hire her."

"Fuck, Jennair. Oh my God!" I said, burying my head in my hands. "And UD?"

"I sent a letter to Glenn," she admitted. "I told him you were having an inappropriate relationship with your boss."

"Fuck!" I said, taking a deep breath. "Okay. Okay. Okay. Go home. Drive. I have to think."

"One more thing," Jennair added.

I steeled myself for the worst.

"You didn't call me back. I got worried. So I called her husband to see where Meredith was."

"I told you she wasn't with me!" I shouted.

"I know," she said. "He was in the Bahamas. He told me to stop calling him."

"Well, no shit," I said in frustration. "Stop contacting him. Just stop."

I had to tell Meredith. Or did I? What good would it do her, except to worry her, I reasoned. She was already on edge, anxiously waiting to hear if she had gotten the job. Either she did or she didn't. Nothing I could say or do was going to change that, and would actually only further enrage Meredith to despise Jennair, who it seemed had come to a moment of conscience, waving a white flag in her war. I decided to keep the peace.

Two days later, while driving home, Meredith called me.

"Hey!" I said to her. "How are you?"

"Hey," she said back. "Life was not easy today."

"Why? What happened?" I asked.

"Ha," she replied, wondering where to begin. "I called him to ask if he'd be home, what he was doing. And it just so quickly turned to, 'I told you not to have him at our house and you had him at our house.' And I was like, whoa, what are you talking about? He said he was tired of my lying, and said, 'I don't need his wife calling me to tell me she can't find him and the two of you were together, and she's asking, 'Where's Meredith?' So it turned into an epic fight about that."

"I'm sorry. How is it that I was at your house when I was in D.C.?" I asked.

"I know, and that's what I told him, and then I told him I don't owe him an explanation for this. Nothing happened and I wasn't involved in anything," she told me. "He said he can't trust me because of you, and we're going to have to figure this out. And I told him, 'You know what, I just signed my papers today and in my counter to you I chose not to put all my questions in there about finances or anything else, because I thought we both agreed this isn't going to work, and let's move on."

"I'm sorry," I said to her. "I've told her not to do it. I can't control her fingers. I don't know what else to do."

"I know," she assured me. "I'm just making you aware that we were good before we went away and now it's like a switch has flipped all because of that call. Like he couldn't wait to bring it up. This is about to get really nasty," she said, her voice starting to crack. "He told me he doesn't want to see me again. I know this isn't your problem, but you're the only one I can talk to about this."

"Your problems are my problems," I told her. "We're in this together."[4]

Less than a week later, on March 12, as I was driving home from work, Meredith sent me a text.

M: *Guess who's Villanova's next AVP of Marketing?*

Mark: *Seriously? That's awesome. Congrats babe.*

M: *Thanks.*

Mark: *Where are you?*

M: *Getting in my car. Headed to gym.*

I grabbed my phone to map her gym, then immediately diverted my course to surprise her. Ten minutes later, I pulled up alongside Meredith's car, just as she was getting out.

"What the..! What are you?..." she shrieked in excitement, as I ran to her and lifted her up off the ground and into my arms.

"You deserve this. You've earned this," I told her. "And you are going to make a great AVP."

"I know I am," she laughed and then kissed me. I was so proud of her. At least one of us had made it to safety.

---

[4] Recorded conversation March 9, 2018

The next day, Meredith scheduled a late afternoon meeting with Glenn and with great delight, she handed him her resignation letter. While she had graciously offered to stay on for four weeks, Glenn had decided that she should finish out the week and just go.

That Thursday, I and members of the team joined Meredith at one of all of our favorite campus bars to bid her farewell and wish her luck. An hour into the celebration I had to excuse myself. "Sorry guys, I have to go to a St. Patrick's Day party in our building," I told them. "So, sadly, duty calls. Meredith, we will miss you. Please don't be a stranger," I told her, playing the part of the forlorn coworker.

"Oh, I won't," she said, raising her glass and sneaking a quick wink in my direction.

When I got home, I rushed into the apartment. "Sorry I'm late," I told Jennair. "I have time to change?"

"Yes, take your time," she said, primping in the bathroom.

I walked into my bedroom closet, threw on a sport coat, and ran into the guest bathroom for a quick wash up. I dried my face and hands and made a quick adjustment of my jacket lapel when I felt a familiar thud near my pocket. "No. No. No," I said, reaching into the medicine cabinet for a pair of barber shears, then slicing haphazardly into the lining of my jacket. I reached inside and pulled out the USB flash drive-sized device and looked down at the familiar green blinking light.

I flung open the bathroom door and walked into the living room where Jennair was waiting for me. Holding it in my hand, I thrust it into her face. "I thought we were done with this shit!" I yelled. "Is this all you do all day? You're supposed to be looking for jobs, trying to make a go of it!"

She stood there silently, shaking like a scared child about to be punished.

"If this is what you've become," I screamed, grabbing the glass coffee table and flipping it on its side, "if this is all you can do then you are nothing to me! *Nothing!*"

The look on her face turned to pure terror, her bloodshot eyes gushing tears.

I practically ran out of the apartment, letting the door slam behind me. I was done.

CHAPTER 18

SHE'S LIVING MY LIFE

When I got back from Costa Rica early on a Saturday morning, I decided it was time to get serious. The bills were starting to pile up and I still didn't know much about what Jennair had been doing with our finances for years. The stacks of phone logs and bank credit card statements were still laid out neatly on my desk, reminding me just how much I still didn't know. Without even bothering to unpack my suitcase, I dove headfirst back into it all.

The one place I hadn't even begun to look into was our checking account from our bank in South Carolina. I had opened my own account in Pennsylvania to start separating our finances, and Jennair had opened her own as well. Apparently, however, Jennair had left the joint S.C. account open, and our bills were still being automatically paid through that account.

After downloading the statements from the past year, I went through each one line by line and began transferring automatic payments Jennair had set up to my new account. But one recurring charge from Google that had started back in January stood out to me. *What is that?* I wondered. She has a paid Google account? For what? I had to find out. I knew that in her long suicide note, Jennair had included her login credentials. But because she wrote the letter to her family, I didn't have a copy. So I sent a text to Jennair's sister to ask her to send me the login info. Almost immediately she responded, and within a few seconds I was logged in.

"You are using 150GB of 200GB," it said on her account dashboard.

"A hundred and fifty gigabytes?" I said out loud. "She told me she didn't know how to use Google apps." I clicked on a folder icon titled, "Computers," which exposed a folder titled "Surveillance."

"What the hell?" I said under my breath, trying to understand what I was looking at. Hundreds and hundreds of files, photos, and folders, one of them titled, "Sounds of Silence." I took a deep breath and opened it. Inside were dozens of audio files, a backup of every recording she had ever made, some as far back as January and as recent as mid-April. Some files were labeled with auto-generated names from the various devices she had in her arsenal, others she had named herself, like "Philly-edited-1.mp3," "Saturday-morning.mp3" and "032818fightend.WAV."

I clicked on "Saturday-Morning" dated March 10, and it began to play. At first it sounded like just a lot of static. Then I could clearly hear the sound of a car door opening, and the unmistakable ping, ping, ping of my 2015 Honda Accord. Then, very distinctly, I could hear the sound of Velcro as Jennair secured the recording device into place inside my car. The car door closed, followed by five seconds of clicking. Then the door opened and closed again. The ignition engaged and the engine whirred to life. The passenger door opened and then quickly closed and then I heard Jennair's voice. "She have a cold?" she asked, and I instantly recalled our conversation. She was referring to an open box of cough medicine on the passenger-side seat. I had been fighting bronchitis and a sinus infection for weeks.

"No, that's mine," I responded, as I shifted the car into drive. For nearly two minutes, the transmission revved up and down as I navigated several stops and starts. Not a word was spoken.

"I want to know your plan, where you guys are going with this," Jennair insisted. "She gets a job and you're going to get an apartment. And then what? You stay here in an apartment and then see each other evenings and weekends?"

"I guess," I answered. "If that happens, she's going to live up there, and I'll live down here." The audio got rough, as a train rumbled by.

"So," I could hear her plainly again. "She talked about marriage again last night."

"She did not," I said in frustration.

"The fuck she didn't!" she yelled. "I'll play it for you."

"Please do," I said.

Jennair began reading from a notebook. "She said it would melt her heart if you would make that offer."

"What are you hearing?" I asked, my voice jumping two octaves.

"This is like the third time she's brought up marriage," she said. "And you didn't say no. You didn't shut it down."

"Because she didn't say it," I replied.

"She did too," Jennair insisted, then looked back down to her notebook. "She said, wouldn't it be great if one day, maybe not this month, maybe in a year you would promise to love her until you die."

I sat in silence, stunned, not knowing what to say.

"Don't deny that," she raised her voice at me.

"What's this place called?" I asked, looking at my phone.

"De La Coeur!" she shouted.

227

That's French for "From the heart," I said to my computer, clicking the pause button. I knew the exact day and time of this recording. We were driving to brunch in Wilmington, back in March, just four days after I had gotten back from D.C. I took a long sip of wine, then marked it on the calendar and clicked the play button again.

"She will get pregnant," she said. And she will trap you. And you will marry her."

"One of the things we both have in common is that we don't want kids," I shouted back at her, all the while knowing that part wasn't completely true. For about a week in January, Meredith thought she might have actually been pregnant. She had shared the news with me at lunch one day and neither of us could stop smiling at the prospect.

"Oh my God," was all I could manage to say. "Oh my God." Since Jennair hadn't wanted to have children, I had grown so used to the thinking I'd never have kids that, after a while, I thought I hadn't wanted kids either. But the truth was, Meredith and I were both a little disappointed when she found out she wasn't pregnant. I knew that little scare had opened up an unexpected door, a door that had been slammed shut in my face for twenty-four years. And no doubt Jennair knew as much about those conversations with Meredith as I did.

"That's what she says," Jennair scoffed. "She wants to say the things that make you happy. Hook you in. Then accidentally or using it to keep you, she will make you feel bad enough that you will get married. Keep pushing and pushing." She paused and then continued. "I can't watch that happen. I can't watch you have a happy life."

"What does that mean?" I asked.

"We can't be friends," she said, now tearing up. "We cannot talk. It's too painful for me to see you living your life happy." Again she paused and wiped her tears. "She's living my fucking life!" she screamed at me. "I can't have that."

"Stop," I said, trying to console her. "She's not living your life."

"She took my fucking husband away and broke up my family!" she shouted. "And ruined my life."

"I did that," I said to her.

"You both did," Jennair replied,[5] and then abruptly the audio ended, the end of the file.

I didn't realize it until then, but I had been crying for several minutes, reliving that moment in time in such excruciating detail, my nose running and tears spilling down my face. I closed my computer and walked out onto my balcony for fresh air and sun to collect myself. I just wanted to scream. I wanted to break down, curl up on the floor and just cry. Every word I'd said. Every place I'd gone. Everything I'd done. For four months. Captured forever in time. It was all so overwhelming. But somehow, I kept it together. It was the only way to know what she knew, what she felt, and to remember the things we'd said to each other—not as I recalled them, or wanted to recall them, but as I'd actually said them. And as she'd actually said them.

I spent the rest of the day in my favorite leather chair, headphones in my ears. A full glass of wine always at my side, scrubbing through months of recordings, hundreds of hours of audio. Jennair and me. Meredith and me. UD colleagues and me. But eighty percent of it was deafening silence, or the sound of my en-

---

[5] Recorded conversation March 9, 2018

gine droning as I drove to work day in and day out down I-95 between Wilmington and Newark, Delaware. Tragically, the name of
the folder Jennair had labeled became abundantly and painfully
clear. "Sounds of silence" contained an abyss of nothingness, and
we were both obsessed enough to listen to every maddening silent
second.

I woke up the next morning, still sitting in my chair, headphones still in my ears. Looking down at my computer, I logged
back in. "Okay," I said. "What else is in here?"

"Logs? Ipad Upload? GPS Maps?" *What the hell is that?* I wondered, clicking open the folder. Inside were thirty-seven PNG files,
screen captures of maps with two car-shaped icons, each one
showing its exact location, whether it was moving and in which
direction, and each was distinctly labeled so she could see which
was which, "Mark Liar" and "Whore." She had also named each file
even more distinctly, such as "liar-asshole-not-coming-home.png,"
"1st-day-fuck-at-her-house.png" and "Jewelers-040718.png," the
day I had gone to pick out the ring to give to Meredith.

"How is this even legal to sell to someone?" I wondered, shaking nervously. The police had told me the night that they had released me that they had found a GPS device mounted to the passenger-side front wheel well of Meredith's Audi A3 convertible, but
they couldn't find one on mine. *But wait,* I thought. There's a map
from that morning, titled, "look-whos-going-to-merediths-today."
If the police didn't find it, then somehow she had taken it off my
car later that day. I stood up, walked to the kitchen and began to
make a pot of coffee. As I turned on the power button, another
switch flipped. "It's still there!" I said loudly.

I grabbed my keys and ran out the door. Standing anxiously at
the elevator, I could barely keep still. "Come on. Come on. Come

on," I yelled, clicking the button again repeatedly. When the doors finally opened, without even looking, I stepped in.

"Oh, you startled me," a voice said. I looked up and saw my elderly neighbor. Agnes was about to get off at our floor, her walker in hand. She was looking sharp in a periwinkle blue cardigan and pants that matched her perfectly maintained coif of snow white hair. "You going for a walk?" she asked, still standing in the elevator as I held the door open for her to step out. "It's a nice one out there this morning."

"Something like that," I told her, nervously fiddling with my car keys, anxious to get to my car. "Need any help?"

"No, I can manage," she said proudly, and then with her shaking left hand she managed to inch her walker forward as she braced herself against the elevator wall with the other. Sliding one foot forward a few inches, then the other, then the walker again, she slowly but surely crossed over the elevator threshold as I continued to hold the door open, wishing to God she could move faster. Not quite out the door, she stopped and looked back over her shoulder at me. "Where's that beautiful dog of yours?" she asked in the sweetest voice.

"Oh, he's still sleeping," I told her. "He doesn't do mornings."

"Ha," she laughed, and then looked forward again. "Dog doesn't do mornings," she repeated, giggling. As she made her final step out of the elevator, clearing the door, I removed my hand from it to let it close.

"Have a nice day," I told her.

"Oh, I will," I heard her say as the door closed behind her.

"Crap!" I said out loud once she was gone. I couldn't get to my car fast enough, as if the GPS might vanish if I didn't get to it in time. I nervously pushed the button for the first floor half a dozen

231

times, as if that would make it come faster. "It's got to be there. It's got to be there."

When the elevator door opened on the first floor, I ran out, through the lobby and into the parking lot toward my car, clicking my fob repeatedly to unlock it. Instinctively I went to my knees and reached into the passenger-side front wheel well, frantically feeling for the device. Nothing. I stood up and scurried to the driver's side and again reached in to feel for the device. Still nothing. Then to the back, bracing myself with one hand on my tire and reaching in as far as my arm would allow. "Dammit," I said. "One more." Walking around the back of the car I again assumed the position, feeling every inch of the rear wheel well. "Shit," I said and then sat down onto the asphalt, sweating. "Nice, my ass, Agnes," I said panting. "It's hot as hell out here."

But I wasn't done. I laid back and slid my body under my car as far as I could go. My eyes darted around, looking for anything that seemed out of the ordinary. Again I found nothing. I opened the driver's door to pull the hood release, and then stuck my hand into every nook and cranny where I could think to look under the hood. It had to be inside the car, I thought.

For close to an hour I meticulously searched every inch of that car, under each seat, the trunk, the glove box, the fuse panel, deep into the recesses under the dash and along the steering column. The police couldn't find it and neither could I. She'd outsmarted me again.

Sitting in the driver's seat, I closed the door and started the engine to cool off in the air conditioning. As I sat there, I thought about all the phone conversations I'd had in that car in the past few months, each and every one of them recorded. Then it hit me. The time and length of each call, as well as the location where each call had originated, would be documented in my cell phone bill. That meant that every call Jennair had made would also be documented. What if, I wondered. What if she made a call that day? I'd be able to see where she was. Did she come to my office and remove the tracking device for some reason? I shut off my car, ran back inside and up to my apartment to the stack of cell phone bills I had printed out. Grabbing the one for April, I scanned down the page to the 23rd, looking closely at the time and location of each call. Wilmington. Wilmington. Wilmington. "Wait. Haverford, PA at 1:49 p.m. A toll-free call for twenty-eight minutes." I said. "Who'd you call, Jennair?" I grabbed my phone and dialed the number.

"Thank you for calling SpyTec technical support," the automated voice said. Instantly, I hung up. I had seen that name before. I went to the other end of my desk and began looking through the six different piles of credit card receipts, stacked in chronological order. And there it was. April 9, 2018, SpyTech $408.75. I went to the company's website. Sure enough, for the first time I could see the GPS tracker I had been looking for, a sleek black rectangle with LED lights and a single button on the front, just twice the size of a dime, complete with a magnetic mounting case. *Okay,* I thought. So why did she call technical support for twenty-eight minutes? Why was she in Haverford? And where was I?

"Wait," I said "1:49? No." Again, I began searching through the credit card receipts and bank statements. April 23, 2:37 pm, $21.00. That was when the team had taken me out for late lunch. It was also the day that Jennair had killed Meredith, then herself.

Was she sitting outside in the parking lot for twenty-eight minutes with a loaded gun? Did she remove the tracker from my car? Did she think I was inside with Meredith? There was no other proof. This is as close as I would come to knowing. Or was it? Again, I called tech support for the GPS tracking system.

"Technical support," a live human voice answered. "How can I help you?"

"Hi. I'm wondering if you keep a detailed log of tech support calls?" I asked.

"We do. Are you a customer?" she asked. "Do you have an account with us?"

"Well," I said. "My late wife does."

"And do you have her email address?"

"Yes, of course," I said and gave her Jennair's email address.

"I'm sorry, that's not an email we have on file for any account," she said. "Is there another one?"

"No," I said in frustration. "The police told me that my wife used more than twelve different email addresses, most of which I don't know." Another dead end. I hung up the phone and sat back down in my chair with my computer. Again I began to dig around in the hundreds of files from the backup of Jennair's computer.

A folder labeled "Logs" contained a detailed history of my work computer, including every application I used, when, and for how long, my browser and search history, and a spreadsheet of every keystroke I had made for months, with every username and password I'd entered for every account I used, including, among others, my University of Delaware email account and calendar.

A folder titled "House Pics" contained eight photos showing every angle of the outside of the house Meredith had moved into just two days before she was murdered inside of it.

A folder titled "SC" I thought might be something pertinent to when we lived in South Carolina. But no. Inside were more than

400 photos Jennair had somehow taken of the many personal conversations Meredith and I had had on SnapChat.

Inside the folder titled simply "Photos" was a menagerie of
photos from our past, including a wedding photo, recent photos of
herself crying outside in a park that she titled "despair-1" and "de-
spair-2." There was also a photo of a Valentine's Day card from the
early days of our marriage, titled "Mark's Love for Jennair Past"
including the note I had written to her inside.

*I know you'll say that you don't deserve it, but you're wrong. You
do and so much more. This is for putting up with all of the late
nights and me working all the time. But just know that I'm doing it
for us. I believe in us and most of all I need us. I would be lost without you and your love.*

*I could have gone the traditional route of flowers or chocolates,
but I wanted my Valentine's Day gift to be practical and mean something. Every time I see you in this dress, my heart will melt, not only
because you will look beautiful in it, but because I will think of this
very moment and how filled with love I am for you. You keep me
going. You give me a life to look forward to. And most of all, you give
me you. What a wonderful gift I get every day. Now and for the rest
of my life.*

Your Loving Husband,

Mark

She looked stunning in that dress. I remembered that day like
it had happened yesterday. But it wasn't yesterday. It had been
close to twenty years ago, before much of the worst fighting and
years of tearing each other apart. It tore me up to read that card
and to think of how perfectly wonderful our future had looked
back then. *I can't dwell on the past right now,* I thought. I dried my
eyes and pressed on.

The last folder from the cloud backup, titled "Movies," contained more than sixteen video files that had been uploaded automatically from Jennair's phone. Six of them had been recorded on March 15, the night of the St. Patrick's Day party in our apartment building, the same night I had found yet another recording device sewn into one of my jackets. The night I had found my limit. "You are nothing to me," I had screamed at her, and then stormed out.

On my way out of the building, Jennair had run after me, catching up with me in the lobby. "Where are you going?" she had asked, distraught and crying. "Don't go. Come back and talk to me. Please." She grabbed my arms.

"I just can't be around you right now," I said in disgust. Forcefully pulling my arms from her hands, I walked out the door. Without even knowing where I was going, I got into my car and recklessly sped through the parking lot, pounding on the steering wheel to the beat of the music. When I got to the first red light, I sent Meredith a text.

Mark: *Where are you?*
M: *Out with friends? Why?*
Mark: *Just left home. Headed to 2S. Join me?*
M: *Seriously? BRT*

Back in our apartment building, Jennair took the elevator to the seventh floor and opened a window in the hallway that overlooked the front entrance and the parking lot I had just left. With her phone, she took photos and video of the scene below, the wind whistling in the mic.

When I got to one of Meredith's and my favorite meeting places, a bar in Hockessin, I ordered a beer and by the time Meredith walked in five minutes later, I was already ordering a second.

"Wow," she said. "Everything okay?"

"Nope," I replied and showed her the hole I had cut in my jacket.

"Oh shit," she said and ordered herself a beer.

"I don't know if I can take anymore," I told her.

"You need to get out of there," she said. "Now."

"I will," I explained. "It's just not that easy. She doesn't have a place to go. I need to make sure she lands on her feet."

Meredith turned from me and shook her head.

"What?" I asked.

"Nothing, it's not my place," she said.

"I'm making it your place," I insisted. "What?"

"Women. Me. Everyone," she said. "We have a responsibility to be independent. To take care of ourselves. Not rely on others."

"I know," I said. "But it's not that easy. She's been looking for a job for eighteen months."

"Sorry," she said, shrugging her shoulders. "Just how I see it."

Meredith couldn't possibly know what it felt like to be forty-seven years old and unemployed, so I didn't press it. I needed to keep the peace with both of them. And that night, after my blowout with Jennair, what I needed most Meredith's support and what she did best — help me envision the man I wanted to be. We raised our glasses in a toast, a toast to Jennair's independence.

Jennair sat down on the couch, and with her phone in her hand, she pushed the record button. She had been crying, her eyes red and puffy, her face tired from stress.

"His car is still there," she began in a monotone voice. "Who knows if he's even there. She could have picked him up. He's not coming home tonight. I just didn't want to do it this way. I can't get the momentum to do it. It's so unnatural and I'm so afraid of falling and heights. This is the worst option for me. Instinctively I can't get my brain to make me do it. I don't want to hurt anyone accidentally. I don't want some poor neighbor to find me.

"I'm not sorry. I know everyone wants to hear me say, mom, dad, that I'm sorry. But I'm not. In my heart I had a great love. And it doesn't even matter anymore if he ever loved me back. It doesn't even matter anymore. I'm nothing, I'm nothing, I'm nothing. I don't matter," she said crying, wiping her nose.

"She used to be so independent," I told Meredith. "She had two jobs. She was going to school. She wanted to do so much with her life. Then I don't know. It's like she lost her confidence. And then she started wrapping herself around my life, controlling me. Telling me I wasn't good at this. I couldn't do that. I hated it, but I just let her do it."

"I thought I was a pretty special person," Jennair said to the camera. "But really I'm not. I can't hold a candle. I will never measure up. I have been totally extinguished, like a candle, a flame. He blew me out. I can't go on. I can't see the future. I'm too broken, I'm too broken. And I don't matter. He is right. He is right. I don't matter. I am nothing. I am nothing."

"Then she started breaking into my email," I said. "Going through my things, reading everything. She had to know where I was and who I was with at all times. We fought about it all the time, but she continued to do it. And I let her. It was just easier than fighting. There were so many times I wanted to just leave, Meredith," I told her. "I just wanted to start over. But I just couldn't do it. I imagined what a different life might be like. How much better it could be. But I just couldn't do that to her. Does that make any sense?"

"You are a horrible, horrible man," Jennair said through her tears. "And I am so ashamed that I loved you. I deserved so much better. I wanted to be adored and I wanted someone to pursue me and protect me. And have my back like you did with Meredith.

"My life is such a waste. My life was such a waste. I don't deserve him anymore. My life is over really. Everybody keeps telling me I will be okay and I will go on, but look at me, look at me. Look at me. I'm so ugly. I'm so worn, I'm stupid, I'm pathetic, I'm jobless, and apparently, I don't have anything to offer anybody. Love isn't enough.

"You are so horrible. And I am so ashamed. You beat me down. I am no longer who I am. I am no longer a viable person. I am not worth it. This is too hard. It is too hard and I can't even. I can't even.

"Why does it have to end this way? Why does God make me suffer like this? I can't accept that it's over. I can't do it. It's just so hard to accept that it's over. What did I do? What did I do to my life that God would let this happen to me? Why do they get to be happy and why do I have to suffer? I just love him so much I can't take it. I don't want anybody else. I don't want anything else. I just want him back. Please, God, why?"

"This past year, oh my God, it put such a strain on us," I told Meredith. "I still love her, but she was so depressed. We both were. It felt like we were just going through the motions most of the time. We were more like roommates. But then she would bounce back. We'd have a great dinner. We watched the eclipse back in September and I can remember us smiling and laughing. And then two weeks later, we held each other and cried. I still love her. I don't want to hurt her."

"No, I get it," she replied, nodding.

"I told her I would always love her. Does that make sense?" I asked her.

"Of course," she said, "Twenty-four years is a long time."

Yes, it was. It was most of Meredith's entire life. Could she truly get it?

"Why now? Why couldn't we do this twenty years ago, ten years ago," Jennair cried. "Why now? I don't want to feel."

"She almost left me eight years ago," I confided in Meredith. "She almost didn't move to South Carolina with me. We were fighting so much back then. Would she have been better off? I don't know."

"I tried to go up on the roof," Jennair said, like it was a totally normal thing to do. "I couldn't pick the lock for the door. I tried so hard. I was going to get a hammer and knock it off. But I would get caught. I could have waited here a little longer, I could have done what I wanted to do. If I had a gun, I would kill her, right in the face, right between her eyes. And then I would kill me. He can't have her. And he has to live with that for the rest of his life.

"I tried. I couldn't get a gun. I'm not a resident. I couldn't get a driver's license. Just got my birth certificate to do that and wait the waiting period out. Now it's too late. This is not the way I wanted to go. Loving someone unconditionally is a true gift, and he shit all over it. I have nothing to offer him."

"But this spying thing. It's out of control." I told Meredith. "She said she would stop. She promised. 'No more,' she told me. She just keeps hurting herself. I don't know what else to do."

"I'm not making excuses," Jennair said soberly. "I will take accountability that my investigation for the truth, recording them, hacking into their phones and computers, and tracking them, it's not me. It's not what I wanted to do. But it was the only thing I knew how to do to get the answers. At first it was the truth that he was having an affair. That was very clear right from the start. And then I wanted to know what I was up against. Was it really love for him, or was it just sex or an affair? I needed to know the strength and the parameters of what this was about because he wouldn't tell me anything. He just lied.

"I had potential and I was a good person and I loved life and I was so looking forward to a future. It's not in the cards for me anymore. You extinguished me. So, I'm just going to finish it, finish it for you. I just wish I could have taken her away because you don't deserve any happiness for what you did to me."

"Thanks for listening," I said to Meredith, then kissed her. "I have to go. Congrats again on getting out of UD. It was time. But I know saying goodbye to everyone tomorrow will be a tough day. I'll be around if you need me."

At 1:30 a.m, now completely sober but exhausted, I got into my car and drove home. I felt so bad for what I had said to Jennair. I needed to apologize. I needed to try to take back those words.

"I have nothing to offer him. That's what he said," Jennair repeated, sounding completely exhausted. "No one will ever love him like I did. I hope he gets sun cancer and it ravages his face and he ends up in a nursing home alone. Please, somebody, erase this bitch from the world because I can't do it now."

I walked into our apartment, not expecting what I found. Every light in the place was turned on, and Jennair was gone. I assumed she had gone out or she had gone up to the second floor to talk to our neighbor Alicia, with whom Jennair had forged a friendship of sorts, one pretty much based on an alliance against me as the heartless, cheating husband. I turned out the lights and lay down on the couch to fall asleep. Less than an hour later, Jennair burst through the door in a huff.

"I'm not here when you get home and you don't come looking for me?" she asked, obviously upset.

Half conscious, I sat up and tried to collect myself, grabbing my glasses from the coffee table. "What? What are you—"

"I'm going to do it," she said and ran back out the door.

"What the hell?" I said looking over at Huck, who was sitting on the chair next to me, looking every bit as bewildered as I was. I walked out the door and into the hallway, standing right next to the door that led to the back stairwell. Hearing heavy footsteps running up the mesh steel treads, I opened the stairwell door and started my ascent after her. Above me I could still hear the heavy footsteps speedily making their way higher and higher. With every floor, I picked up my pace, but I couldn't catch her. Finally, the stairs stopped, and I saw a large number seven painted in grey on the dark red door in front of me. Straining to catch my breath, I opened the door to the seventh floor and stepped into the hallway. At the end of the hall, I could see an open window, which seemed odd for the middle of March. As I walked down the corridor toward the window, my mind started to wander. "No. No," I said and then picked up the pace, finally reaching the window and looking down. Nothing. *Where did she go?* I ran to the elevator and nervously pushed the button for the first floor. "Come on. Come on. Come on," I grumbled, as the elevator slowly made its way down. When the door opened, I ran out and down the hallway toward our apartment and flung open the door.

Jennair was standing there in the kitchen. "I'm going to do it!" she yelled again and tried to push past me toward the door. I grabbed her and held her tight in a bear hug, the two of us falling to the floor. "Let me go! Let me do it!" she cried. "Let me go!" But I wasn't about to.

After two minutes of screaming, crying and trying to escape me, I felt her give in, her body going limp. "Let me go," she whispered one last time, panting, exhausted from the struggle. "I'm fine."

I believed her and slowly I released her. We both sat up, still trying to catch our breaths. "Please don't tell anyone," she pleaded. "And please don't institutionalize me." The thought hadn't even crossed my mind. I was still trying to figure out what the hell had just happened.

"I won't," I said to her. "But you have to go see someone. See a psychiatrist. Get medication."

"Okay," she said, nodding.

"And I want you to call your parents in the morning and tell them what happened tonight. "Okay, I will," she agreed.

In that moment I had no idea what had taken place, not having yet seen the video diatribe she had delivered on the couch that evening. I had no idea how desperate she had become. In my gut, in my mind, I only knew that the act that had played out when I had gotten home was a plea for help. However staged or contrived it may have felt to me at the time, I knew Jennair needed counseling and professional care beyond anything I was equipped to provide. My wife was sick. And it was all about to get worse. Much worse.

CHAPTER 19

A SPECIAL PLACE IN HELL

"I actually had a mental breakdown, which was pretty bad," Jennair wrote to a total stranger named Samantha on the public forum NextDoor.com. "But maybe that was rock bottom to go up. Not sure. I'm scheduled to see a psychiatrist who can prescribe something. I do need it. All my other therapists can't give me an RX. Not really sure if I'm healing."

I was getting ready for work in the morning and I felt absolutely awful. After worrying about Jennair's breakdown all night, I had slept maybe a total of an hour and a half and I could feel the effects weighing heavily on my body. I had been fighting a late winter sinus infection for weeks and trying so hard not to succumb to it. But it was a fight I was losing. I could feel an infection swelling from my throat to my sinuses and my inner ears cracked and popped in pain as I strained to clear my head of an unending surplus of bright green mucus. "Just stay home," I told myself. But it was Meredith's last day at UD. I felt like I needed to be there.

As I slowly struggled to get dressed in the bathroom, Jennair walked in uncharacteristically chipper, proudly proclaiming she had made reservations at an Irish pub in West Chester, Pennsylvania, to celebrate St. Patrick's Day. Neither of us were even remotely Irish, but for twenty-four years we used this holiday as an annual excuse to gorge ourselves on fish and chips and Guinness. I was just grateful to see her smile and look forward to doing something together. It seemed she had turned a corner. I didn't want to disappoint her. But my body wanted so badly to just shut down.

"Sounds great!" I lied. I finished my coffee and forced myself out the door as Jennair settled in at her computer. She was smiling as she bid me goodbye and started typing away. I was relieved to see her already busy and returning to normal, looking for work. Maybe finding a job would change everything for her.

An hour later I arrived on campus and got my usual morning coffee at the bookstore across the street from the OCM office. As I took my first gulp, the steaming hot liquid burned the back of my throat and shot a lightning bolt of pain into my inner ears. In that moment, everything went silent with the exception of a high-pitched tone that, in and of itself, was deafening.

"This is going to be a long day," I said out loud. But I could only hear the words as low muffled tones coming from the vibrations in my skull. I wanted nothing more than to crawl under my desk and sleep. But I wanted to be there for Meredith. She had made the decision to leave, but because she didn't get to do so on her own terms, I knew she was feeling emotional about her last day.

By late morning, as I struggled to get through a meeting and read my never-ending stream of email, I still hadn't seen nor heard from Meredith. I sent her a text message.

Mark: *Where are you?*

M: *I'll be in by 11:00 I'll turn in my computer and phone and then that's it. I'll let you know when I'm done. Let me know if you want to get coffee.*

Mark: *Sure. Let me know when*

Shortly before noon, Meredith sent me a message to meet her at the bookstore for coffee. As she walked in, I could tell she had been crying after saying goodbye to everyone. Now in public, she was trying to keep her composure. I myself could barely hold it together, but for a different reason. I could barely hear anything she said and I was struggling to keep my balance and my own composure. The infection in my ears was taking its toll.

"I've been up all night," I told her. "Jennair threatened to hurt herself."

She shook her head. "I'm sorry," she said, seemingly unfazed by the news, obviously distracted by the bittersweet emotions of her last day at UD. Her mind was elsewhere, and it was apparent that neither of us was in a good place to talk. After just fifteen minutes, we decided to cut our discussion short, agreeing to catch up later. I walked back across the street to get ready for a 1 p.m. meeting. As I struggled to climb the stairs to the second-floor conference room, I could feel myself getting more and more woozy. I couldn't fight it anymore. I walked into my office across from the conference room, closed my door and lay down before I collapsed. The world was spinning.

Minutes later, I awoke to footsteps and voices filing into the conference room across the hall. I took a deep breath and steadied myself as I got to my feet. Shaking off the cobwebs of my twenty-minute power nap, I opened my door and greeted everyone in the conference room, taking a seat at the end of the table. As I sat down, I could feel myself falling backward on my chair then and I managed to right myself at the last minute.

"I'm sorry. I can't do this. I'm sick. I have to go home," I announced to the room, and walked out. I made it down the stairs to the VP's office and told him I was going home. And then I realized,

"Shit. I can't drive like this." Seeing that I obviously wasn't feeling well, Glenn insisted I go to the clinic on campus, and asked his assistant to drive me there.

On the way, I called Jennair. "I'm sick," I told her. "I need to go home. They're taking me to the campus clinic. Can you pick me up?"

She hesitated. For more than five seconds, she said nothing.

"Nair? Are you there? Did you hear me?" I asked.

"Okay," she finally said after a deep sigh. "I'll be there."

An hour later, as I was being released from the campus clinic with a prescription for antibiotics and eardrops, I looked around the waiting room for Jennair. I didn't see her.

"Are you close?" I texted.

Jennair: *I'm in the parking lot. I'm not coming in there.*

As I opened the car door of her SUV and climbed in, she looked at me suspiciously. "Are you really sick or was that just a ploy to have me institutionalized?" she asked, repeating her fear from the day before.

I would never do that to her. "What? No. Of course I'm sick. I can barely hear you or sit up straight," I snapped as I offered my prescription to her as proof.

"Just please take me home," I pleaded. "I just want to go to sleep."

Five hours later Jennair woke me up, standing over me, calling my name. "Mark. Mark. Wake up. You need to get a shower. We're going to be late. We have a seven p.m. reservation."

"Oh my God," I said in my head, struggling to open my eyes and rejoin consciousness. As much as I wanted to pull the covers over my head and go back to sleep, I knew I couldn't back out now.

"Okay. At least let me take a shower," I begged.

As the hot water was beating down on my sore neck and shoulders, I happened to look over and could just make out the hazy silhouette of Jennair through the steam-covered glass door. She was frantically moving about. I wiped away the steam to get a better look and saw her rummaging through the laundry hamper.

"Where are they, Mark?" she asked.

"Where are what?" I asked in return.

"Your underwear from the other night. You destroyed the evidence, didn't you?"

"Destroyed the evidence?" I said. "I... I have no idea where they are. I don't have the days of the week written on them."

Without saying another word, she just shot me that "you're so full of shit" look, then turned around, picked up the clothes from the floor, put them back in the hamper and walked out in a huff. I knew exactly what she was up to. She was looking for another specimen to send to the DNA lab, just like she revealed she had done weeks before with my clothes, prompting me to come clean with my feelings for Meredith, when she had also revealed she had cloned my phone and shared audio evidence with Meredith's husband. But why? I had already told her about my relationship with Meredith. Why did she continue to obsessively compile evidence to prove what she already knew?

An hour later, the episode put behind us—as had become our routine—we were driving to West Chester, a small quintessential college town twenty-five miles due west of Philly. As we drove by beautiful homes and the shops of downtown, Jennair remarked how cute and quaint it was, adding, "Well, isn't this nice? You and your girlfriend can visit here once you find a job."

I didn't say a word. I wanted and badly needed to keep the peace. After passing the restaurant a few times without finding a parking spot, we opted for a parking garage a few blocks away. While spring wasn't far away, we both froze as we walked from the garage to the front door, sharing idle small talk. My ears burned with the frigid March wind as I struggled to take in what she was saying.

Finally escaping the cold, we were warmly greeted inside Kildare's Irish Pub. On stage we could see a young woman with an incredible voice loudly belting a variety of indie music favorites with an acoustic guitar strapped to her shoulder. As if my ears weren't already at a disadvantage, our hostess sat us in the only table available, right next to the stage.

After ordering dinner and drinks, Jennair wasted no time sharing what was on her mind. Over the music, she shouted into my ear.

"You know you look ridiculous with her, don't you? It's disgusting! Everyone I talk to agrees. You're seventeen years..."

"It's fifteen years. And if she doesn't care, neither do I," I replied. "It's not about age. It doesn't make a difference." I was too sick to wonder who "everyone" was that she was talking to, but couldn't imagine it was many people, as Jennair had few relationships with anyone other than me and her immediate family—and she kept them at a distance. And I sure didn't care about Meredith's age. She was a mature adult with a successful career, not some twenty-something I'd plucked off a college campus.

I spent the rest of dinner fending off a barrage of put-downs about my feelings for Meredith and the unlikelihood of it going anywhere. While I understood her sadness and frustration, I felt like I was under attack and I was too sick to deal with it. If this was somehow an attempt to win me back, it was having the opposite effect. But despite the ineffectiveness of her argument, I knew Jennair was fighting to save our marriage. And as much as I was head over heels in love with Meredith, I continued to wrestle with the thought of ending it. Divorce felt so permanent, so wrong. But the more Jennair monitored my every move, put me down and insisted she had no life of her own outside our marriage, the more I wanted out.

Four days later, on March 20, according to her bank statement, having met the legal residency requirements for Delaware firearms sales, Jennair walked into a gun store and purchased a matte stainless steel Taurus Tracker .357 Magnum. She was the last person on earth I would have ever thought would own a gun, much less use one to take not one life, but two. Jennair was tough. She was strong willed, outspoken and difficult to deal with at times. But she had never been violent. And she certainly was no killer. Except for one time, and the incident shocked me as much to recall as it did to witness it.

On a hot Indiana summer day in 2004, Jennair was mowing the front yard with a garden tractor when a mother robin swooped down in front of her to grab food for her nearby nest of babies. Jennair was going too fast to stop and ran over the bird. Turning around in the tractor seat, she saw that the mother robin was still alive and flailing around in agony. Immediately she shut the mower off and began crying and screaming at the top of her lungs, "Oh my God! Oh my God!" all the while running to the garden shed. She quickly returned with a pair of pruning shears and, with only slight hesitation, she asked the mother bird for forgiveness and then thrust the shears into its chest until it was still. I stood there, stunned. I could have never done that. But that was Jennair—brutally compassionate when she had to be. For the next two weeks, she cared for the babies in the nest, feeding them until they were old enough to fend for themselves. She never once spoke of killing their mother with the pruning shears. It was just her instinct. But it scared the hell out of me.

Nearly ten years later, in South Carolina, Jennair and I had lived in a gated neighborhood that backed up to a horse farm with green rolling hills and a beautiful serene pond. We would sit at our table or on our back porch and watch the horses and other wildlife every morning and evening. It wasn't unusual for the property owner to fire his rifle over the pond just for fun. Occasionally we would hear a rogue bullet whizzing through the trees in our back-yard, prompting us to ask him (loudly) to stop. Jennair and I were not fans of hunting or guns. We didn't understand the culture and we wanted nothing to do with them.

On a clear Saturday afternoon, Jennair was sitting on the back porch with her iPad when she happened to look up and see the horse farm owner next door with a handgun. He was walking up on a gaggle of geese that had landed to forage for food. Something didn't seem right about this scene. Instinctively she pulled up the iPad and began recording video. He walked up to within ten feet of the geese and began indiscriminately firing. Pop. Pop. Pop. Pop. Pop. Five rounds had gone off, scattering dozens of geese, while one goose lay dead.

Still recording on the iPad, Jennair could be heard exclaiming, "Gotcha!"

Within an hour Jennair had called the county sheriff and the Department of Natural Resources. Killing Canada geese was a fed-eral offense, and the horse farm was technically within the city limits, where firing a firearm was forbidden. In the end the owner was fined five-hundred dollars and warned never to fire his guns on the property again. One more gun had been silenced. But more importantly to Jennair, justice was served for one dead goose.

On March 22, 2018, the same day Jennair had sent the message to a woman on NextDoor.com about her mental breakdown, I told her I was going to the coffee shop to prepare for a job interview I had the next day. The antibiotics had kicked in and I was feeling better than I'd felt in days. On the way there, Meredith sent me a text message.

M: *What are you doing tonight? Haven't seen you all week.*

Mark: *Prepping for that interview. You?*

M: *Having dinner with a friend in Greenville*

Mark: *At coffee shop. Come say hey later if you want.*

Two hours later, as the coffee shop was closing for the evening, Meredith sent me another message.

M: *OTW*

Mark: *They're closing. Drink next door?*

M: *K*

Copperhead was a quaint little neighborhood wine bar right next door to the coffee shop and less than five-hundred yards from our apartment. I knew it was a bit of a risk to meet so close to home, but it was never intended to be anything other than a quick visit. By the time I packed up my things and walked in, Meredith had already ordered two glasses of wine and was sitting at a small round pub table near the back, but with a clear line of sight to the front door. She waved, though I had spotted her the second I walked in the door. Her long straight hair fell elegantly over her brown leather jacket. Her face beamed radiantly. With the exception of seeing her briefly on her last day at the office, I hadn't really seen her since that night at the bar in Hockessin, exactly a week before.

I leaned down, kissed her cheek, and took off my olive-green insulated winter coat and draped it over the back of my chair. Meredith said something to me, but I didn't quite catch it.

"What?" I yelled, leaning in toward her. "Sorry, this music!"

"I love that coat," she yelled back. "I've never seen you wear it."

"It's cold out there," I said. "Winter is back."

"Did you check it for recording devices?" she yelled, laughing out loud.

"Ha ha," I replied, reaching back and putting both hands into the pockets. "No, I seriously doubt—" Then I froze and closed my eyes. "Fuck. Seriously?" I raised my left pocket to show Meredith the small rectangular shape protruding through the lining of my coat. Just as I did, I froze again.

"Jennair just walked in the door," I mouthed calmly to Meredith.

Since the day Jennair had moved to Delaware in December, she and Meredith had never actually been in the same room. Now three months later, she was walking right toward both of us, glaring daggers.

"Look what I just found," I said to Jennair, displaying the protrusion in my coat as she approached the table. Jennair turned her eyes away from me and stared Meredith down. She leaned in to whisper into her ear, while pointing her index finger and accidentally striking Meredith in the head. I couldn't hear what she said. Meredith didn't move a muscle.

Jennair then looked at me and demanded loudly, "Come. Home. Now!"

"I'll walk home when we finish our conversation," I said firmly.

As Jennair stormed away from our table, I could feel every eye in the place on us. When the door closed behind her, there was a collective and audible gasp.

Meredith sat there stunned, laughing nervously.

"What did she say to you?" I leaned over and asked.

"She said, 'There's a special place in Hell for women like you,'" Meredith repeated, tasting the bitterness on her tongue. The look on her face turned to anger and she began rocking back and forth in her chair.

"I'm sorry," I told her. "You okay?"

"Oh, I'm fine. I just need a few minutes," she assured me. Shortly after, we resumed our conversation, and before we knew it, ten minutes had gone by. Again I could feel every head in the place turn back toward the front door.

"She's back," I told her calmly.

Before she even reached the table, I stood up and intercepted her. "I'll be home in a few minutes. Just go," I said firmly. Without saying a word, she turned and walked briskly out the door.

"I'm going to go," I told Meredith.

"Okay," she replied. "I'm going to hang out here for a few minutes."

I walked out the front door and cut across the parking lot toward our building.

As I opened the door to our apartment, I expected an immediate confrontation with Jennair. But she wasn't there. Then my phone rang. It was Meredith.

"Where are you?" she asked.

"I'm home. Why?" I replied.

"Jennair has me parked in and won't let me leave," she said, frustrated. "Can you please call her and tell her you're home?"

I sent Jennair a text. "I'm back. Leave Meredith alone."

There was no response, but Meredith called me back to let me know Jennair had gone. As Meredith prepared to leave, some of the staff had gone out ahead to make sure it was safe for her. That's when they saw Jennair, sitting in her car, parked directly behind Meredith's.

Eerily, one of the images I found on Jennair's computer backup was a photo of Meredith's car taken as she was parked directly behind her. But at the time, I wrote off the confrontation as normal, given the context. What married woman wouldn't confront her husband's lover given the chance? Yes, she'd glare. Yes, she'd say mean things. And yes, she'd hang out in the parking lot until her rival was gone. If the tables had been turned and it was Jennair meeting her lover, wouldn't I have done the same? But the tables weren't turned. Normal or not, I was thinking of Meredith, not Jennair. And I was thinking of finding another recording device sewn into the lining of yet another coat.

Five minutes later when Jennair walked in the door of our apartment, she was no longer the one enraged—I was.

"Why the hell did you do that?" I screamed. "We were just having a conversation." Our relationship had so deteriorated that I was unable to put the event in perspective. I was unable to see Jennair's perspective. I was so desperate for my independence from her that it didn't matter to me that I was bringing my lover to a place so close to home, a place where my wife would surely find us. What mattered was that no matter where I went with Meredith, Jennair's eyes were on us. No matter where I went without Meredith, Jennair's eyes were on me. I so desperately had to get away from her.

I grabbed my keys from the hook near the door.

"Where are you going?" she asked.

"For a drive to cool down," I told her. "And no, I'm not going to see Meredith. She's probably pissed at me right now. My God, what the hell were you thinking?"

Minutes later, I found myself driving aimlessly down dark country roads somewhere in rural Pennsylvania. I called Meredith to check that she'd made it home okay. She had made it home, but she was still pumped up. One of the patrons she talked to in the bar after I left was a lawyer. He encouraged her to consider filing a PFA (Protection from Abuse) against Jennair, but she wondered if that would do more harm than good. I agreed and asked her to sleep on it.

When Meredith called me the next day, I could tell she was torn. While she and her husband were getting a divorce, they remained on good terms. And he and a friend were lobbying her hard to file for the PFA and she wanted my support to do it.

"Look," I said to her, "I need for Jennair to get a job. If you file a PFA that's going to show up on her permanent record. I'll leave it up to you though."

Reluctantly, she agreed, at least somewhat. She asked her attorney to proceed with the paperwork, but ultimately decided not to file.

Two days later, Meredith called me at work—this time distraught. Someone had vandalized her car, carving deep scratches all the way around it. Since the night of their confrontation, it had been raining, which had made it nearly impossible to see the gouges in the dark grey paint of her A3 Cabriolet. We both knew who it had to be and when. The only other time Meredith had left her car out in public was at the gym.

I called the bar and the coffee shop next door to ask them for security footage from that night. They didn't have cameras in place. Meredith also struck out with the gym, because their security cameras weren't pointed toward the area of the parking lot where she had parked.

When I got home from work, I thrust open the door and immediately unleashed on Jennair.

"What did you do?!" I screamed.

"What?" she replied innocently.

"You know what. You keyed her car. And now she's going to file a restraining order against you."

Jennair sat there for a moment to let that sink in. Then she said coldly, "Physical damage and violence isn't my style. If I wanted to fuck with her, I would ruin her precious reputation online."

So was that what she'd do next? Troll Meredith online?

I wanted to protect Meredith but I didn't know how. Jennair emphatically denied everything and we had no evidence to prove otherwise. Again, Meredith's husband pleaded with her to file the PFA. But without physical proof, Meredith couldn't bring herself to do it. In the end, of course, it wouldn't have made a bit of difference. That piece of paper would never have stopped Jennair nor changed the violent tragedy that occurred almost exactly one month later. A tragedy I never once anticipated, as I worried that Jennair would ruin Meredith's online reputation.

CHAPTER 20

NOT EVERYONE GETS OUT ALIVE

I never thought she would actually talk to me. But I said, "What the hell? Why not try?" Sheila, Jennair's divorce coach, was described to me by Jennair as "a real ball buster," somebody who would "absolutely chew me up and spit me out."

I had never even heard of a divorce coach before, but I thought if she could help Jennair through the most difficult time of her life, I was one-hundred percent behind it. "She's not a lawyer. She's not a therapist. She kind of does both," Jennair explained to me. "Her background is accounting and she's great at negotiating, especially messy divorces. She's like a wedding planner for divorces." Just what we needed. Someone to plan our divorce, in style.

After her first meeting, I could tell Jennair saw Sheila as an ally she could trust. I offered to meet with them together, but Jennair rejected the idea. "No fucking way," she said.

One Saturday morning I left our apartment to go to the gym. As I neared the lobby I heard Jennair's voice. I could tell she was talking to Sheila on the phone. "He's going to screw me. He's just so bad with money and so disorganized. Like I told you he has ADD. And now he's going to..."

I stopped in my tracks and doubled back. I didn't want Jennair to think I was spying on her. I suppose one could argue I had every right, given the weeks of espionage she had so flawlessly executed. But I didn't know how to play her game, and certainly not at her level. I didn't want to either. Not once during our twenty-eight years together did I ever look through her purse, read her email or try to break the code on her phone. To me it was common decency, an instinct. Something stopped me, like it would most people. She had every right to express what she was feeling to her divorce coach. She needed support and I was glad she was getting it.

Conversely, her obsession with shattering my privacy continued to escalate. On some bizarre level, finding surveillance devices had become commonplace. I became unfazed by this annoying game of cat and mouse. But she continued to step up her game, her techniques and the sophistication of the technology she used. Every morning before leaving for work, I did a sweep of the inside of my car. Among the many devices I found were a tiny microphone clamped under the passenger seat and a high-def digital recorder Velcroed to the bottom of my steering column, deep under the dash. When I found them, I either smashed them, pulled them apart by hand or submerged them in my coffee to soak on the way to work. And then I left them in place for her to find.

But with Jennair now gone, I reluctantly and with very low expectations sent an email to Sheila.

Sheila,

This is Jennair Gerardot's husband. As you might imagine, I am still devastated about her death, as I'm sure are you. I'm still trying to make sense of it all, especially after the email she sent you that morning. Despite what you might think and what Jennair may have shared with you, I still loved her and told her that every day. Would you be willing to meet for coffee or lunch in the near future? Or entertain a phone call? Please let me know.

259

Respectfully,

Mark Gerardot

To my surprise, Sheila replied to my email the very next day.

Hi Mark,

I'm happy to talk to you, for sure. Maybe we could schedule a coffee after that.

You're in my prayers. I can't even begin to imagine what you've been going through.

Best,

Sheila

We made arrangements for a phone call later that week. That morning, I sat in my car in the parking lot of the office park where I worked, waiting nervously for the 9:30 call. Suddenly, I didn't feel well. I had been so pleasantly surprised by her willingness to talk, I hadn't even considered what earth shattering news Sheila might be prepared to drop on me. I'd discovered so many things about Jennair I'd never suspected that there was no telling what she'd shared with Sheila, true or false. Was I really ready for that? The phone rang. Shit! My hands began to sweat.

"Good morning, Sheila," I began.

"Hi, Mark, how are you feeling? I can't even imagine," she replied in a reassuring voice, likely honed after years of on the job training. As a divorce coach, she speaks with hundreds of distraught couples a year, especially women, giving them compassion and hope, but with a dose of hard reality. As she will remind her clients, she gets paid by the hour, so as pleasant as she can be, she is also quick to get to the point.

"Jennair lied to me," she said. "She never told me she had a gun. I didn't ask her but it was an important fact to leave out."

Without mincing her words, I could tell in Sheila's voice that whatever alliance or pact she had with Jennair had shifted. "I don't care what she did, Meredith didn't deserve to be shot in the face for it," she said. "And you certainly don't deserve the aftermath you've had to deal with either."

Now comfortable and feeling we were on the same side, I asked Sheila if she had talked to the police. I could barely believe her response. Of course it would make sense for the police to want to talk to her, I thought. She had intimate knowledge about Jennair's state of mind, having spoken to her for weeks about her fears and anger concerning our divorce; she was even one of the last people Jennair texted before the killings.

"I offered," Sheila said, "but the police didn't contact me. I went to the police station the following night to speak to someone. The detectives were off duty for the day but I was told someone would contact me. But I never heard from anyone."

Then in the week or so following the tragedy, a story came out in the news about a neighbor who saw Jennair scoping the neighborhood with binoculars two days prior, but she didn't report the mildly suspicious activity. The police seized on this moment to make an example of her, publicly scorning the neighbor for not reporting what she had seen.

"That was bullshit!" Sheila told me. "That poor woman didn't deserve that. And yet I have relevant information to offer, and they don't even bother to talk to me?" This time, she contacted the Chief of Police by email and questioned the irony of making an example of the neighbor, yet not contacting her at all. The detective in charge of the investigation contacted her within 30 minutes of the email to the Chief and tried to set up a time and place for an interview. The detective offered to meet at her office but, Sheila rebuffed him. "No, I'll come to you."

Sheila told the police that Jennair seemed to be overly fixated and very concerned about getting in trouble for illegally planting devices and recording someone against their wishes. "It's a federal crime," Jennair had told Sheila.

"It *is* illegal," the lead detective confirmed.

But Sheila had told Jennair that planting recording devices paled by comparison to some of the other things she had done. At one point, Jennair had bragged to Sheila about how she found out intimate details of my plans for a new job. Sheila had stopped her. "Wait—how do you know this?" she asked.

"Because when Mark goes to sleep at night, I take his keys and go into his office at UD," Jennair said nonchalantly.

"*That's* a crime!" she had told a perplexed Jennair. "You can't do that. That's breaking and entering, maybe more! UD will press charges. Mark has nothing to do with that. He can't say yay or nay."

As Sheila recounted this new detail with me, it made me think. "It's as if Jennair had no sense of right and wrong," I said. "But the more I think about it, it really wasn't all that far from how she normally acted. Rules didn't matter to her. Justice mattered to her. At any cost."

Sheila pondered the thought, but didn't respond.

Before I knew it the thirty minute conversation Sheila and I had scheduled was over. I asked if she would be willing to talk again in the future. She agreed. A few weeks later, Sheila and I met again and picked up the conversation where we'd left off.

"I talked to her for five hours," Sheila told me. "And I didn't pick up on anything."

"I lived with her for those four months, and I didn't pick up on anything," I replied. "She had a gun at our place for a month. A gun."

"A few days before I first met her in person, you met Meredith for drinks at Harvest, right?" Sheila asked.

"Yeah. That's right," I confirmed.

"Well, she texted me photos of the two of you, and told me you two were there right then. Jennair suggested I go there and see what the two of you looked like. I wrote back, 'Not going over there, but how do you know where they are?' And she told me, 'I'll tell you on Monday.'"

When they met face to face that following Monday, Jennair confided in Sheila that she had been tracking and recording us for weeks. As she rambled nervously, Sheila could tell that Jennair was completely obsessed with knowing my every move and pleaded with her to stop, for her own sake.

"You already know he's having an affair," she told her "He admitted it. Stop torturing yourself. I think it would be great for you to get a job, any job. Maybe try something at Starbucks. Structure would be so beneficial to you where you're not thinking about Mark, Meredith and what they're doing all the time."

But Jennair couldn't stop thinking about it, constantly and incessantly. The more she thought about it, the more she carved a cognitive trail in her brain that made it impossible for her to think of anything else, to have any other goal other than to gather more "evidence" to justify her rage. Just as my thoughts went straight to Meredith no matter where I was, no matter what I saw or heard, Jennair's thoughts went straight to Meredith as well. My thoughts brought me to love. Jennair's brought her to hatred—a hatred like

I'd never before seen in her. And discovering that dark side of Jennair left me wondering what else there was about her I'd missed.

Now sitting across the table from Sheila, I asked her point blank, "Did you ever see anything....off when you first met her? Different?"

"I just thought she was distraught, never thought suicidal or homicidal," Sheila said. "There's a book called Crazy Time that, as a coach, I tell my clients about and I myself reference it. Because it is crazy. During a divorce everything you knew to be true is changing."

I had to admit something to Sheila. "Look. To me I had probably become socially conditioned to the idea of divorce over the years. I didn't really know what I was getting into. I didn't understand how big of a deal it was. How devastating it can be. But then again, I never told Jennair, 'Hey, let's get a divorce.' She was the one hell bent on divorce! Divorce! Divorce! I guess she thought the enormity of the decision would scare me. And I'm like, okay... you see celebrities getting divorced all the time. You see it in movies and on TV... people get divorced. It's just one of those things, I thought. But I had no idea the impact it would have." I told Sheila that, looking back, one of the things that makes me most sad for Jennair is that she didn't have the support of friends to help her through it.

Sheila nodded. "She had just moved here and didn't have friends. I tell people, when you're going through a divorce, you can't have just one friend. You need a team of friends. And she had nobody." At least she gave Sheila that impression.

"I know. I know," I said sadly. "And she didn't want to move back with her family in Indiana and surround herself with the support they were offering her."

"Yeah, but when you don't live near your parents and family, you often make friends who become like family, sometimes even better." Sheila said.

"But she didn't," I replied. "She refused to make friends."

"No, because she had you. She built her whole life around you," she said.

"And is that healthy?" I asked Sheila, "not wanting friends?"

Sheila didn't think so. "But it wasn't her unwillingness to make friends," she said. "She just didn't need more than you. And that was the situation/relationship the two of you had built."

We both paused, looked at each other and took a deep breath, letting the sadness of that statement sink in.

"Like I always say, if you don't have that balance," Sheila added, "that you're a sister and an aunt, and a friend, and a neighbor, a colleague, all the different pieces of your pie, so when one of your pieces falls apart, you have support from other areas....And it's scary to think, what would have happened if you had died? What would she have done?" she asked.

I looked up, paused and said very directly, "I think she would have been happy. Or happier," I said.

"What?" Sheila said surprised.

"It's true," I said, "Jennair told me it would be different if I had died. With the divorce, she felt the past twenty-four years of our marriage had been a complete waste of her time. But at least if I were dead, she could look back and remember it all as sweet memories."

Sheila nodded, her eyes sad and sympathetic. "Jennair was convinced that you and Meredith were going to get married and have babies and live happily ever after," Sheila shared. Jennair's thoughts weren't different from most women who find out their spouse is having an affair. But most of all, her greatest concerns were money and insurance. She was sure you weren't going to support her. She thought she might end up homeless since she had been out of work. She thought you were going to punish her because she didn't have a job and wasn't contributing anything."

"Punish her?" I stopped her. "That's the word she used?" I shook my head. "That's crazy," I told her. "I don't know how many more times I could have told her I was going to support her. But even if I wasn't willing—it's the law."

"And I told her," Sheila related, "You've been employed. You're employable. You're going to be okay. You'll find a job." She constantly reassured Jennair, trying to make her see even the slightest of silver linings. "As awful as this is," Sheila said she had told Jennair, "it's your unique chance to decide where you want to live, what you want to do and where you want to be, without being someone's spouse."

"But she just wasn't capable," I said.

I had been badgering Sheila with questions for more than an hour. Then she turned the table. "Did she get along with your family? Was she on good terms with them? I'm not judging her, just asking."

I paused, wondering how deep into my chest of dysfunctional memories I needed to go. "Jennair was different. So different than my family," I told her. "My father loved her and she loved him. But my siblings and their spouses, they were all so quiet and reserved. Jennair was so outspoken. Loud by comparison. She said what she thought, often without thinking of the consequences," I said. And then I recounted a story, one that I had rarely, if ever, shared with anyone before.

In 1995 my brother went to the hospital on Christmas night. Both of his kidneys were failing. While working as a groundskeeper at a golf course for months, he had been exposed to highly toxic herbicides and pesticides they used to keep the grounds immaculate. Months later, his kidneys had shriveled up to the size of dates, as my brother graphically told us all. So for the next few months my brother had to be on a dialysis machine a few times a week. But long term, that just wasn't sustainable. Fortunately, he had ten siblings which made him a great candidate for a possible kidney transplant.

At the time, Jennair and I lived in Indianapolis, while my brother and most of my family lived two hours away in Fort Wayne. The IU Hospital was in downtown Indianapolis, so my entire family rented a passenger van and made the trip down to be tested as possible kidney donors. We were all more than willing to give up a kidney to save my brother. No question.

In a presentation room, doctors explained to us how a transplant worked, and how humans can live very normal lives with just one kidney. It was a major surgery and a huge decision, but they told us it had become a very common surgery with a long track record of success stories. And then the doctor opened it up to questions.

Not surprisingly, we all sat silently, looking at one another, afraid to ask questions or completely satisfied with what we had learned and ready to learn more about the next steps. But then Jennair held up her hand. "I have a question," she said.

Oh God! I thought, squirming in my seat. I stared her down, hoping she would read what my face was saying, "Please don't. Please don't." But she ignored my silent plea. As she began to speak, I braced myself for what she was about to say.

"Just because you're a match doesn't mean you have to do it, right?" she began. "I mean, I'm assuming my husband is the closest match because he's male and just two years older. But what if he refuses?"

"Jennair!" I interrupted. "Stop." But she kept going. No filter.

"I don't want him to do this," she stood up and said loudly in front of the group. "Why should he have to risk his life? What if he dies? What do I get? I mean, look if he has to do this, then I'm at least going to have his sperm frozen before—"

I stood up. "That's enough! I'm doing this." I said firmly. I sat back down, embarrassed.

"That was just two years into our marriage," I told Sheila. "For the first time my family got for themselves a taste of what it was like to live with Jennair. On the two-hour trip home, my older brother Ernie later told me that everyone was in shock and couldn't stop talking about her little 'frozen sperm' diatribe. And she never really regained their respect again."

"What? That was a medical emergency," Sheila said in disbelief. "Decisions are made differently. That's harsh...really harsh."

After several more stories and vignettes of our lives together, Sheila pondered before she asked, almost rhetorically, "You were in an abusive relationship. You know that, right?"

"Me? An abusive relationship? I would never say that. Why would you call it abusive?" I asked naively.

"That she would stand up in front of your family and embarrass you like that...this was your brother who would have died... so yeah, I do think what she did to you was abusive," Sheila said emphatically. "She needed to control things, seems most things. You don't have control like that over your kids. In a relationship, that's just unusual. Did you think at the time it was more than just pure embarrassment?"

"Wait. It gets worse," I warned, sharing another story with her. Our family cultures couldn't have been more different and holidays, especially more somber family occasions, revealed stark contrasts. In 2009, less than eighteen months after my mother's death, my father passed away. In his will he named the oldest of my eleven siblings, Jeanne, as the executor of his estate. I love and respect all of my siblings, and Jeanne was the first born—the default family matriarch. It was a responsibility she didn't take lightly and we all trusted her implicitly. She sent us all regular updates, including a letter from the estate attorney that outlined the process and terms by which the estate would be equally divided. The letter also offered each of us the opportunity to respond if we had questions or concerns. I had none. As expected, Jeanne had everything under control.

When someone died on Jennair's side of the family, however, like clockwork there would be this sort of frenzy-like feeding among siblings, cousins, nephews and nieces over who got what. It caused full-blown heated arguments and so much stress that I refused to even be a part of the conversation, much less engage in the live in-person brawl.

Until my father passed, there hadn't been an occasion for my family to even consider dividing someone's personal belongings. But to their credit, Jeanne and my other sisters took an orderly approach to the task. My two brothers and six of my sisters got together at my father's house to organize his belongings. Unfortunately, unlike my siblings, I didn't realize that wives, husbands and significant others weren't expected to be there. But Jennair was there.

While my father and my mother had moved into the home less than ten years before, they had amassed a considerable amount of furniture, tools and other keepsakes. I had my eye and my heart set on one item in particular that had sentimental value to me. During my childhood, my father had showed me how to use his Craftsman wood router to make beautifully rounded and sculpted edges on hand-made furniture. That's all I wanted and I let my siblings and Jennair know.

But when Jennair saw my brother was loading up his SUV with a drill press, a wood lathe and a number of other power tools, she couldn't resist. I should have known better, but she convinced me to start loading up with as many tools as we could before he took them all. Before long the entire back of Jennair's Nissan Pathfinder was packed so full, the tailgate wouldn't even shut. I'm sure my siblings were shocked, and rightly so.

Just then my oldest sister Jeanne approached me in the living room. "So you don't trust me?" she said.

"What are you talking about?" I asked, perplexed.

"The letter. You sent a letter to the attorney asking for more details of the estate," she said.

"No I didn't," I said in my defense.

Jeanne pulled out a letter from an envelope and pointed to the signature and said, "You signed it!"

I looked down at the piece of paper she was brandishing and sure enough, it was a letter written to the estate attorney, ostensibly from me, and signed by me.

"No. I didn't," I said as I held the letter in my hand, shaking my head in embarrassment.

Immediately, I found Jennair and confronted her, trying to keep my composure in front of the entire family. I told her I knew about the forged letter and that she needed to apologize to my sister. Jennair reluctantly went into the house to talk to Jeanne while I unloaded all the tools from the truck back into the garage and waited for her to come out.

She told Jeanne that she forged the letter because she was looking out for me. I had A.D.D and I didn't understand how to deal with money, she explained. Jennair also challenged Jeanne that she and my siblings had said, "welcome to the family" when we had gotten married, so she shouldn't be left out and be treated like she was on the outside.

Needless to say, my sister wasn't buying it.

When Jennair opened the door and sat in the passenger seat, she started to say something, and I immediately held up my hand.

"Don't. Just don't," I told her, and then we drove back to her parents' house without saying a word. For the next nine years, she would never see or speak to anyone in my family again.

"She wasn't normal. Probably for a long time." Sheila said. " It probably had become so normal for you. I believe that mental illness gone unchecked gets worse. Like diabetes, heart disease, cancer. If it's not treated, it gets worse. From constantly checking your phone to alienating colleagues, siblings, your staff...abusive," she said convincingly. "You were so limited in your life. Then when you experienced your relationship with Meredith, you felt great compared to feeling like shit. I agree with you. That's really tough to overlook and pass by – although I don't ever condone affairs."

I was speechless. I didn't know what to say. I didn't hire this woman. Jennair did. And here she was concerned about me and what I had been through, not just in the past few weeks, but the entire course of my marriage.

As we wrapped up our conversation, Sheila shared an important insight. "My biggest takeaway or what I've learned the most from all of this is that everyone has a breaking point and you need to be aware of that. This situation just confirmed that. I didn't see it at all, but she totally hid what was really going on. Yes, she was distraught," she said. "But distraught pretty much goes with the territory."

Sheila then shared with me a number of stories about divorces she was familiar with that ended badly. Murders. Suicides. Destroyed lives. It was of little comfort and disturbing, actually, that my story (our story) had been added to a list of marriages/divorces that ended so tragically.

"This story is absolutely tragic," Sheila said. "It's so hard to fathom the far reaching effect of losing someone suddenly, shockingly, like they were plucked off the Earth. It devastates family, siblings, friends, roommates, cousins, and everyone who loved that person. It just never goes away. It's so painful and awful."

"Do you think Jennair gave that even one thought at all? Would that have stopped her?" I asked.

"Not sure," she answered immediately. "But she was on a mission."

She paused. "I tell all my clients, divorce is huge. It's not as easy as it sounds. Happens to 50% of marriages. Yes, that's true." Sheila warned ominously. "And not everyone gets out alive."

We both sat in discomforting silence as her words hung in the air.

CHAPTER 21

THIS MEANS WAR

Sitting in my favorite leather chair in my apartment, I opened my laptop and looked at the entries on my calendar. For no particular reason, one day in particular caught my eye. "March 27 - Interview 9:00 am. Offer - 5:20 pm." The memories of that day came flooding back.

"Hey," I greeted Meredith on the phone from my office at UD.

"Hey," she replied, walking out of her gym.

"So…. I got it." I told her. "I got an offer letter."

"You what? Oh my God," she said. "That's fantastic. Are you going to take it?"

"Uh, yeah," I said without hesitation. "And get this—two free vacations for two people per year at any of their resorts. *Our* resorts, I mean."

"So where are you taking me first?" she laughed. "Oh wait, I'm getting another call," she said. "Oh my God. It's Villanova. I'll call you right back." While Meredith had gotten a verbal offer from her immediate boss weeks before and had already left UD, she had still been waiting for the official written offer after a standard background check and a phone interview with an administrator who she said had interviewed her about her knowledge of the Catholic church and her beliefs as a Christian woman. "Pretty sure I aced that interview," she told me a week before, proud of herself after stressing about it and studying up on it for days.

Less than five minutes later, Meredith called me back. "Guess who else just got an offer letter?" she said, barely able to contain her enthusiasm.

"Congratulations! Again," I exclaimed. "Although we both knew you were going to get it."

"Thank God," she said with a sigh of relief. "And you got yours too? Five minutes apart? When do you start?"

"April 16," I told her.

"Me too!" she screeched.

"Fuckin' bananas!" we both said in perfect unison, then began laughing hysterically. We couldn't believe it. It was as if the stars were aligning, we both thought. Just weeks before Meredith and I had sat in my car and mused about the circumstances of how we had met and the destiny we were certain was somehow at play.

"I know this is really weird to say, but I'm just going to say it," Meredith began. "So, when I was a teenager, I had a dream that my Prince Charming was at UD and he just..."

I put my hand to my mouth, trying not to laugh.

"Listen to me," she said. "...and he just swept me off my feet. And I couldn't figure out what the dream meant. And my mom said, 'Oh, it means you're going to meet a guy from Delaware.' And I said, 'I don't know. But in the dream there was this guy and we worked together..."

"You are bull—" I started to say.

"Nope. I'm not bullshitting you," she said, cutting me off. "Ask my mother."

"Get out of my car," I yelled out loud, laughing.

"Stop!" Meredith pleaded with me to take her seriously. "And my mom said, 'Oh, you worked on a project together?' And I said, yeah, that must be how we meet."

"Get out of my car," I yelled again.

"Stop!" she pleaded, embarrassed. "From the time that you and I have been in this 'well, maybe there's something more' phase, that's all I can think about. It's all I can think about. Look, I had no intentions of this happening when I interviewed you obviously. At all."

"Of course not," I said.

"I didn't think while working at UD that this would ever happen. I thought I was already there [meaning: found her destiny]. But I remember getting married and thinking, 'This isn't quite it. There's something else.' I just feel like all the things I did to stay at UD were for a reason. I kept sticking it out and sticking it out. And if you were to ask anybody, I have felt more joy, more excitement starting this past fall than I ever have before. Because of this guy," she said, pointing at me. "This guy."[6]

As her voice echoed in my mind, I looked back down at my calendar. There were several invitations and entries made directly by Meredith. "March 31: M+M Running," April 16: First Day Drinks." After she left UD, I had given Meredith administrative access to my UD office calendar so she could not only see what I was doing on a day to day basis, and when I was available, but she could also add events to it whenever she wanted.

Then one evening while at home with Jennair, I received a few strange emails that were forwarded from members of my team.

---

[6] Recorded conversation, March 2018

"What is this? What does this mean?" one of them asked. "Is this a mistake?" asked another. Confused, I scrolled down to the email they each had forwarded.

"Aw shit," I said.

"Jennair Gerardot is now the sole administrator of Mark Gerardot's calendar," it read.

I immediately sent an email to my entire team. "Sorry for the confusion, guys. Ignore that previous email. It was a mistake." Then I checked my email settings and, to my surprise, Meredith was no longer an administrator. And somehow neither was I. But Jennair was.

"What did you just do?" I yelled to Jennair, who was in bed with her iPad.

"What?" she asked innocently.

"My calendar," I scolded. "Obviously you hacked in."

"Yeah, so?" she yelled back, "Why does she get to put things on your calendar and I can't?"

"Seriously? Because I invited her to," I argued. "Change it back now! And stay the hell out of my accounts."

The next morning, still asleep on the couch, I received a text from Meredith.

M: *Did you remove me from your calendar?*

Mark: *No. Jennair did. I told her to reinstate you.*

M: *Looks like she's still an administrator. Want me to remove her?*

Mark: *Yes. Please do.*

Minutes later, Jennair came storming out of her bedroom. "Are you fucking kidding me?" she yelled. "Are you fucking kidding me? That fucking bitch!"

"What?" I jumped up, startled. "What are you yelling about?"

"Meredith Sullivan has removed me as the administrator for Mark Gerardot's calendar!" She screamed, reading the email she had just received. "This means war!" she proclaimed.

"Stop. I told her to do it," I yelled. "Calm down. I didn't know you were going to get an email."

She just stared blankly at her computer screen, seething, crying. I told Meredith that Jennair had gotten the email. She felt awful. "Oh my God," she said. "I had no idea that would happen. I feel so bad. Please tell her I'm sorry."

Meredith's response surprised me. She wasn't usually empathetic with Jennair and in this case, she had every right—in fact, it was her responsibility—to remove Jennair from the calendar. But something about it struck a nerve with her—she knew that in Jennair's mind, it was a personal confrontation, and that was a boundary she respected. She wasn't going to confront Jennair in any way, even in cyberspace.

Before I left for work, I walked up to Jennair who was pounding away on her laptop keyboard, writing a response to Meredith.

"She didn't mean it, Jennair. The system sent the email, just like it did when you made changes. She feels awful." Jennair stopped typing, glanced up at me, and then clicked the cancel button. Ultimately I caved and reinstated Jennair as an administrator. If I hadn't, I knew there would never again be peace.

Caving in to Jennair's outrageous demands had become our routine for years, our dance. She would cross a line that would somehow become the new norm—a new line I retreated from to draw and redraw again and again. It was a fight I didn't want to fight, not wanting to lose to someone who had nothing to lose. So I would just back down. She was a master at making the extreme seem normal. At making my opposition to her extreme behavior seem cruel. Me. I was always the bad guy. And she. She was always the victim.

But the fact is, while I didn't know it at the time, Jennair insisted on me giving her access she already had. Sitting alone in my new apartment, poring over the purchases, phone calls, and plans she'd made in the last few months of her life, I discovered she had already secretly installed keystroke recording software on my computer months before we'd had that argument. And in the middle of the night as I slept, she had placed my thumb on the Touch ID sensor on my phone and then added her own thumbprint, so she could log in whenever she wanted without my even knowing. If I had changed the password to my calendar, she would have known it in an instant.

When I got to work that morning, I told my team again that it was all just a stupid mistake. "I had been trying to let my wife view my calendar and I must have just checked the wrong box," I explained. But the way they all looked at one another, I could tell not everybody was buying it. The cracks were starting to show. I needed to do something quickly.

"I can't continue to do this anymore," I told Meredith. "We need to start the ninety-day break we talked about. Immediately. This is just getting out of control."

Although she wasn't happy about it, she understood and reluctantly agreed. She needed time to get ready for her new job and move up to Villanova. And Jennair and I needed to come to terms with our relationship and make some difficult life decisions.

It was a lazy spring Saturday and if I was going to get through the first day of the break and then the next eighty-nine, I needed a distraction. I needed to stay busy. I went to the gym. I got a haircut, filled my tank with gas, dropped by the neighborhood coffee shop, picked up my dry cleaning, even went grocery shopping. Nothing seemed to take my mind off Meredith. I lay down on the couch and turned on the NCAA tournament. I couldn't care less about the game. I tried to take a nap but just tossed and turned.

Tired of seeing me mope around the entire day, Jennair finally couldn't take it anymore. "My God, you're pathetic," she scowled. "You can't even go a day without talking to her."

It was true. I was a mess. Since the holiday break in January, Meredith and I hadn't gone a day without talking or texting. Clearly I had underestimated my ability to go cold turkey. I was miserable. And selfishly, I hoped that Meredith was too.

The next morning, I heard a text alert on my phone—a message from UD. It was the first weekend of spring break and there had been an accident involving students on the way to Florida. For weeks I had been collaborating with my team to coordinate photographers and videographers to document a story about a group of students who were on a volunteer trip to clean up hurricane damage. The accident was a big deal that made local news. My team had to make a call whether to proceed or pull the plug. Meredith had always been my go-to for something like this and I couldn't fight my urge to send her a text message about the news. That started a flurry of text messages back and forth, first about the story, but then it turned personal. Before long we admitted to each other that the previous day had been miserable for us both.

Jennair saw me texting and lost it. "That's her, isn't it? I knew you couldn't fucking do it."

"It is. It's about work," I said, and then paused, thinking of just how miserable the next eighty-nine days would be. "You're right though. I can't do this. I don't want to. I'm not happy. And I'm in love with Meredith."

Days later my divorce attorney Jennair had insisted I needed to hire pleaded with me, "You have to get out of there. You need to file a PFA."

I stood up and began pacing in the conference room, looking out at the skyline from the fifteenth story window. "I'm not in any danger," I insisted, looking down at the floor, still pacing. "Jennair isn't a dangerous or violent person. And if I filed a restraining order, or I left or forced her to move out, it would just escalate things. Make things worse."

"Then file a petition for a divorce," she said soberly. "The way you are living is just crazy. Once you meet your six-month Delaware residency requirements in thirty-five days, you can file."

I stopped in my tracks and paused. The more Jill spoke, the more I came to realize just how unhealthy and far beyond repair my relationship with Jennair had become. Nobody deserved the self-inflicted pain that Jennair was enduring. And nobody, no matter their transgressions, deserved a daily existence spent looking over their shoulder, sweeping their car for bugs and patting themselves down to simply have a private conversation. This was the reality check I had needed. I looked up at her. "Okay," I said, nodding. "Okay."

"But don't wait to tell her," she warned me. "Don't surprise her on May tenth when she gets it in the mail. You need to tell her now."

The lump in my throat suddenly doubled in size. My heart felt like it might jump out of my chest as I rode the elevator down to the ground floor. But it was time. I couldn't conceal, much less get over, my love for Meredith, and I couldn't take anymore of Jennair's surveillance of my every word and movement. Jennair needed a life of her own, a job of her own, a focus of her own—something that wasn't me. We both needed it.

On the way back to my office at UD, I called Meredith and recapped the highlights of my meeting with Jill. She was at home, packing for a trip to Miami that she and a girlfriend were taking the next day, a quick getaway before she started her new job two weeks later. She was happy and proud I had taken this huge step forward—a necessary step for us to start a new life together.

When I got home that evening, Jennair was anxious, almost excited, to find out what I had learned from my meeting with the attorney. We sat down calmly on the couch and I told her everything I had just learned about divorce law in the state of Delaware. Then I had no choice but to tell her, "On May tenth, I'm filing a petition for divorce. A couple of days later you'll get it in the mail, and you need to sign it." I explained that this would just start the clock. We had at least six months of separation to figure things out financially, or even to reconsider.

Jennair sat there stunned. She had wanted me to go see an attorney, but somehow she didn't expect this. She began to cry and I grabbed her tight and held her.

Months later, sitting in my favorite leather chair, I started looking through the folder of videos from Jennair's computer backup again. There was one I hadn't noticed before, dated April 6, that very night I'd told her I'd be filing for divorce. The thumbnail image was completely black. I clicked on it and it began to play. Very shakily, the camera panned up from the floor while the auto-focus lens struggled to zero in on an object. Then I recognized the patterned upholstery of the chair in the furnished apartment that Jennair and I had shared. As the camera panned up over the chair, the lens found an object to settle on. It was me, fast asleep on the couch, a half empty wine glass on the end table. For the next three minutes and thirty-five seconds, the camera watched as I slept, stirred, and at one point, reached up to scratch an itch on my face.

I didn't understand. What was this I was looking at? I played it back again, this time turning up the volume as high as it would go. At first all I could hear was a dull hum, white noise or perhaps warm air flowing through the vent from the furnace. As I stirred, she ducked and quickly covered the lens with some sort of fabric. After a couple of seconds, she uncovered the lens and she refocused it on me. Then, at roughly the 01:30 mark, I heard a metallic click. Then another. A ten second pause and then a third click. Then eventually the video again goes black.

Perplexed and more than a little freaked out, I sent the video to a film producer I knew for her opinion, who sent it on to her friend, a homicide detective. A couple of days later, she sent me a message to arrange a three way video call with the detective. "I want you to hear this directly from him," she told me.

I was literally sitting on the edge of my seat as the detective began, "I didn't know what this was when Barbara sent it to me. But the second I heard it I knew exactly what it was."

"And?" I asked nervously.

"It's a revolver," he said without hesitation. "Absolutely an unloaded revolver firing and then advancing and then firing again. No question. It's a very distinctive sound."

After another thirty minutes of hearing him describe the mechanics of a handgun, I had had enough. I could hear my own breath deepen and the growing sound of my heart beating in my chest. "Thank you," I said and then set my phone facedown on the table, my hand trembling.

Was there a bullet loaded? Were there two? I suppose I'll never know.

CHAPTER 22

PLAYING HOUSE

Jennair's reaction had taken me by surprise. She's the one who sent me to the divorce attorney; surely she knew we'd discuss divorce. And the next day she offered yet another surprise. Overnight she seemed to have come to terms with our new reality.

"If we're inevitably headed toward divorce in May," she explained to me, with a notebook in her hand, "I have some terms I want to discuss for our 'wind-down' period."

"Okay…." I replied, with some hesitation.

"We're going to continue to live together in this apartment through the end of our lease on May 31."

"Right. Agreed," I said.

"You and I will spend as much time together as possible, taking walks, going to dinner, hiking trails with the dog."

"Sure," I said. "We can do that."

"I'm going to look for jobs back in South Carolina, Indiana or anywhere."

"Okay, great," I said.

"You can spend time with Meredith," she said, and then looked up from her notebook. "But it needs to be kept to a minimum. And you have to be completely transparent about when and where you're going."

"To a point," I said. "I'm not going to check in and tell you every time."

"Mark, you owe me that much," she argued.

"Okay, okay. Whatever…" I said, gesturing with my hands to move on. Telling my wife every time I saw Meredith didn't seem like a good idea, and it certainly wasn't good for Jennair's mental health, but I was tired of arguing. "What's your next point, demand or whatever you call it?"

"Terms," she corrected me. "I will have sole custody of Huck and Gypsy," she said, saving the biggest bomb for last, and then closing her notebook.

"Jennair! No!" I refused that one. "I can't do that. You know I can't do that."

"Tough shit!" she said. "You made your choice. You chose Meredith."

"So, this is retribution?" I asked, then stood up and walked to the kitchen for coffee. I couldn't imagine losing Huck. He and I were as bonded as she was with her cat Gypsy. And now she wanted to take him away from me out of sheer spite.

"Call it whatever you want," Jennair said, following me. "These are the terms."

The idea of losing Huck, who we had rescued in Atlanta in 2012 and raised together for six years, was absolutely heart-wrenching for me to even think about. And she knew it. We both loved Huck like he was our child.

"Just stay here. Stay close," I reasoned. "Let me have visitation. You're going to need help. Just stay in the area."

"No!" she said in defiance. "If I ran into you two," she paused. "I.. I… just couldn't handle it," she said, putting her hands to her head. "Do you want me to blow my head off?"

"Don't say that," I said, repulsed. "That's an *awful* thing to say."

To some, I suppose, that statement should have been a red flag, especially given her recent unstable behavior. But exaggerated, dramatic, over-the-top declarations had always been a part of Jennair's vernacular. She loved to drop histrionic bombs then sit back and watch people's reaction to them. She had no filter. No boundaries. No rules. It had been one of the things that had originally attracted me to her. But twenty-eight years later, the act was old and I was tired of it. On a weekly basis she would tell me she was going to kill me for something I had done, or "fuckin' murder" the person who had cut her off in traffic. "You're a fucking asshole. You're an idiot. You're a pussy..." and a quiver-full of other put-downs and insults she would fire at me, all designed to get a rise out of me or whoever was on the receiving end of her verbal wrath.

Clearly she was using Huck as a ploy, a bargaining chip. I think she thought I would call the whole thing off if it meant losing Huck. And I almost fell for it. I almost caved. But I knew I would find a way to see him. She thought she had played her best hand and won. She hadn't. I wasn't going to let her take him from me. And I wasn't about to go ten rounds with her, yelling about it, only to lose the argument. I'd deal with that issue when we came to it.

"Okay," I said.

"Okay, what?" she asked.

"Okay, you can have Huck," I told her, then walked out of the room.

As far as I was concerned, all the other conditions she had proposed seemed fair. We needed to stay in Delaware through May to establish residency anyway. As long as we could get along, spending time together sounded like the amicable end to our twenty-four-year marriage I had hoped we could have, anyway. So I agreed to her terms.

With the prospect of moving at the end of May, I started to look at houses and apartments to rent within ten miles of my new employer across the border in Pennsylvania. But true to form, Jennair couldn't resist her urges to want to control the situation. She began her own search for apartments and houses for rent—not for herself, but for me, and about as far away from the Villanova campus where Meredith would be working as you could get. Then she started sending me decorating ideas and promotional sales on furniture, rugs and household items.

"Jennair. Enough. I can do this," I told her.

"Just trying to be helpful," she said, sounding unappreciated for her efforts. But it didn't feel like help she was offering. It felt more like trying to continue to control how I lived. Or maybe she was just clinging to her role as wife and homemaker in some small way. Whatever it was, I knew I had to draw the line.

Ultimately, I decided to enlist the help of a realtor and made an appointment to look at homes and apartments in the Philly suburbs on April 4. Meredith told me she was heading up that way to measure her new place to make sure her furniture would fit and asked if I would help. So, per our new agreement, I told Jennair our plan. I was going to meet Meredith for lunch and then help her measure her place. On the way up to Bryn Mawr that morning, however, my realtor called me to cancel my appointment with her because of an unexpected personal crisis. But I was already halfway there, and I had taken a vacation day specifically to look at places. Instead, I met Meredith early and she rode along to help navigate the list I had created of places to see. I didn't think a deviation this minor warranted a check-in with Jennair.

After Meredith and I had lunch together, her new landlord let us into the house so we could measure all her rooms. Her new home was a charming three-story red brick twin with white trim, a basement, a cute little backyard and a sunroom in front, all within walking distance to campus and her new office. It was perfect for her and she was excited to share all her decorating ideas with me. Meredith had always wanted to be an interior decorator on the side and now she had this big blank canvas to paint however she wanted. She also insisted I have a say, since we had hoped to spend a lot of time there together. But I didn't have much experience with decorating, Jennair having made those decisions, so I just agreed with all her ideas. On top of her many talents, she made beautiful decorating choices. And it was her home, after all.

It was a joy to watch her light up talking about her first home as a newly single woman. We talked about dinners we would have, the wine we would drink on the front porch and the walks we would take in the neighborhood. But we agreed that we both also needed to maintain some independence and have our own spaces to retreat to.

That afternoon we looked at a brand new apartment for me in Bryn Mawr that I just couldn't wait to see—a modern top-floor flat that overlooked the city and the Villanova campus in the distance. And the best part was that it was less than a mile down the street from Meredith's new home. We couldn't wait to go running, shopping and lounging at the corner coffee shop on a lazy Saturday. And I couldn't believe it was finally happening—I was finally going to be with the woman I loved, and bring an end to an unhappy marriage that had been dying for years.

When I got back to Delaware late that afternoon, Jennair wasn't home. Twenty minutes later, from inside the apartment, I saw her outside, talking on her phone. She saw me through the patio door, hung up, and joined me inside.

"Did you two have fun playing house today?" she asked.

I didn't respond.

"You're such a liar. You spent the whole day together. Freddy told me all about it," she said.

"Freddy? Who's Freddy?" I asked.

"He's part of my team watching you," she warned.

Oh, God. Here we go again, I thought.

I didn't believe her for a second. But whenever she inferred that she had a team of coconspirators, it made me uneasy, which was one of her goals I supposed. Or was she literally that delusional? I had to wonder.

I explained that the realtor had cancelled on me and I apologized to her for not keeping her in the loop. To keep the peace with Jennair I told her I would do a better job of holding up my end of our deal. It was only the fourth of April. May 31 seemed so far away.

A week later, I needed to go back up to Bryn Mawr to follow up on a couple of places that had come on the market and make a final decision on the fourth-floor flat that was my top contender. I asked Meredith to go with me and, following the rules, I very clearly disclosed to Jennair that Meredith was tagging along. I told Jennair I would try to be home by 9 p.m.

After looking at the new properties, which took less than an hour, I still felt good about the decision to sign a lease on the flat. "I want it," I told Meredith.

"It's awesome," she told me. "Are you going to do it?"

"I'm going to do it," I said, then sent a follow-up text to the realtor telling her I was ready to sign a lease.

It was still early in the evening so Meredith and I decided to celebrate the decision over sushi and a glass of wine, finding a cute little place just off campus.

"This will be our place," she told me, walking in. "We can walk here."

"Our place," I repeated. "I like the sound of that."

As had become our habit, Meredith and I found a spot at the end of the bar and after a couple glasses of wine and gorging ourselves on spicy tuna rolls, I looked down at my phone.

"Crap," I said. "8:39." I sent Jennair a text message.

Mark: *Lost track of time. Leaving now. Not going to make it home by 9*

Jennair: *Okay. Thanks for letting me know.*

But later, I would discover how she really felt, in a letter to her family.

He just left at 8:40 pm and it takes 45 minutes to get home. He said he would be home at a respectable hour on a Monday work night. Well drinking and coming home at 10:00 pm is not a respectable time nor condition. And he will fix himself some food and sit in front of the TV and fall asleep and be in no state to talk or spend time with me. And I will most likely just go to bed because that's what normal respectable people do on a Monday night.

Driving home, Meredith and I laughed and sang to our favorite songs on the Pandora station we had created, titled "Green Hearts"— her signature sign-off emoji. We both had new homes to look forward to and new lives to start.

When I got home, Jennair was standing in the kitchen in her coat, heading out to walk Huck.

"Sorry I was late," I said. "I just…"

"It's okay," she said calmly. "I'm not mad." Then she walked out the door.

"Okay…" I said to the refrigerator, "that's new."

As I started to hang up my keys, I noticed the spare key fob to my car was missing from the hook where it normally hung. I instinctively walked over to the patio door and parted two of the vertical blinds to peer into the parking lot to watch. Jennair was headed straight for my car and I heard the distinctive chirp-chirp and saw my taillights flash. I knew what she was going to retrieve.

With my keys still in hand, I opened the door and stepped through the blinds and onto the patio. I then clicked the lock button on my fob, which again flashed my taillights. And then again, just for effect. Jennair stopped, looked back over her shoulder and saw me standing on the patio.

"I already found it," I shouted. "It's not there."

I was bluffing of course, but she bought it. Immediately, she changed course and headed toward the front door of our building. When she came back in, she was unapologetic.

"Give it to me!" she demanded.

"I can't. I already destroyed it and threw it out the window on the way home," I lied.

She just shook her head and turned away. And that was that. Or so I thought. She walked over and picked up her laptop off the kitchen counter. "I've been working on our finances tonight. I want to go through them with you," she said.

"Okay," I said bewildered, unsure of what just happened or what was about to happen.

She then proceeded to open up a spreadsheet populated with every detail of our financial picture. She had divided up our assets, our expenses, personal belongings, our debt... Our finances weren't all that complicated, but clearly this was more than just a few hours of work. She had spent days contemplating our financial future. Jennair had put the bulk of the debt burden in my column, and I was okay with that. She wasn't working and I was the sole breadwinner. In the short term, it was my responsibility to take care of her, and I accepted that. Eventually though, I expected her to work and bear her fair share of financial responsibilities.

It wasn't our first discussion of finances. Weeks before, Jennair had tried to persuade me to agree to pay her forty percent of my salary, with no set end date. I was hesitant to agree. My fear was that it would set a dangerous precedent, letting Jennair live off the forty percent for the rest of her life. She had already suggested several times that she did not want to work anymore. But I wanted so much for her to pick herself back up, find a new career path and make a go of being the independent, successful woman I knew she could be. Of course, I knew and accepted that I would owe her some financial support in the form of alimony, likely for the rest of my life.

In the meantime, I told Jennair I would pay one-hundred percent of the monthly expenses until we had reached a settlement agreement. That I would continue to pay her car lease. That I would pay her insurance. That I would give her money for groceries. And that she would need to find some work—just as she needed to do if we had stayed married. She was a skilled and talented woman with an impressive professional record and was decades from retirement. Yes, she was facing age discrimination, but she could go to graduate school and gain new skills. But she refused. She could go to work for herself in some way. She refused. Or she could just try harder to find work. But she was too busy monitoring me to do so. In short, I felt like she wanted to retire at the age of forty-seven. As for me, I was finally taking control of the finances as I should have done so many years before. And she was fighting me every step of the way, and of course, as I discovered later, had already hacked her way into the new bank account the day after I had opened it, in order to track my every deposit and every withdrawal.

But now we sat together calmly and respectfully talking it through for almost two hours. Despite our obvious dysfunctions and constantly second guessing each other's motives, the discussion was strangely amicable. This emotional roller coaster, this dance we did with each other, had become our new normal.

The next morning before the sun came up, I quietly snuck out to my car to retrieve whatever device she had planted. After several frustrating minutes, I couldn't find anything. But I knew it had to be there somewhere. I pulled the driver's seat back as far as it could go, and with my left hand and knees planted firmly on the blacktop, I reached as far under the dash as my arm would go. Paydirt! Strapped to my steering column, I recovered one of the largest, most sophisticated recording devices yet. I pulled the SD card and crushed it into the pavement with my foot.

When I walked inside the apartment, Jennair was sitting at the kitchen counter waiting for me. "Where were you?" she asked. I set the empty digital recorder on the counter, as if daring her to try it again. I just walked into the bathroom to get ready for work. We didn't say another word to each other.

It was May 21. Almost a month after the killings. Sitting on my desk next to my computer at my new job was the iPhone I had just purchased and ported Jennair's phone number to. The police had confiscated her phone that evening and twenty-eight days later their digital forensics team was still trying to break the code to comb it for evidence. Suddenly, the phone pinged. I picked it up. It was a text.

Jennair, it's Freddy. . .

CHAPTER 23:

DID I SCARE YOU?

On Saturday, April 14, Jennair had planned an outing for us at Brandywine State Park in Delaware to go hiking with Huck. On the drive there, she made an announcement. "I have a hair appointment on Monday," she said. "I'm thinking of getting my hair dyed purple. What do you think?"

"Why?" I asked, hoping she wasn't serious.

"Cause I like purple."

"No," I said. "Why would you do that? You're going to have a hard time with people taking you seriously in a job interview."

She didn't say another word. Neither did I.

When we pulled into the park, the parking lot was already packed. It was a beautiful, breezy spring day and, unbeknownst to us, it was the park's annual Kite Day. We sat in the grass eating the lunch we had packed while hundreds of kites flew overhead. It was mesmerizing, nearly cinematic to see the myriad of colors, shapes and sizes as the wind whipped the kite tails this way and that like a beautiful orchestrated dance. But then a sad, familiar sound brought me back to earth. Jennair began to whimper and sniff as her face welled up with tears.

"Why are you doing this to us?" she asked. "We can fix this."

"Jennair," I said softly, "it's too late. You can never trust me again. I can never trust you again. We're too broken. Maybe in a few years, we..."

"No! You will never see me or hear from me again," she bawled.

She lay her head down on the ground and began to sob uncontrollably, the tears flowing freely onto the dry brown grass. I stroked her soft blonde hair and pulled it away from her face so it didn't get wet with her tears. I felt so awful for the pain she was going through. I wanted to make it go away. I could, in an instant, of course. But even if I had been willing to end my relationship with Meredith, it would have just delayed the inevitable and caused more years of pain and mistrust between us. We both needed a fresh start. I was confident she would get through this pain and be even stronger once she was back on her feet. And I wanted to help her and support her through the process, though it was naive to think she would accept any help from me, other than financial. So I just held her as she cried.

After a couple of hours, we packed up and returned to the car. Jennair had gathered herself and seemed to be her normal, strong self again.

"Let's go to Kennett Square and get ice cream," she said with a final sniff while wiping her eyes.

"Okay, sure," I said, surprised but glad to see her make such a quick recovery.

Kennett Square is a quaint, historic town, just across the Delaware border in Pennsylvania. Dozens of restaurants and shops bring a mix of locals and tourists to the downtown square. It was just the place to go for some distraction and exploration.

On the way there, we came to a four-way stop in Centerville, a charming little town known for its antiquing. "Wait," she said. "I've been wanting to go there." She pointed to a cute little gourmet store and café nestled behind one of the antique shops. "I've heard it's great."

"Alright," I said and turned left into the drive. As we walked up to the store, however, a woman stood in the doorway, flipping the "Open" sign to "Closed."

"Sorry," she said. "We're closing."

"Can we just get..." Jennair started to say.

"No. Sorry," the woman told her, turning away.

"Crap. I'm never going to get to go here," she said, disappointed.

The comment struck me as a bit melodramatic, since surely she could go another time, but I didn't give it much thought.

When we arrived in Kennett Square fifteen minutes later, Jennair walked into a crowded ice cream shop to stand in line while Huck and I sat on a bench outside. To pass the time, I flipped through my phone to check for any new emails or texts. I glanced up and couldn't believe my eyes. A green 1970 Triumph Spitfire rumbled by. I looked down at my phone to launch the camera app and when I looked back up, the car had already gone by, and there stood Jennair with her hands and face pressed up against the store window, her eyes burning at me. I knew exactly what she was thinking: "I'm watching you, asshole."

She came out five minutes later and joked, "Did I scare you? How's Meredith?"

"I'm not. I just—" I stuttered, then having second thoughts, I stopped talking. This wasn't the place nor time for the confrontation she seemed to be inviting. I just took the ice cream she was handing to me and walked away.

We found an old metal table on the sidewalk and sat down across from each other. After a few minutes of awkward silence, the conversation turned completely normal as we talked to passersby who couldn't resist doting on Huck. To them, we must have looked like any other happy couple hanging out in Kennett Square. I wondered what challenges they might be going through in their own lives. Seemingly happy, sharing laughter, holding hands. But you never know, do you?

Soon the afternoon sun began to wane, so we ordered takeout from a popular restaurant down the street and walked back to our car. As we drove out of town, I inadvertently made a left turn on a street clearly labeled Meredith Street, hoping Jennair hadn't noticed. But she did, prompting an immediate visceral reaction from her.

"You must be fucking kidding me," she moaned. "Get us off this street."

At the next corner, I gladly obliged.

The next morning was a Sunday. I awoke to the sounds of Jennair getting ready in the master bathroom. When I walked into the room I was surprised when I saw her putting the finishing touches on her makeup, all dressed up to go out. "Wow," I said. "You like nice. Where are you headed this early?"

"Brunch," she replied. "It's a divorced women's support group."

"Good," was all I said. It seemed like a good sign and I didn't want to ask any questions or upset her.

After she left, for the first time in a long time, I had the whole place to myself. I walked into the kitchen to make coffee and was surprised to find a sink full of dirty dishes. That wasn't like Jennair.

"This place is trashed, Huck," I told him, who looked up at me with his big innocent brown eyes. "Did you have a party last night? Well, while Mommy is out today, we're going to clean, brother," I said, trying to sound excited. I wouldn't go so far to say that I ever actually enjoyed cleaning the house or doing laundry. The thing I hated most was being told I wasn't doing it right or my efforts weren't good enough. But nobody was there to tell me that. So I cranked up the music and got down to business, starting with the sink full of dishes. Next the bathrooms. Then vacuuming. And finally, a bath for Huck. When I finished and was putting the vacuum cleaner away, I heard my phone vibrating and saw it dancing across the kitchen counter. When I picked it up, there must have been fifteen text messages, all from Meredith.

It was day one of Meredith's move to the Main Line, a wonderful historical and social region of suburban Philadelphia. She had enlisted the help of Keith, a good friend and former UD colleague, to move in the first wave of essentials she'd need to live in the house for the week while she began her new job at Villanova. A bed. Some clothes. A coffeemaker and some food. But from the look of her texts, things were not going so well. It was pouring down rain. Her new place hadn't been cleaned at all. Her queen-sized box springs wouldn't fit up the stairs. It was one thing after another. I felt bad that I wasn't there for her.

Mark: *Sorry. I feel helpless*

M: *Thanks. What a mess. I'm having a mini-meltdown.*

Mark: *Call you later?*

M: *Yes. Please do. I need my person.*

Just then Jennair walked through the door. She was crying. "What's going on?" I asked.

"Nothing," she said, obviously hiding something.

"Jennair? You okay? What is it?" I asked.

"It's fucking hopeless," she said.

"What is?" I asked.

"My life," she said and then broke down in tears, laying her head on the kitchen counter.

"What happened?" I asked.

"These women," she started. "They're all divorced, but they're all rich. They were like, 'Oh, you'll be fine. Look at us. We're happier now.' It's not the same. I don't have their resources. My life is fucking over," she kept saying over and over and over.

"No, it's not," I told her, stroking her hair. "You're going to get through this. We're going to get through this."

A month later, looking through Jennair's receipts and bank statements, it just didn't add up. April 15, 9:42 a.m. Dunkin Donuts $1.99 in Wilmington? Why would someone who was driving to a brunch stop for coffee at a donut shop? And another: 2:33 p.m. $4.00 for a salad at a grocery store that was a mile and a half from Meredith's new house in Bryn Mawr. Two hours later she walks into our apartment, crying. Had she spent the whole day in Meredith's neighborhood, watching her move in?

I pulled the cork on my second bottle of wine. The text from Freddy had me shaken up—it was as if Jennair herself had contacted me from the grave. She had been watching me and Meredith for so long, it never struck me as possible that there really was a Freddy. But here he was, a month after her death, texting her.

Jennair, it's Freddy. . . Sorry it took so long to get back to you. I was on vacation. I'm still interested in doing your window tint and helping you out in any way with your husband. Call me back.

What window tint? She'd been following us in a rental car so we wouldn't recognize her. Had she planned on tinting the windows of a rental car? As for the rest of the text, helping her out in any way with me, well, that seemed pretty obvious. Unless he was a hitman, I presumed she meant follow me. Get pictures of me with Meredith for her attorney? But to what end? She had plenty of audio already, I didn't deny the relationship, and it was a no-fault state. What was the point of hiring Freddy?

Whatever it was, I had to find out. So I texted him back:

Hi Freddy, this is Mark, Jennair's husband. I'm sorry to tell you that Jennair took her own life, and the life of the woman I was seeing. Call me.

He never called. And I couldn't bring myself to call. When a cable network show later sought him out, he vehemently denied ever meeting or knowing Jennair.

But they must have met or at least talked on the phone. Who was he? With some Googling of auto window tinting, it wasn't long before I found him. He wasn't a private eye, but he clearly was willing to "help." What did that mean? And if there was a Freddy, had there been a team all along? I crossed the room and looked out the window to the cars parked along the street. I had assumed no one was watching me now, but I couldn't shake the feeling that Jennair's mission wasn't done. I imagined a white, windowless van pulling up alongside me as I walked down the street, shoving me into the back and slipping a dark hood over my head as I was whisked away.

I finished the bottle, with each dwindling glass taking me deeper into the darkness of my mind and memories. Those final days had been so strangely normal.

A week after Meredith had moved into her new house and Jennair had gone to "brunch," I awoke on the couch where I had become accustomed to sleeping alone since January. It wasn't yet 5 a.m., the sun barely wobbling into view. Something felt strangely familiar. As the fog of sleep began to lift, I felt Jennair wrapped in my arms. At some point during the night, she had nestled in next to me and put my arms around her without waking me. I laid still, not knowing what to do. Then I carefully extracted myself and walked toward the spare bedroom.

"Where are you going?" she asked.

"To my bed," I replied.

"Why?"

"Because it's not right, Jennair."

Looking back at that moment, I regret not holding her longer, giving her the comfort she was seeking. Would it have changed anything? I doubt it. But I was afraid it might mislead her or escalate into sexual advances from her that I wasn't prepared to handle. And for all I knew I was being recorded and a video of us spooning on the couch would have been all Jennair needed to wreak havoc with Meredith. I didn't trust her any more than she trusted me. Without making a conscious decision, my loyalties, my heart, now belonged to Meredith.

I laid in the guest bed thinking of all the things I needed to do that morning. It was Saturday, April 21—the big moving day for Meredith. For weeks this day had been clearly marked on the Google calendar I had shared with Jennair. I told Meredith I would help her coordinate the movers she had hired and put together furniture she had bought for her new place.

Later that morning, keeping to our agreement to tell her when I was going to be with Meredith, I told Jennair I was going to the hardware store to buy tools for Meredith. Of course, Jennair wasn't happy about it.

"Make her buy her own tools," she said, annoyed.

I ignored her and drove off. On the way to Meredith's new home in Bryn Mawr, I stopped at the hardware store to purchase the essential tools that someone living alone would need: cordless drill, hammer, screwdriver set, wrenches and a level. Meredith had never lived alone or had to do any real handiwork around the house, so I looked forward to helping her.

At the time, I didn't think I was doing anything wrong. It wasn't anything I wouldn't have done for a friend who had asked for help. But Meredith was more than a friend. To Jennair, however, Meredith was her replacement. For almost a quarter of a century, Jennair and I had spent probably hundreds of weekends at the hardware store to get supplies and tools for our many home projects—fixing windows, cutting tile, laying hardwood and painting walls. And while any home improvement project almost never failed to spark an epic fight, looking back we had fond memories of what we had accomplished together. Helping Meredith with her house was surely a wound that cut deeper than I knew. But at the time, my focus was on the joy I'd have helping Meredith, not on the wound my doing so would cause Jennair. We'd inflicted such deep wounds on each other by that point that it wasn't even on my radar.

But it was on hers.

When I pulled up to the house with tools in tow, the movers had already arrived and were starting to unpack the truck. Even better, the rain was gone, and in its place, a bright sun lighting up the sky. What a perfect, warm spring day to move, I remember thinking. Meredith was buzzing around the kitchen with as much energy as I had ever seen in her. She was happy, excited and moving at a frenetic pace as she directed the movers where to put things. She stopped briefly to give me a hug. "Oh wait," she said, "Wait. Wait. Wait," then walked over to a kitchen cabinet. "Ready?" she asked, then paused. "Tada!" she said proudly, opening the cabinet to reveal the green glow of the model Triumph Spitfire I had given her.

"It was the first thing I brought in," she said. "Well, that and Indy."

Indy was Meredith's dog she had gotten as a pup when she moved into her first house with her now ex-husband. She walked me to the back door to show me Indy in the yard enjoying her favorite pastime—playing with a rock in the long green grass. Through the hedgerow that separated her yard from her neighbor's, we heard the ferocious bark of a dachshund, who was quickly corrected by its owner.

"Stop," he said in a corrective but gentle tone. "Be nice."

"Hey, Tim," Meredith said to him cheerfully.

Tim brought his dog over to introduce him to his new neighbor Indy. Meredith introduced me to Tim who lived next door with his wife. Meredith expressed how helpful and kind they had been as she spent the first week there alone with nothing but the bare essentials.

One of the movers poked his head out the back door with a troubled look on his face. "It won't fit through the door," he said.

Meredith and I went back inside to investigate. Three young men stood in the doorway holding a buff-colored, oversized sectional. Clearly, when this home was built in 1888, the builders had not envisioned the girth of 2018 furniture. In an instant, Meredith's optimistic energy turned to disappointment.

CHAPTER 23 | **DID I SCARE YOU?**

"Well, gentlemen," I said, "we're just going to have to take that jam off. Who has a crowbar?" They looked at each other and shrugged.

Earlier, while buying tools, I never imagined we would need a crowbar. But refusing to accept defeat, I made a mad dash to the local hardware store. Upon returning with Meredith's new crowbar, I chipped through 130 years of paint to disassemble and remove the wooden door jam. After a few minutes of acrobatic maneuvers, we squeezed the couch into the living room and gently set it into place.

Meredith and I spent the rest of the afternoon unpacking and assembling her new furniture while the movers brought in the rest of her things. After they left, we plunked onto the sectional to relax. We were both exhausted but content.

"I want to spend every Saturday with you," she said.

I smiled back. "Let's get some food."

"Later," she said, then grabbed my hand and led me to the third floor.

Later that evening, I sent Jennair a text message.

Mark: *Wrapping up here. Be home after I get gas.*

Jennair: *Not there. Home after 9:00*

Her not being home close to 9 p.m. didn't strike me as odd at that moment. But a month later, I found a lottery ticket Jennair had purchased from a convenience store just down the street from Meredith's house. She also took a fifty-one-minute incoming phone call sitting in that same spot in Radnor.

Later, when Jennair got home, she slammed the front door of our apartment. "How was the sex?" she asked. I didn't answer. "Talked to Rose tonight," she told me, referring to a phone call she had with her favorite aunt.

"And?" I asked.

"I asked her how long before she felt better after her divorce. She said it took ten years to get over it. Ten fucking years," she yelled and then walked into her bedroom and slammed the door.

The next morning, I awoke alone on the couch in our Wilmington apartment, and after a cup of coffee to shake off the cobwebs, I went for a run. Jennair had another all-day outing planned for us, including a hike at nearby Alapocas Run State Park, so I cut my run a little short to conserve energy. I didn't see Jennair when I returned to our apartment. Then I heard crying. In the bathroom, I found her curled up on the floor of the shower with the water running over her. She was overwhelmed with grief, and it was hard to see her like that. I wanted so much to take her pain away. But as difficult as it was to see her suffering, I thought it was a natural and necessary part of her grieving process.

I opened the shower door and extended a hand. "Come on," I said. I wrapped her in a towel and held her until she stopped crying.

Later when we got to the park, it was another warm and sunny spring Sunday. After enduring our first grey Mid-Atlantic winter, the bright sun and budding trees and flowers in the park were a welcome sight. The faces of passing hikers and bikers reflected how much they were enjoying being outside again. So were we. Especially since it might be awhile before we could enjoy another weekend hike like this.

Jennair had scheduled surgery for two days later, to have some painful fibroids removed. Because her doctors had advised her they might have to perform a hysterectomy as well, she was concerned she'd be off her feet for a while. She was also concerned because she didn't think I would be there to take care of her. As we crossed under a concrete underpass heading toward a historic family farm that was part of the DuPont estate, Jennair asked me, "You're going to go back to work and just leave me there to fend for myself, aren't you?"

"No, I'm not," I assured her again and again, while she insisted I would indeed abandon her. "Why do you keep saying that? I already negotiated three days off when I signed the offer letter. And if I need more, I'll take more."

"Mom wants to come and help me," Jennair told me. "Just in case."

"In case what?" I asked. She's obviously more than welcome to come, but I'm going to be there. Of course I'm going to be there, Jennair."

She gave me no response, and we continued our hike, quietly taking in the wildflowers and the welcoming feeling of the warm sun on our faces and the brisk early spring breeze into our lungs.

Other than this briefly dramatic but innocuous exchange, our hike was otherwise uneventful. No arguments. No tears. No deep, substantive discussions. Just an easygoing Sunday hike. Later, when we got home that afternoon, Jennair made a routine grocery trip to load up with some of the usuals—orange juice, apples, spinach, hummus, salmon, almond milk and bread. Everything seemed normal, like any other night. But it wasn't any other night. She already knew it would be our last night.

CHAPTER 24

I'VE DONE A BAD THING

One of Meredith's neighbors spotted her. It was Saturday, the day I helped Meredith move in. A dark-haired woman with a grim look had stood near the neighbor's driveway, clutching a pair of binoculars, gazing down the block. She looked as if she was searching for a lost pet or something. It never occurred to her to call the police. Only later, when the homicide detectives had found the ammunition, the rubber gloves, the ear plugs—and the binoculars—in the rental car parked down the street did she realize there was no lost pet.

How did I not see her? How did I not know she was there? A block away, in disguise, watching Meredith and me through the binoculars as each piece of furniture, each box, was carried into the house, as I ran to the hardware store to buy a crowbar, as I stepped inside to tear down the door jam. She saw it all. And that ticket. The damn lottery ticket she bought that night at a gas station just down the street, hoping for one last chance to change her fortune. If only she had picked some winning numbers, won just enough to give her hope, to give her some security, it would have changed everything that happened that awful day. But the odds were against us all.

While I was in the shower, getting ready for work that Monday morning, Jennair sent me a text message:

Can I get the gas receipt for Saturday night? Seems high for gas at $42. Did you move the next deposit from UD to your new checking account? We're going to bounce the bills soon and May rent won't be paid. I'm trying to get on top of this.

I stepped out of the shower, dressed, and Jennair didn't say a word about the gas, the bills or the rent. Her request documented in the text I'd yet to see, she sat down to her computer to look for work, just as she did every morning. Yet something was off. She seemed oddly despondent, far away. But I didn't ask. For months she'd been sinking into that space, and I'd learned to just accept it. She was understandably angry, understandably enraged, understandably grieving. Any effort to intervene in any way, ask her what was wrong, hold her as she cried, would only hurt her more.

The minute I walked out the door, Jennair sent an email to Sheila, her divorce coach, copying the divorce attorney who she had retained three days before on Friday.

April 23, 8:04 a.m.

Good Morning, Sheila.

I'm not sure we need to meet today. I'm not sure what else we can do at this point. But let me know. ......My surgery is tomorrow morning and I'll be out of it recovering for a few days. Here's an email exchange below with Mark from last week about the support discussion we had and about calling the PA lawyer for a second opinion. ......

Regarding the finances, he alludes to in this email that he is not going to do the support agreement. He stressed in a conversation, that HE would pay the bills as HE sees fit and will not put money in the joint account. He also did not say one way or the other that he would provide me with any money for support because I was already being supported by the rent, bills, etc.

...... Judy and I are meeting Friday to go over the numbers so we can immediately file the interim support once he files. But this is just a waiting game at this point.

Oh, and Mark mentioned to me that he would be open to attending our meetings (his lawyer even said it would be good). I told him I did not hire you as a mediator and that it would probably be a conflict of interest at this point.

Please advise on this and what if anything we can plan/meet at our scheduled 2:30 meeting today. Otherwise, we can cancel that.

Thanks,

Jennair

Minutes after hitting the send button on that email, Jennair logged into the SpyTec realtime GPS dashboard on her computer. She watched as the icon she'd named "Mark Liar" made its way up I-476, passing the exit that would have taken me to my office. At 8:20 she captured a screen shot and named the file, "Look whos going to Merediths today 042318.png"

Fifteen minutes later, at exactly 8:35 a.m., Jennair captured another screen that showed "Mark Liar" parked in front of Meredith's house, naming the file, "Working today question mark 042318.png." My car was parked there for all of two minutes, just long enough to hand Meredith the venti blonde roast with extra soy I had bought on the way, wish her a good day, and give her a peck.

When I sat down at my desk in the office twenty-five minutes later, I sent Jennair a reply to the text message she had sent me earlier, prompting a mundane exchange not unlike we had had on any other day.

Mark: *Didn't print the receipt. No I didn't change the deposit. Will hit old account on 4/30. Let me know where you want to do dinner. I'm out by 5:30.*

Jennair: *Did Huck go this morning? He's asking to walk and I'm about to get in the shower... wondering if I can wait.*

Mark: *He did*

Jennair: *K*

Mark: *But that was pretty early. I cut it short because he insisted on eating goose poop*

Jennair: *Walked him. Diarrhea with mucus (hand over mouth emoji)*

I had to chuckle at her timely use of the emoji. With it, she added a little levity to an otherwise unenviable and often messy situation. But that's the kind of shit (no pun intended) we dealt with day in and day out. Even after everything we had been through, there was still an unbreakable bond, a connection and a language that often went unspoken.

For the next two hours, Jennair made a flurry of phone calls to at least five separate pet stores, trying tirelessly to locate a specific prescription digestive health cat food for Gypsy. When at 11:08 a.m. she finally found a store that carried it, she grabbed a scrap of paper, wrote a short note and taped it to the bag, "I got the wrong one. You can get it from Petco."

Gypsy was my problem now. Jennair wasn't coming back.

Then she did the laundry, cleaned the kitchen, the bathrooms and the rest of the apartment until the entire place was spotless. She laid out her bank account information on the dining table, all clearly labeled in a neatly organized pocket folder, writing the account number, username and password on the pockets. After almost twenty-five years, Jennair was finally relinquishing control over the finances, a constant source of pain and epic arguments between us.

Sitting at her usual spot at the kitchen counter bar, Jennair put the finishing touches on a letter she had been writing for weeks, a twelve-page graphic explanation to her family for what, how and why she felt compelled to what she was about to do. And then, it was time to say goodbye.

Five weeks before, on the night of her failed suicide attempt, Jennair had recorded a video of her tearful goodbye to Huck and Gypsy. "Please don't hate me," she asked them. "Please don't hate me." I can only imagine she repeated that tearful scene again, telling her beloved pets just how much she loved them. Now, in her final letter, she had shared with her family an emotional final plea, an excerpt her mother would later share with me. "Let Gypsy go to the rainbow bridge to be with me. I know you think this is an awful request and what kind of terrible person I am for putting down this healthy cat, but it really is the right thing to do in her case. If I had the opportunity and the time, I would have done it myself." But part of her must have known or hoped we wouldn't do it, because she included detailed instructions for Gypsy's care. As much as she wanted Gypsy to cross the rainbow bridge with her, she wanted her to live.

Next, not wanting Huck's sour belly to ruin all her hard work cleaning, she coaxed him out onto the patio and closed the screen door behind him. Then she walked into her bedroom, removed the gun from the gun box she'd stashed in the laundry basket in her closet, and walked out the door.

It was lunch time. And Jennair knew right where she wanted to go. She walked through the parking lot and climbed into the black Cadillac XTS sedan she had secretly rented almost two weeks before and drove seven minutes away to the gourmet food store and café in Centerville that had been closed two weeks before. The sign hanging from the door now read "Open." She walked in and made an eighteen-dollar purchase. What did she order? What is the last thing she wanted to taste on her tongue? It's a silly thing to wonder. Yet I still wonder.

After she finished her last meal, Jennair got back into the Cadillac, her gun likely in a bag in the passenger seat beside her, and drove five and a half miles across the Pennsylvania border toward the firing range where she had been honing her skill for weeks. I had driven that same twisting and turning back country road on the way to my new job every day for a week. It's the kind of drive you see on car commercials, the driver speeding into the curves, putting the car through its paces, the smile on their face full of contentment. Spring had finally come to the Mid-Atlantic and it was shaping up to be a beautiful, warm sunny day. The grass so green, the yellow wildflowers creeping up the split rail fences and stone walls that separate the road from the fertile rolling hills, while century-old oak trees stretch themselves over the road, their young buds bursting in the warmth of the sun. Nature's beauty had to have given Jennair at least some pause. She had to wonder if she should pull over and turn back. I want so badly to believe she did. But some other force compelled her to press on.

After paying $33.74 for an hour of target time and a pair of earplugs, she sharpened her skill one last time, the woman so opposed to guns now firing shot after shot into a paper target of a human outline, aiming right between the eyes. Her aim perfected, she was back on the road again.

At 1:49 she calls SpyTec technical support from Haverford. That was the twenty-eight- minute call I'd tried to find out about. The place that had sold her the GPS device for nearly five-hundred dollars. What did she want to do with the data? What had she done with the device? Clearly there was something she wanted to know from them about how to do something with that device, the device she'd never need again. Another detail I'd never know, another loose thread I want so badly to tie up but likely never will.

While she was on the phone with tech support, Jennair's mother left her a voicemail, her sweet loving voice full of concern for her daughter who was scheduled for major surgery the following day. "Hey hon, it's Mom. I was just calling to see if you got everything ready for tomorrow. Um, give me a call. Love you. Bye-bye."

Her next stop at 2:40 p.m. was a gas station, exactly .6 miles from Meredith's front door, where she paid twenty-five dollars to fill her tank. Why? Why fill the tank unless you plan on driving back home? Unless you are planning an escape? Unless you are having a change of heart? Why? I'll never understand it. Maybe she did it because that's what you do when you return a rental car. She'd agreed to return it with a full tank of gas, and so she would.

Seven minutes later, Jennair returned her mother's call. It was only three minutes long, so I can only assume she left her a voicemail. It would be the last time she would hear the voice of her first-born child.

Exactly what Jennair did next and at what time is anyone's guess, really. She had been closely studying Meredith's new home for more than a week, downloading a map of Villanova's campus, a satellite photo of the block, and photos of every angle of the house. "Her house is situated weird in the back behind other houses with a long driveway and has a lot of windows that I might not be able to do it there as I wanted," she wrote in the final letter to her family. "I really can't hide well or surprise them without getting caught. I can't have them see me and call the police before I can do what I need to do. In public they will see me coming."

She decided to park just around the block and then, carrying a bag and once again donning her clandestine, secret opps attire— black running pants, black hoodie, black shoes, and now, a dark wig—she walked up to Meredith's front door, broke a single pane of glass and slipped inside.

Just back from lunch, I was having my first one-on-one meeting with Tony, one of my two direct reports. After just a week on the job, he went out of his way to share all the ins and outs of the job, including the strengths and weaknesses of every team member. As we walked up the stairs from one of the conference rooms, Tony noticed something not many people did.

"You're married, right?" he asked. "I noticed you don't wear a ring."

"You're right, I don't," I confirmed. "My wife and I haven't worn rings in years. She needs hers resized, and I, well, I don't like the way mine fits either. It's kind of a long story." We changed the topic, but my own words lingered in my mind. Our rings didn't fit any more than we did.

Safely out of public view, Jennair removed her wig. Her keen sense of detail missed nothing. She swept up the broken glass to not alert Meredith to anything remiss when she came home. For the next two hours, she likely cased the house, still full of unpacked boxes and power tools strewn about from moving day. She probably went through Meredith's drawers, gawked at her photos scattered about, looked inside boxes to see what was inside, wanting to know more, wanting to know everything she could about the life and mind of the woman whose life and mind she was about to end.

At 5:25 p.m., my new colleague, Tony, stood up in his cubicle adjacent to mine. "Have a great night," he said.

"I will, thanks," I told him. "Do the same." I then hit send on my final email for the day and closed my laptop.

Making her way up the steep, creaky wooden stairs to the second floor, Jennair must have discovered Indy, asleep in Meredith's closed bedroom. Having only lived there for two days, Meredith kept her safe in her room because she was afraid Indy would fall down the unfamiliar stairs. While later that evening I would briefly worry about the health and safety of Indy, Jennair loved animals too much to harm her. I can imagine Jennair talking to her sweetly, asking her forgiveness for what she was about to do.

Jennair then walked down the narrow hallway to discover the bathroom, and then peering into the trashcan, she made another discovery. She dumped the contents onto the grey tile floor, and with her phone, she took a photo.

At 5:28 p.m., Sheila sent Jennair a text message:

Sheila: *Good luck with surgery tomorrow*

Jennair: *Thanks*

But Jennair knew there would be no surgery, no need to recover.

Five minutes later, walking out of the office and into the parking lot toward my car, I sent Jennair a text message:

Mark: *So where did you decide for dinner?*

Jennair: *The new place—Firepoint*

Mark: *K. See you there*

Jennair: *K*

While I was driving to the restaurant, Meredith was just six miles away on campus, standing in front of St. Thomas of Villanova, a church and a campus landmark, smiling for a selfie. Moments later at exactly 5:42 p.m., she posted the photo to Instagram. "Couldn't be more excited to be Villanova University's new Assistant Vice President for Marketing and Creative Services! Just a week on the job and I'm already feeling the love from #NovaNation! #GoingNova #HigherEdMarketing #NewAdventures"

"She is a parasite. A blood sucking life sucking parasite and she needs to be destroyed," Jennair wrote in her final letter. "It's all I can think about. I just want to blow her face off and destroy her. I want Mark to have lasting memories of the visuals of us both like that. It's all I dream about."

Five minutes later, I arrived at the restaurant.

Mark: *Here. Sitting at bar outside. Get you a glass of cab?*

Jennair: *Sure*

I ordered her a Cabernet. Moments later, Jennair sent me another text message.

Jennair: *I'm running late. I made a wrong turn.*

Mark: *K. I'm ordering food*

At 5:49 p.m., while Meredith was making her way home, Jennair's phone rang. She didn't answer, letting it go to voicemail. "Hey, it's Alicia," she said. "I just wanted to let you know I went down to see Huck and he's not down there. His leash is on the counter, but he's not in any room. What's going on? Give me a call. Talk to you later."

After playing back the voicemail, Jennair immediately called me, but with my ringer turned off, I didn't hear it and missed the call. A minute later when I looked down and saw the alert, I called her back, but I got her voicemail. When I hung up, I looked down at my phone again to find that Jennair had sent me a text message.

Jennair: *Where is Huck?!!*

Mark: *What?*

Jennair: *Where is Huck? You took him. I knew you would do this. I asked Alicia to let him out, but he's not there.*

Mark: *I didn't take him. He's there. Have her check again.*

Five minutes later, Jennair sent me a reply.

Jennair: *She found him. But now I'm too upset. I'm turning around. Just go home.*

Mark: *Can't. I ordered food*

Jennair: *Go home now!*

Mark: *No. I'm going to finish*

Through the window, Jennair saw Meredith pull into her usual spot in the driveway behind the house. Meredith got out of her car, keys in one hand, her phone in the other, her white leather Kate Spade bag over her shoulder. As she walked up to her back door, I imagine Meredith could barely contain her joy. A new job. A new home. A new future. She couldn't believe this was her incredible new life. She unlocked the door and walked into her kitchen, not bothering to close the door behind her completely. "Indy, I'm home," she likely called to her.

"I need justice for my pain and destruction. Their immoral, unethical and cruel actions have consequences," Jennair wrote. "He doesn't grieve for me now. He won't grieve for me then. So, maybe he'll grieve for her. Yes, this is payback."

Left to eat my dinner alone, I texted Meredith. When she didn't answer, I tried again. And again. That wasn't like her.

Mark: *Where are you? Home yet?*

Finally, I tried calling. But she didn't answer.

Meredith made her way through the kitchen and stepped through the threshold of the next room, toward the front stairs. But before the sound could even reach her ears, a .357 caliber bullet traveling at 1,440 feet per second pierced her left cheek and lodged in her spinal cord, instantly taking her life and all the promise it had to offer.

Lowering her gun and reaching for her phone, Jennair dialed a number. After four rings, she waited for voicemail. "I've done a bad thing," she told Alicia.

Minutes later, Jennair sent me a text message with a photo. It was a pile of trash, strewn onto what looked like a concrete sidewalk. In the center was a used condom.

Jennair: *You fucked her.*

Mark: *I don't know what you're talking about. This photo is disturbing in so many ways.*

Jennair: *Then she was cheating you*

I didn't respond. Jennair must have been going through Meredith's trash outside her home, I figured. I had to get there.

Jennair: *You ruined my life*

I was already asking for the bill, nervously tapping my credit card on the table so I could get out of there.

Jennair: *I hope you never find happiness*

I hurried across the parking lot to my car.

Jennair: *Bye Mark*

Okay, she left, I thought. Was this goodbye forever? Where was she headed? Back to Indiana with Huck and Gypsy? No, she was just telling me she was through with me. If she had the nerve to go through Meredith's trash, she had the nerve to start a fight with her. I had to get there before the two of them went at it. Meredith would surely call the cops if she found Jennair at her house, and God knows what Jennair would say to Meredith to turn her against me.

I put the car in gear and tore out of the parking lot toward Meredith's house.

Standing just ten feet from where Meredith now lay surrounded by a pool of blood like a sanguine halo around her hair, Jennair raised the gun to her own head.

And once again, she pulled the trigger.

CHAPTER 25

SO DAMN MAD

It came in the mail. A laminated news clipping of Jennair's obituary from our hometown newspaper, noting a private family graveside service that had been held. Her mother had sent it to me after burying her ashes in a family plot. I wasn't there. I wasn't invited. Sitting in my chair, the announcement still in my hands, I sent her mother a text message.

Mark: *Thank you for sending the announcement. I love that photo of her. If you only knew how much I miss her and love her. I still tell her that every day.*

She didn't send a reply.

Meredith, too, was buried in a private family service a little more than a week after I found them both lying on the floor of the kitchen in her new home. Having no contact with our mutual friends or her family, I had no choice but to read about it online. "Private Funeral Held for Meredith Sullivan Chapman," the May 4 headlines read. "Friends, colleagues and the community will remember social media pioneer and community leader Meredith Sullivan Chapman on May 14." That was the day Meredith would have driven me to the airport for a company meeting in Costa Rica. I would have done anything, dropped everything to be there to remember her. But I knew I wouldn't be welcomed, much less allowed through the doors of the campus memorial. Days before, the UD police had threatened a restraining order if I even contacted my former colleagues. Just showing up to the "invitation only" event would surely have escalated the situation and just caused an unnecessary scene.

My former colleagues at UD had shut me out and I hadn't yet met Meredith's family, and it didn't feel appropriate to reach out to them. With no way to publicly pay tribute or memorialize her, spontaneously, I did the only thing I could think of at the time to be close to her.

"Can I help you?" a youthful, energetic salesman asked the minute I stepped through the doors of the dealership.

"I want to order an A3 Cabriolet," I told him. "Monsoon Grey." It was the exact same car Meredith had driven. The same car my boss on whom I'd had a professional crush had first picked me up in to take me to her favorite pizza place. The same car we had driven to the Notre Dame basketball game the night we could no longer restrain our feelings for each other. The same car she was driving when she captured her last image in the selfie she'd sent me on her last day on this earth.

And now it was my car. Our car.

The two women I loved most in this world were gone and I didn't have the opportunity to properly and formally say goodbye to either of them. So instead, I made room in my life to say hello to them every day, whenever I climb into Meredith's car, whenever Gypsy crawls onto my lap for affection, knowing at least one life had been spared.

In the shock of the days that followed Jennair's death, I did my best to stay busy, taking on the responsibilities that naturally fell to the next of kin. One of those responsibilities was making arrangements to go through the personal belongings we had shared. Days before she died, Jennair had made arrangements for the belongings we still had in storage in South Carolina to be shipped to her family in Indiana. After her death, her mother and I agreed we should reroute the shipment to my new apartment in Pennsylvania and her immediate family would come out to go through our belongings together. I called the shipping company and made the necessary arrangements.

"Okay, so just to confirm," Angela, the woman at the moving company, said, "that's twenty tons of cargo now being shipped to your new place in Pennsylvania on…. Let's see here… May fifth."

"Twenty tons?" I asked. "Is that a lot?"

"Oh, it'll be a big truck," she answered. "It's a lot of stuff."

"Okay," I said. "I guess I don't have much choice."

Forty thousand pounds of stuff. What was it we had really been hanging on to all those years? It was never the stuff. It had always been the joys, the anticipation, the uncertainty, the fears, that the stuff came to represent. The joy we'd felt when we'd bought our first house and filled it with the furniture and things we loved. The anxiety we felt when we couldn't quite afford the lifestyle we had aspired to but found comfort in the small indulgences we could buy. The plans we had for traveling the world, trips we both knew we could never afford but could imagine with the exotic knick-knacks we came across.

Instead of letting go and accepting that we were growing—as individuals, and as a couple, both closer together and further apart —Jennair clung to the stuff as if each object constituted our lives. As if it defined us as a couple. And now she had left it all behind for others to give meaning to.

323

And what it meant to me was forty thousand pounds of stuff I didn't need.

The next morning, after agreeing to the shipment, I received a call from the legal department of the shipping company that was based out of Indiana. "Mister Gerardot, one of my associates here saw the story of your wife's death on the news and brought it to my attention," he said. "I've notified the authorities in Pennsylvania. So until I get clearance from them, your shipment is on hold."

In other words, all that stuff was now potential evidence. Evidence not of our lives, but of Meredith and Jennair's deaths. Even if I'd wanted any of it, I no longer had a right to it, not until others had scrutinized it. The irony wasn't lost on me. All those years of clinging to all that stuff, paying for moving and storing all that stuff, hauling each pound of it from room to room, from house to house, and still it wasn't mine. Not until strangers conferred their own meanings upon the stuff of our lives.

Fortunately, however, after days of exchanging emails between Jennair's mother, her sister and the shipping company to prove that I, the surviving husband, wasn't trying to pull a fast one and steal my own belongings, the Radnor Police finally relented and released the shipment.

On a cold, overcast Saturday morning, I stood in the parking lot of my apartment, at least fifteen feet from Jennair's mother, father and sister, who stood together, waiting in awkward silence for the moving truck to arrive. Before I could see it, I heard the diesel engine rumbling and the gears shifting as the driver negotiated his way through the winding streets of the complex. As it made a final turn into the parking lot and came into view, my eyes must have popped from their sockets like giant marbles. Before the truck came to a complete stop, I let out a "Holy…"

"Tsssssht!" the airbrakes made a final hiss. It was the biggest semitruck I had ever seen. Standing next to the cab, I felt like a dwarf. The cab opened up and out stepped a man who made me feel even smaller. He had to be six-foot-seven, and 320 pounds, dressed in overalls, a red plaid shirt and a worn, dingy Carhartt cap that looked like it had seen him through many miles on the road.

"You Mark?" he asked in a deep south accent.

"Yep," I replied. "How much stuff is in there?"

"Oh, it's a bunch. Packed bottom to top. Front to back. Barely fit it all," he snickered. With a smile, he extended a hand that could have easily crushed mine by accident. "I'm Randy, by the way."

In what had to be size fourteen work boots, Randy plodded his way to the back of the truck and rolled up the door. That's when I lost it. All that stuff did constitute our lives. And there it was, right before me. Overcome with emotion, tears started rolling down my face and I just had to walk away and duck behind a nearby trash dumpster. I began sobbing harder than I ever had, shaking, bracing myself with my hands on my knees as my tears fell, soaking into the dry blacktop. After a couple of minutes, the breakdown passed and I coaxed myself to stand up. "Come on," I said. "Get your shit together."

When I returned to the truck, the movers had already opened up the side door, and for the first time I could truly get a sense of the enormity of the task before us. The movers, a group of four local Philly guys hired by the trucking company, stood by the truck, cigarettes in hand, enjoying a laugh. With a final wipe of my eyes and nose, I walked up to them, and out of earshot of Jennair's family, I asked them nicely, "Guys?" Then I paused. "I just lost my wife. And they," I said, pointing over to her family, "they just lost a daughter. A sister. So…" They all stood at attention, dropping their cigarettes to the ground and stepping on them out of some unspoken universal sign of respect.

"We get it," one of them replied. I nodded at them, unable to say another word.

For the next seven hours, we unloaded every piece of furniture, every kitchen appliance, every garden tool, every box, carefully inspecting the contents and making gut-wrenching split decisions whether to keep it, give it away or pitch it. Twenty tons. Twenty tons of purchases, of memories, of arguments over twenty-four years, now strewn about a parking lot into three piles—one pile to keep, one pile to give to her family, and one pile to give away. For six straight hours, Jennair's sister loaded and unloaded her mother's Jeep Cherokee with things I donated to a charity down the road. It had to have been nearly half of the truckload, maybe thousands of dollars' worth, but much of it worthless.

"This is really nice," one of the movers said, wheeling an oversized Xerox all-in-one printer, copier, scanner that had once sat next to Jennair's desk. "I told my sister she needs to get one of these for her business."

"It's hers," I told him.

"What?" he asked.

"It's hers," I said. "Take it." He looked at me and then back down at the oversized grey machine. I gestured in a sweeping motion with my hand. "Seriously, it sounds like she needs it more than I do," I reassured him.

He smiled as if he'd just scammed me out of a priceless gem and set it aside in his own pile.

For some things, it was an easy decision. For others, like our six-piece bedroom suit, and Jennair's beautiful armoire desk, I just couldn't bear to part with them. She was gone now, but I could still feel her disappointment weighing on my every decision. "Sorry, Jennair," I would say, looking up to the sky so many times that day. I had begged her for years to part with so many things. Yet she refused.

"I don't know when or if we'll ever be able to buy nice things again," she'd rationalize when buying something we didn't need or hanging onto something we no longer used, not only justifying the accumulation but painting a bleak picture of her future. Of our future. A future of downward mobility marked by the life we'd once had.

Anticipating that I would actually keep some of the nicer, larger pieces we owned, I had rented a ten-by-ten-foot storage unit just a mile down the road. And when the "keep" area we had cordoned off into one of the parking spots began to overflow, I was forced to make the call. "That's it," I told the movers. "No more in the keep pile. Everything else goes." When the trailer had finally been emptied, the movers loaded the items I decided to keep back into the truck and took them to the storage unit. Like a giant Jenga puzzle, they packed it all into the one-thousand-cubic-feet metal box, leaving just enough room to shut the door. As I pulled down the door and secured it with a padlock, a sick, uneasy feeling came over me. Again, I began to sob uncontrollably. It felt as though I was burying her all over.

It would be a year later before I could bear to open that door again.

When I returned to the apartment, Jennair's father and sister had gone to get something to eat. In a rare moment, standing in the parking garage, going through a few remaining boxes, I stood alone with Jennair's mother.

"What did the letter say?" I asked.

"I can't tell you," she replied. "Her father and sister don't want me to share it with you. She sent it to us, not to you."

"Okay," I said. "Okay." I could tell it was a sensitive topic, and I didn't want to push her. But minutes later, her resolve began to soften.

"It was twelve pages of rambling," she said. "Didn't even say I love you. I'm just so damn mad at her."

I didn't say anything, but that really struck me. While I had every reason to be just as mad, if not more so, I hadn't yet experienced that step of the grieving process. I was still stuck in what seemed like perpetual shock and sadness for her loss. Anger. Bitterness. Blame. We'd already had enough of that. As for feeling those feelings once again, well, it would have to come later. Now all I could feel was a bottomless sadness and loss.

After moving the last few boxes into my fourth-floor apartment, I found myself alone in the elevator with Jennair's father for the first time that day. For the first time in years, actually. It was a long ride down. He didn't say a word. He wouldn't even look at me. "Thank you for all your help today," I said simply.

"Mm-hmm," he replied without even moving his mouth, his eyes fixed straight ahead on the stainless-steel door, waiting anxiously for it to open. When the door finally did open and as the three of them got into their car, I offered a final thank you and waved. They all looked straight ahead and drove away.

That stung. But I didn't blame them for blaming me. After all, especially in their eyes, my love for Meredith had caused the death of their daughter. The woman with whom, twenty-four years before, I had stood before them and my own family and friends and promised to be faithful. To have. To hold. For better, for worse, for richer, for poorer, in sickness and in health, to love and to cherish, till death do us part. But instead, I had betrayed her. I failed to take care of her. And in her darkest hours, I wasn't there to save her, even from herself. I had seen Jennair in the depths of her sorrow, sobbing openly, lying naked in the shower. And yet still I actively pursued putting an end to our marriage. I saw her take desperate measures to discover what I tried so hard to conceal, and then blamed her for her violating my privacy. I put my own needs, my own desires, my own dreams, over her very survival. And I'd been so determined to do so that I didn't realize her survival was even at stake.

In my mind, she controlled me. Expecting. Wanting. Hoping so much that I needed her. But in the end, and truthfully every step of the way, she was the one who needed me. She relied on me. And I turned my back on her. How do you possibly do that to someone you love and still look at yourself in the morning? How do you look at someone with whom you've shared half your life and say, "Eh. I've had enough. I want something else?" The fact is, as hard as it is to say and to write, the love I had for Meredith didn't even come close to the love Jennair and I had built and shared. It just didn't. How could it? Twenty-four weeks will never be equivalent to twenty-four years, despite the ups, the downs, the suspicions, the mistrust and the late-night knock-down, drag-out verbal battles Jennair and I had shared, and the laughter, excitement, and intimacy Meredith and I had shared. It just won't.

This is why I found myself wanting so desperately to climb to the seventh floor of a building, open the window and hurl myself onto the pavement. This is why I wished I had the courage to walk back into that gun store and actually buy it, and then do what Jennair had both the weakness and the courage to do. Yet each time I found my mind wandering to that ledge, to that trigger, I pulled back. I knew that such an end was not my future. Yet despite the hell I had already been through, those thoughts were just the beginning of my darkest days. I was walking deeper into a darkness I'd never imagined, a darkness not even Jennair had wished on me.

CHAPTER 26:

IF ONLY YOU WERE DEAD

"I started journaling," I told Sam, my therapist, a couple of months after the tragedy. "I feel so alone and like I'm such a burden to my friends, constantly pouring my heart out to them. I just have this overwhelming need to tell what actually happened. To tell everyone."

"I think that's great," Sam said. "I think that'll be a good outlet for you."

"Do you want to hear some of what I have so far?" I asked.

"Absolutely," he replied.

I pulled my phone from my back pocket and opened the app I had been using to write whenever I had a private thought or a very public panic attack at the airport, at the grocery store or any number of places it came on. Those attacks followed me as relentlessly as Jennair had done, catching up to me when I least expected it, when my guard was down. When my guard was up. I couldn't escape them, no matter how I tried. Writing out my pain, telling my story, however flawed and imperfect, became my only defense against them.

I cleared my throat and began to read out loud. A few pages in, I paused and looked up at Sam, who was staring back at me with an expression I couldn't quite discern. "What?" I asked.

"You need to write this," he said. "This should be a book. Your story is one in a hundred million. Nobody, or certainly very few, have ever experienced what you are feeling right now. But there is so much to learn from it. So much to share with others."

"I don't know," I said. "That was never my intention when I started this."

"I know this guy," he said. "A screenwriter, a producer."

"I'm not doing a movie," I interrupted. "No way."

"No, just a book," Sam replied. "Let me connect you with him. See what he says."

"Okay," I relented. "I'll talk to him."

That afternoon, I sent Sam's writer/producer friend an email to ask his advice. As I told him, "My intent is in no way to exploit what had happened, but to set the record straight, shine a light on mental health, on guns and hopefully humanize the two women I loved and give them both the respect they deserved." When I hit send, I never really expected him to reply. But the very next morning, he did.

"Tell the story using the barest facts that reveal the emotional truth," he encouraged me. "Get obsessed. Keep driving through the pain until it's finished."

So for the next few weeks, sometimes five, six hours a night, I spilled my guts in an exhausting, often tearful, emotional catharsis. I'd get home from work, walk Huck, make myself dinner, pour a glass of cabernet and then just start writing. I had no real expectations. No clear agenda. Just raw, unconstrained emotion, telling whoever might listen my every feeling, my every thought. My marriage to Jennair. My relationship with Meredith. And my obsession with trying to piece together how and why Jennair was driven to kill. But something felt like it was missing. Jennair. How could I honestly tell her story if she wasn't here to tell it?

I hadn't gone looking for it. It had happened quite accidentally, actually. About three months after the tragedy, culling through the hundreds of files in Jennair's cloud backup once again, this oddly yet purposely named file stood out to me, just inviting me to read it. "Letter of Discontent," it was titled. I opened the document and within seconds of reading the first paragraph, I realized what it was. Immediately I closed it. It was *the* letter. I closed my laptop and pushed it away from me on my patio table and walked away. I was in no way prepared to read those words, to hear Jennair's voice, to feel her pain. And her mother's words still echoed in my mind. "She sent it to us, not to you."

Inside my apartment, I anxiously paced back and forth, never taking my eyes off the patio table that overlooked the busy pool and a courtyard full of neighbors four floors below, a leap to my death still tempting me. Minutes later, spontaneously summoning the courage, I rushed to the balcony, and took the leap. No, not over the ledge, but into the past. Jennair's past. Our past. I again opened the letter, scrolling, scanning the text for anything that jumped out before I lost my nerve.

"Tell everyone and anyone," Jennair wrote. "I want everyone to know what they did to me… I want her parents, her grandma, his family, their coworkers and friends and everyone in Newark, Delaware to know what they did and how they did it and what they did to me to cause this."

What had we done to Jennair? We knew our relationship was forbidden. We knew it had consequences. We just didn't know how great. Our relationship had killed her. It had killed Meredith. And though I lived, it was killing me, one cruel memory at a time, one cruel thought at a time, one cruel insight into my own words and choices at a time.

Unsure of what landmines might still lie ahead, I again closed my laptop, carefully playing and replaying her words in my mind. She wanted people to know. If I was truly committed to telling this story as it actually happened, I reasoned, I really needed to give Jennair a voice, a chance to share her point of view. After all, this wasn't *my* story, it was *our* story. And unknowingly, yet quite purposely, the letter, the videos, the audio recordings, had all captured not only her words but my words and a window into her thoughts from the darkest recesses of her mind.

Each and every night, I forced myself to read short passages of the letter, letting her words cut me, but not so deeply that I couldn't recover. It was profoundly sad, poignant and visceral, full of anguish, anger, revenge, painful truths and half-truths and figments of her own imagination, lamenting the death of her marriage, unable to imagine a future that wasn't filled with darkness and crippling pain.

However much I disagreed with what she had written, this was her truth, what she believed, and the lens through which she saw her wasted past and her foreboding future. Reading the words she had never meant my eyes to see touched me deeply, making me question how we fell in love in the first place, what we meant to each other, and why we had stayed together for so long.

"I lived a lie this entire marriage," Jennair wrote. "I feel so foolish for devoting my entire self to it now. I got nothing. I am here now because I was so stupid in love and careless with my own life." Soon after I had told her I would be filing a petition for divorce, Jennair had expressed a similar regret directly to me, as only she could. "The past twenty-four years were a complete waste," she said. "All the memories we made are too painful to remember. If only you were dead. At least then I could remember them fondly."

"Our past wasn't a waste," I insisted. "We made a lot of great memories together that I will never forget. And neither should you." But now that she's gone, I feel the stabbing pain of those memories all too well. Yet somehow, and as painful as they are to recall, the images, the feelings, the kind and loving words we had shared for each other are forever etched in my mind. And I hope they never fade. I know in my heart that our life and the love we shared together was never a lie.

For forty-nine years, I had lived my life determined not to have regrets but rather to view the mistakes, bad decisions, and wrong turns as learning experiences. The wrong job. The wrong words. The wasted opportunity. All just steps toward becoming a better, wiser person. Despite her words, wishing to have never met me, I will never regret falling in love with Jennair, marrying her and building a life together. Life isn't perfect. There is no perfect person for us out there. Falling in love with someone, despite their imperfections, is a gift not to be squandered nor to be regretted. But now I do regret having carelessly wounded Jennair so deeply, for not recognizing her sickness nor the depth of the wounds I'd caused, and not foreseeing the lengths to which she would go to relieve her pain and exact her revenge.

It confounds me and pains me deeply that she would regret us, thinking had she just followed another path, married someone else, life would have been perfect.

"I wish I had never met him, nor fallen in love with him," Jennair lamented in her letter. "Having another life with another person who truly loved me and appreciated me in a supportive relationship would have been a better life for me. I suppose that I

335

would have had kids and been a great mom. I suppose I would have been more confident and happier."

While it's a tempting exercise to ponder "what if," I just don't think it works that way. Had she married someone else, would her life have been so different? Possibly. But better? I'm not sure. What life doesn't come with setbacks? Would she have been better able to handle them? Better able to bounce back? She had so internalized her insecurities and resentments by the time I'd met her that I doubt she would have been a stronger person, no matter who she'd married. But maybe I am wrong.

She prayed for guidance, she hoped for success and expected prosperity. She was a hard worker, but when success and reward didn't come, someone else, something else, or the universe was to blame. There was always another to blame.

As she entered her thirties, she often blamed her age as the reason why she didn't get what she thought she deserved, for not being where she thought we'd be in life. From the moment I met Jennair at the age of sixteen, until she left this earth at the age of forty-seven, I thought of her as the most beautiful person I knew. But as she started showing signs of aging, as we all do, she became self-conscious about how she looked. My constant assurances and compliments about her beauty would sometimes bring a smile to her blushing face, but it would be fleeting. When she looked at herself in the mirror, she didn't like the woman who was looking back at her. To her it was the reason she wasn't getting the jobs she interviewed for. It was the reason I would leave her. It was the reason she would never find love again.

"We all know what happens to the older wives," Jennair wrote. "They hardly ever get their lives even close to what they once had and usually live a lonely life. There is no great love that comes afterwards. I am so ugly and old. I look so bad for my age. I look like an old wrinkly lady. No amount of exercise or eating right is going to help that. I'm so ugly and unattractive. I can't stand looking at myself in the mirror. I can't blame Mark for running away because I look like shit. I won't attract anyone but ugly losers like me."

She was far from ugly. She was beautiful. But she *was* facing age discrimination with every résumé she sent out, revealing the year she'd received her college degree, her many years of working. Just enough for employers to see, not a seasoned pro, but a middle-aged woman, someone past her prime.

Some contend it's easier for older men to attract younger women. I don't know if that's true. Had she told me she was leaving me for a thirty-three-year-old man, I would have thought she'd lost her mind. Maybe she was right that her options for love were far different from mine. Society has far different standards for women than it does for men, and far different standards for aging women than for aging men. And Jennair was crumbling beneath those weighty standards that devalued her with every passing birthday, with every line etched onto her face.

And given Jennair's self-doubt about her looks, my falling in love with a younger woman was a crushing blow and a confirmation to her that she was no longer beautiful, no longer viable. But Meredith's age and her beauty were not what had attracted me most to her. It was her uniquely positive outlook on life and the future and how she made me feel about mine. The same qualities that had once attracted me to Jennair.

And yet. I was magnetically drawn to Meredith's energy, her vitality and sexuality. I can't deny that. My own advancing age haunted me as well, though in different, far more subtle ways than had Jennair's. Where Jennair felt devalued, I felt concern. Concern that I was running out of time, running out of time to feel that youthful joy and anticipation I'd felt when Jennair and I first met. I don't think I was even all that aware of that concern, as it had wormed its way into my life—into our lives—so gradually that it had come to be our norm.

So by the time I met Meredith and felt again that jolt of energetic promise, I grabbed it. I wanted to feel alive again. I wanted to feel excited about what the future had in store. I fell in love with that feeling—and with the woman who inspired it. I hadn't gone looking for it. But when I felt it surge through my body, I knew I had to have it. And I relished it—even as it ate away at Jennair. Indeed, the more she suffered from it, the more I pulled away. The more she crumbled, the more repelled I was. I was in search of youth—of my youth, of the strength I'd once felt. Of the invincibility I'd felt—in myself, and in Jennair. When she was no longer invincible, when every word and gesture spoke of defeat and spiteful wrath, I became all the more drawn to Meredith, who exuded energy. Who resonated joy. Who sparked a love inside me I hadn't felt in decades.

I believed Jennair would again find love herself, but it would first take a painful journey to find the strength within to again love life and to love herself. It was, sadly, a journey she refused to take.

I hadn't come to Delaware hoping to escape my life or end my marriage. It just happened. After having spent some of the happiest years of our marriage in South Carolina, life had once again thrown us a curve ball when I met Meredith. Jennair had been out of work for more than a year and had fallen deeper and deeper into depression. Yet we were both hopeful, looking for a new start. Finding someone else to have that start with was the last thing on my mind, but it had a devastating effect on Jennair.

"He ruined everything," she wrote. "He ruined my shot and turning this around for us. He tainted this whole town for me. All the places I wanted to explore, all the restaurants, coffee shops, parks, wine bars I wanted to explore with him, he already did with Meredith. All the energy of exploring a new place and making new memories are trashed. He did that with Meredith."

It was true. While it was never my intent, I had selfishly ruined the new start we had both looked forward to. I know I had hurt her, but just how deeply was a shock. The most alarming and tragic part of her letter was hearing the visceral, untethered contempt she had for both Meredith and me. She loved me. She couldn't let go of me. And yet she had so much hatred for me.

In one of the most profoundly disturbing lines of her letter, Jennair chillingly referenced the 1998 murder-suicide of Saturday Night Live comedian/actor Phil Hartman at the hands of his wife, practically admiring what the clearly disturbed woman had done some twenty years before when she murdered him in his bed and turned the gun on herself. "I may need to do a Brynn/Phil Hartman if I run out of time," she wrote. "Which sucks because Meredith needs to be erased and Mark should not get off that easy." Killing me instead of Meredith was Jennair's contingency plan. True to form, she had everything planned perfectly to a T. But plan A was designed to inflict the greatest pain, especially on me, and Meredith's family.

"I hope the results of what I do lead him to a stressful, guilt and shame-ridden existence. I hope all his friends and family reject him. And THIS really is the whole point," she openly admitted. "I hope he spends the rest of his miserable life being rejected, like I was. Rejected for jobs, rejected by love, rejected by friendship, rejected by his family, rejected by financial freedom, rejected by life…over and over. This is true payback for his rejection of me and my love and commitment for us."

Without question Jennair's ultimate goal was to mortally wound me, to strike a blow from which I would never recover, leaving my heart to bleed a slow and painful death. Worse than death itself, my sentence was to subject me to years of my own unrelenting guilt for wronging her, hurting her, and leaving her.

More than a year later, Jennair's plan has been wildly successful. Her words haunt me every day, and I have suffered greater heartache and damage than I had ever imagined possible. Spontaneous panic attacks. Paranoid delusions. Uncontrolled crying. Sleepless nights masked by countless bottles of wine. I still wake some mornings having to remind myself that my new reality is in fact reality. And I can't shake the boulder of guilt that rests on my shoulders for hurting her. For making her feel she had no other choice.

But she did. She had hundreds if not an infinite number of other choices. She just couldn't see them through her own pain, her vitriolic contempt, and whatever force had taken over her mind. That was the simple yet most powerful realization I came to as I wrestled with my feelings. Of all the choices she had before her, she chose the absolute wrong one. And now I and so many others have been devastated by that choice, left to pick up the fragments of our lives and figure out how to move on. But moving on doesn't mean forgetting what happened, sweeping it under the rug. It means understanding it. Learning from it. Learning that the choices each of us makes have consequences we might never be prepared for.

After several unsuccessful calls and emails to the Radnor Police asking for Jennair's belongings to be released, they finally complied. The lead detective emailed me and told me I could come to the station to collect the personal belongings and evidence they no longer felt were pertinent to the case.

I hadn't been back there since the night of the killings and I wasn't sure how I would feel. When I arrived, the detective greeted me and walked me into the same sickly beige room where I had spent hours crying and agonizing just a couple months earlier. I could feel my breath shorten and my heart beating loudly in my chest. A second detective entered the room with a stack of packages wrapped neatly in brown paper and labeled. Meticulously, they watched as I opened each one and read the list of items inside: purse, credit cards, fifteen dollars cash, post office key, USB thumb drive, computer mouse, USB cable, and several spiral-bound notebooks. I signed for the items, shook the detectives' hands and left, hoping I would never have to see that place again.

Back at home, I stared at the stack of more than a dozen notebooks full of pages and pages of handwritten notes, dreading doing what I knew I needed to. I carried them into my bedroom and spread them out, taking up every inch of the duvet that covered the queen-sized bed. Then I dug in. At first I was shocked. Inside one of the notebooks, Jennair had written detailed information about each of Meredith's family members, including full names, ages, addresses and phone numbers. She even knew the make, model and color of the blue Mercedes C Class that Meredith had rented while her car was being repaired for the deep scratches Jennair herself had maliciously gouged. Jennair also listed usernames and passwords for every account and electronic device I owned. Most of the notebooks were full of handwritten scribbles from transcribing hundreds of hours of audio she had recorded over the course of three months. On some weird level, I was impressed and thought, what a waste of time, energy and talent! But the more I thought about it, the more I looked at the hours upon hours of work it had taken to create all of that meaningless, worthless clutter, the angrier I got. "How the fuck? Who the fuck?"

Disgusted and angry, I tore out every page, jamming them into the shredder before throwing them down the trash chute. For some reason, however, I did save one page with a short, haunting handwritten note, as if lines she had been rehearsing to say to Meredith's face.

Not going down w/out a fight. Fighting back – you declared war and fired the first shots underhandedly. I'm defending myself. Can't get away with hurting my family. Fighting for my family/marriage. I won't be a victim to this cruel plan/joke. Don't mess w/my family/ marriage and get away with it – unbruised.

Who was this woman who had taken over my wife's body? I wondered. The next morning, I called her psychiatrist's office, hoping they would speak to me, help me understand what she had shared with them, what they had discussed. But they wouldn't, telling me that would break their patient confidentiality policy that Jennair had signed.

Disappointed, but not surprised, I decided to make a one-on-one appointment with Richard, the marriage therapist Jennair and I had been seeing for weeks. When I told him about Jennair, he was as shocked as anyone. "She had a gun in our apartment," I told him. "I lived with her and never knew it. I saw her break down occasionally. Then she would be fine. Normal. I never thought she was actually going to kill herself."

"And how would you? You're not a trained professional," he said. "You don't know the signs to look for. I've never lost a patient to suicide before, let alone commit homicide," he told me. "This has completely changed my practice. Clearly, she wasn't well. She was upset and agitated. Every session I could see her physical deterioration. Her weight loss. But I never thought she might be suicidal."

What *are* the signs of someone who is seriously considering killing themselves and harming others? I wondered. Did she need to stand up and shout it across the room? If he didn't know, how could I have known?

"When she would come here, she'd get worked up. Angry. But in hindsight, she was actually psychotic," Richard said. "She just hid it well."

"She was what?" I exclaimed, practically jumping off the couch. "Psychotic?" Despite everything she'd done, including murdering Meredith, psychotic is not how I thought anyone would ever describe Jennair—not seriously anyway. It's one of those words in society that we tend to throw around all too loosely to describe someone who was extremely angry. But Richard was using it in a clinical sense. She was experiencing psychosis. She wasn't a sociopath; she knew what she was doing was wrong. She was capable of empathy.

Or was she? As I reflected on our past, I recalled so many times I'd seen her display such great compassion toward our pets, toward other animals. Yet when I thought of her compassion and empathy for people, I drew a blank. Had my wife truly been psychotic?

I don't think so. I also recall the many times she was loving and empathetic toward me. Those times had become so buried in the many years of arguments and lies, of feeling relentlessly controlled and put down, that those years of love and caring had become obscured. When I met Meredith, her caring and empathy for

343

me had filled a void I hadn't really recognized before. My marriage to Jennair had so normalized my emotional isolation that until Meredith came along, I thought that was what marriage was supposed to be.

And was I any more empathetic and compassionate toward Jennair before Meredith had come into our lives? I certainly hadn't been afterwards.

No, Jennair wasn't a sociopath. She wasn't psychotic in the sense of having a psychotic personality disorder, but the trauma of losing me to a younger woman, at the very time she was feeling discarded by society after losing her job and growing older, had triggered a psychotic break with reality.

The reality was, she did have a future. That future wasn't going to be easy, but she could have found work. She could have found a new profession. With her tenacious eye for detail she would have made one hell of a private eye or researcher. She could have found love. She could have recovered.

But she had come to define herself in relation to me. I was the last identity she had left after losing her career, then her youth, and finally me. Each loss chiseled away at her identity, so that by the time I was ready to pull away, she didn't know who she was without me. "I am not even a shell of the person I once was," Jennair wrote. "I used to be a confident, assertive, decisive woman. My husband broke me down over the course of many years. My greatest joy was loving him and making a life with him. It was a joke. I would just forgive and keep loving him. I lost myself. I couldn't figure it out. I'm sorry."

The truth was, the trauma she experienced when she realized there really was no hope for us shut down parts of her brain that would help her to make wise decisions. Just as I had become argumentative and bad tempered when I took the Adderall, Jennair's brain had been flooded with a chemical surge of her brain's own making. My affair with Meredith had traumatized Jennair, and she entered the flight or fight mode, fighting back as hard and brutally as she could.

Yet there was something in her nature that had made fighting back a reflex, even with the small things.

"I wasn't going to put up with his shit anymore," Jennair once told me about the never-ending pattern of arguments she had with her father as a teenager. It was a pattern that followed her into her adulthood and that she then projected onto me, her sister, and so many other relationships. She wasn't going to "put up with shit" from anyone.

That fiercely defensive posturing forged a neural pathway that took her straight from "I hate Mark and Meredith" to "I have to erase Meredith and end my life and make Mark suffer forever and kill my cat, as well."

That's not the Jennair I knew and loved. That was a wounded warrior whose brain had stopped working normally, who had found herself cornered with no visible means of escape. "I am not a crazy lunatic unstable, scorned wife who went off the deep end. I was a prisoner of war suffering a traumatic event and loss," she wrote in her letter, justifying her hatred and the rage that pushed her toward her unthinkable final act.

She couldn't see a future, though she had one. She could only focus on the past she had lost and was losing, and the quest to conquer the enemies she blamed for it.

She was not psychotic. She was trapped in a traumatic psychosis and couldn't find her way out.

And as much as I thought I was offering her an exit—by offering her financial support, by remaining her friend—it wasn't enough. I didn't recognize the psychosis. I only saw its symptoms. The surveillance. The GPS devices. The recording devices sewn into my clothes again and again and again. The computer and phone hacking. The hatred.

I didn't see the building violence, the animal trapped in a corner, preparing its deathly attack.

Perhaps because she was a woman.

I missed the red flags. Her divorce coach had missed the red flags. Richard had missed the red flags. Her psychologist. Her psychiatrist too. We all missed the red flags.

But had the roles been reversed and I had been the one to socially isolate her, to control her money, to follow her in disguise and in a rental car, put GPS devices in her car, tell her I was having others follow her, sew recording devices into her clothes—would others have seen the red flags? Would others have recognized I had the potential for violence?

I believe they would have. But I wasn't the one doing these things. A woman was. And so the flags were missed.

As many clues as my more than a year-long quest for answers has unturned, there are just as many if not more questions that may never be answered. What, if anything, was the underlying condition that caused Jennair to so violently spiral out of control? Was it depression brought on by Hashimoto's disease, a hypothyroid disorder she had been diagnosed with years before? Was it, as multiple people, including two psychologists with whom I have spent many hours, suggested that she may have suffered her whole life from Borderline Personality Disorder, or even experienced some trauma as a child? If I had told Jennair how I felt about

Meredith back in January, would the outcome have been any different? If I had ended the relationship with Meredith when Jennair asked me to, would they both still be alive? If Jennair's psychiatrist had treated her differently and admitted her to a psychiatric hospital, would she have ever recovered? And will I ever recover? I only know one thing. It isn't Jennair I must understand if I'm to heal. It is myself. What was my own role in this tragedy? And what was my own madness?

CHAPTER 27

ALONE

Until three days ago, with the exception of my therapist, no one had dared to ask me the question. The same question I have asked myself for 407 days in a row. The same question that must be on everyone's mind, but they're just too polite to come out and ask or too afraid to hear the actual answer. Three days ago someone asked me the question.

"Do you feel guilt?" my neighbor, a woman who I have only recently come to know, with whom I shared an early draft of this book, asked. "Are you haunted by thoughts of what you could have and would have done differently? Are you at peace with the destiny that brought you and Meredith together?"

So, in short, to paraphrase, do I regret letting myself fall in love with Meredith? The *simple* answer is yes. Because if I had been stronger, if I had been smarter, if I had been able to predict that any of this could have happened, two incredibly vibrant women would still be alive. But it's *not* that simple.

I've played it all back in my mind hundreds of times. And honestly, I know in my heart that there were multiple opportunities for me to pull back, to not pursue a relationship with Meredith and to end it once it had started. But sadly, I failed to seize them. I failed to "do the right thing." I just couldn't bring myself to put an end to something that utterly changed me, making me feel more alive and like myself than I had felt for so long. I didn't want to risk losing Meredith, this person for whose talents and heart I had so much respect. And she, in return, made me feel important. Needed. Good at what I did. She believed in my abilities. She believed in me. On a personal level, I was flattered by her constant adoration, compliments and attention. "You are an incredible and caring man," she would tell me again and again, to the point where I doubted her sincerity. It was just hard to believe. She saw something in me that Jennair no longer did or *never* did. Outside of the occasional greeting card on my birthday or Valentine's day, I don't remember ever hearing anything close to those words from Jennair. It just wasn't how she saw me. For much of our lives together, she saw me, as she stated over and over in her suicide letter, as a series of flaws, a great disappointment, undeserving of her love. Although her letter was written at the height of her rage and despair, it spoke of every flaw she'd ever pointed out in me throughout our marriage, and I came to internalize her perception of me as a lesser man, a weakened man, a man deserving of contempt.

I realize now, as I did even then, that with Meredith, I was high on dopamine and a host of other addictive drugs that naturally coarse through the reward center in your brain when you fall in love. It was intoxicating. But I wasn't so stupid that I didn't recognize what was happening. I was realistic. Would we have made it a year? Would we have made it five? I seriously had my doubts. But not truly understanding the possible risks beyond my own broken heart, I was willing to gamble it all to find out. A selfish thing to do to many eyes. An understandable and justifiable one to others. Do we have the right to seek happiness at the peril of others? Foolhardily, I thought so. And yet, would I have not been foolhardy to resign myself to unhappiness to spare Jennair her pain?

I could have stayed in my marriage, sought ongoing counseling, and made it work, to keep the peace for the next twenty, thirty, even forty years. Many do. "I don't want to be like them," Jennair often said, speaking of her grandparents. "They don't love each other. They're just roommates." Not always, but during rough times especially, Jennair and I acted much the same way. And I could easily see a day when that would become our lives. I think we both did.

I know Jennair didn't just make up my faults, not completely. In many ways she put up with a lot of my flaws, weaknesses and bad habits. I know I failed her as a husband and a friend in many ways. But as many of my friends would admit, I gave up a lot of who I was and what I could have been to be with Jennair.

"Jennair is an acquired taste," I would often explain to people who felt the initial sting of her blunt personality. "You'll learn to like her, or at least navigate her," I'd advise them. Right or wrong, that's exactly what I did. Out of sheer survival, I had to learn to ignore some of her most egregious behavior that many others would have balked at, that many others did—my employees, who wouldn't work with her. My family, who distanced themselves from her after the scene about my brother's kidney transplant. Her few friends in college, who drifted away, never to be replaced with new friends. A stronger, more assertive person would have likely walked away years ago. But that just wasn't who I was.

Even Jennair hated that I didn't stand up to her, that I couldn't bear to argue with her, that my first instinct was to flee, to avoid conflict. It was just easier to give in, let her control me, hold in my frustration and then blow up about it later. I was, and I'm sure I still am, the very definition of passive-aggressive. Would I have repeated this pattern with Meredith? It's quite possible. But she was a very different animal than Jennair. Professionally speaking, she was a strong woman and an assertive leader, but she would much rather let others shine and give them credit than bask in the limelight herself. That takes a certain amount of self-confidence. Similarly, from a personal perspective, she often took a back seat, letting me pick the restaurant, assuming I would make the reservations, and order the wine, and yet she would still offer to pay the bill. The differences between the two couldn't have been more striking.

And yet, as I have come to learn from my therapist, and I guess it's something I've always known on some level, I am attracted to strong, bold and assertive women, often looking to them to make decisions. It probably won't surprise anyone to know that my mother ruled the roost at home, often putting my father down, putting me down, and doubting my abilities, and as I later learned after her death, her mother had done the same to her. My mother also sought to control my every decision under the guise of protecting me. Did I somehow seek out Jennair for these same qualities? Or, as she suggested in her final letter, did I turn her into my mother?

Throughout this book, I have done my very best to be honest and accurately portray how things played out throughout my marriage, and especially during the last four months of Jennair's life, much of which was aided by hours of conversations that Jennair had recorded between us and also between me and Meredith. Still much of the rest I have filled in with my own memories. But I would be remiss if I didn't point out that Jennair saw some of the "facts" and the dynamics between us very differently than I did. I

351

saw her as controlling me, and she saw me the same way. "...He wanted his way on everything and was not capable of compromising," she wrote in her letter. "He interrupts me and talks over me and judges everything I think, say and do." But I couldn't disagree more, which is well documented in multiple audio recordings as she interrupts my every effort to explain myself, share my perspectives, my feelings. Even the moment I described when I found her crying on the floor of the shower and wrapped her in a towel happened quite differently from her perspective. "Mark found me crying on the shower floor (Sunday) after he came back from a run," she recalled in her letter. "[He] asked how long I was like that and then basically 'kicked me out' by standing there so he could use the shower. As soon as I got out, he stripped his clothes to get in. Like 'are you done?' He barely feels bad for me even though he sees the raw pain I'm in."

Did I somehow imagine my version of the events of that day and others? No, I don't think so. But I do believe our memories are filled with gaps and blurs that we fill in to suit our perceptions of the world and of ourselves. I saw myself as caring and empathetic for Jennair's pain. She saw me as indifferent to her, someone who would step right over her as she lay weeping on the shower floor. My guess is that had that moment been among her thousands of hours of recordings, it would be revealed that both our memories had been skewed. Did I kick her out? No, I did not. Did I hold her as she cried? I remember doing so. But maybe I didn't hold her long enough, or lovingly enough, or maybe not at all. I remember holding her because I did. Or because I so desperately wish that I had done so.

Something I think we could all agree on is that all of us, Jennair, Meredith and I, made bad decisions, blindly and foolishly following our hearts much more so than our brains. We all had baggage. We all had flaws. We all had imperfect marriages. And yet we all just wanted to be loved and accepted for who we were. We all wanted better lives, better loves.

When you are blinded by passion it is often hard to empathize with others or put yourself in their shoes. "How would you have reacted if the tables were turned?" I was recently asked. "If you had been out of work for a year, followed Jennair to a city where she had an exciting new job, and she informed you that she was in love with a thirty-three-year-old man and wanted out?"

It's an interesting question. But I'm not sure it's a completely fair one. To be candid, in the back of my mind, I had been thinking about, even fantasizing about what my life would be like without Jennair for some time. For years I felt controlled. Stifled. Denigrated. As symbiotic as we could often be, in the end, I just don't think Jennair and I were working from the same playbook. We wanted different things. We wanted a different kind of life. Clearly from her constant put-downs and the many hateful things she had to say about me in her final letter, she was fed up with my many flaws and weaknesses, as I was with hers. But the underlying spirit in which I think the question was asked, would I have been devastated if the person I had wrapped my whole life around suddenly rejected me, choosing someone else? Yes. Would I have planted GPS devices on their cars? Sewn recording devices into their clothing? Had them followed? Killed her and then myself? No.

My whole life didn't revolve solely around Jennair, and I asked her many times not to wrap her heart so tightly around mine. I wanted her to have her own life. Her own career. Her own friends. I wanted her to be too busy for me sometimes, as I often was for her. I wanted balance, something we used to have when we were at our happiest.

I believe there is merit in looking back at our pasts and at this catastrophic event and trying to understand the many whys, hows and what ifs. But I think the most important question of all is, what have I learned? How will I live my life differently?

The truth is I lied to Jennair. I wasn't honest with her. I began a relationship outside of our marriage and tried to cover it up until I could understand what it was I was feeling and why. We both lied to each other throughout our marriage, but especially me. Lying was something I learned to do at an early age to regain control from a mother whose own instincts were to constrain me. If I had been honest with Jennair and told her how I was feeling about Meredith from the start, would it have changed things? I don't know. But I do know how ashamed I feel now for having been unfaithful, disloyal and deceitful. One of the motivations to write this book was to reveal the truth of what really happened, to stop hiding, to stop avoiding the role my actions played. I don't have a right to stand on a soapbox and tell everyone else to be honest to each other as though I'd found religion. I only have control of what I do in my own life. And I hope that having learned this lesson, I will now have the courage to always be honest with everyone I know, and especially with myself.

Nietzsche once famously said, "That which doesn't kill us makes us stronger." I don't know that that is completely true, and so many parts of me have been irreparably damaged by the loss of the two women I so loved and my own role in the trajectory. But I do know that in facing the fears that have flooded me from the moment I first laid eyes on each of them, I have grown more courageous, far stronger. For all the battering I've taken, the self-doubts and self-loathing that have haunted me since that day, I've found a self-respect I never knew. I've gained self-insight. I've come face to face with the demons in my mind and still I live, still I relish life, and still I look into the mirror and accept the face returning my gaze as undeserving of this fate, and deserving of a life. I've learned that to run from my fears is not the answer, because fear has something to teach us, something to wake us from our sleep.

I didn't really know my greatest fear until recently. Feeling alone and isolated in the hours and days that followed the most tragic event in my life is unlike any horror I had ever known. And yet it was a very necessary lesson. I hadn't been alone for the first forty-nine years of my life. I wasn't sure who I was outside of my family and then outside of my own marriage. I told Jennair I wanted my independence. If Meredith and I didn't work out, I'd be satisfied to be alone, I told her. I didn't know it then, but that was a lie. I likely would have run back to Jennair and asked her for forgiveness, just as I had done when I had broken up with her in college twenty-seven years before. The truth is, I didn't want to be alone. I just thought I did. One of the many reasons Jennair probably spiraled out of control, I am told by my therapist who has read her entire letter and watched videos I don't have the courage to watch, is that she didn't have a sense of self. Not a strong one anyway. Her only identity was our identity. Her only life was our life. And I took that away from her. And it turns out, I didn't have a sense of self, which is why today, I still want nothing more than to turn back time and return back to the comfort of my dysfunctional marriage. But I don't have that luxury. I have friends. I have family. But for the first time in half a century, I am alone. And I'm only now starting to be comfortable with myself. When you are

355

desperate, you look almost anywhere for guidance and for comfort. And while I never expected to quote actor Keanu Reeves, something he said in an interview a few months back struck me and I think about it often.

"Someone told me the other day that he felt bad for single people because they are lonely all the time. I told him that's not true. I'm single and I don't feel lonely. I take myself out to eat. I buy myself clothes. I have great times by myself. Once you know how to take care of yourself, company becomes an option and not a necessity."

I don't know if I will ever get over the pain I am feeling, enough to be with someone again. To love someone again. From here it's hard to see that day. But until that day, or if that day never comes, I have myself. Thanks, Keanu.

A friend of mine recently broke up with his girlfriend he had been seeing for more than three years. It was a tumultuous relationship, full of passion, heated arguments and genuine love. But after multiple fights and breakups, only to then get back together days later, my friend came to the conclusion that what each of them wanted was very different. The relationship, while it had always been up and down, had become unhealthy, doing more damage to each other than good. It was time to put an end to it. After summoning the courage for days, he finally told her, "This isn't working anymore. We have to end it."

He expected that she might not take it well, but after a brief emotional exchange, she drove away crying, but without incident. My friend felt in his heart he had done the right thing. A week later, he was having dinner with his daughter and friends when unexpectedly, his ex-girlfriend, a mature forty-nine-year-old professional woman, showed up at his front door. When he opened the door to speak to her, she unleashed a verbal and physical attack on him, landing punches to his face and scratches all over his body. After the brief but violent altercation, he had the police restrain her and warn her to never step foot on the property again. Later that day, he called me to tell me what had happened and ask for my advice. He was afraid for his safety and for his life. I think my response surprised him.

"Get her help," I told him. "She's not healthy. She's not mentally stable. She needs help." Just eight months before, Jennair had unleashed her own attack on Meredith and then herself. If I had known then what I know now, I would have done anything, given anything, to stop her. To get her the help she needed so badly.

Enlisting the help of friends, my friend has tried to get his ex-girlfriend the help she needs, to try to reason with her, but she has continued to contact him, to spontaneously show up and send him emotional but irrational emails and text messages. I now know he needs a different answer from me. Beware. If a man were doing this to a woman, the potential for greater violence would be clear. But again, because she's a woman, we can so easily dismiss her as "irrational" and not recognize the spiraling danger she might pose. Will she become violent? I don't know. I only know that just because she's female, it doesn't mean she won't be.

Love and heartbreak can unleash an emotional maelstrom few of us are prepared for. I know I was never prepared for Jennair's violence, despite the utter anguish she was clearly in, despite the constancy of her surveillance, her obsessive and controlling behavior as she unraveled and fueled her rage with her mounting "evidence" of my sins.

We all pretend to be strong, to be confident, to hope everything will work itself out in the end. But the truth is, we all have breaking points. As humans, we are all made of the same ingredients and some of us are wired differently. Weaker. Stronger. But in the end, we are all fragile, capable of losing it, of breaking down, of acting out in a way we can't control. What I experienced wasn't the first murder-suicide caused by a broken heart and a fit of rage and vengeance. And sadly, it won't be the last. But I have come to believe we all have a responsibility to take care of the ones we love, and especially the ones we hurt. If not for them, then for ourselves, knowing that we did all that we can do. That we can live with integrity, knowing that we did everything in our power to live our lives with grace, kindness and empathy toward others.

In 2014, in the aftermath of the Boston Marathon bombings, I recall the media trying so hard to get an interview with the parents of the brothers who had planned and executed the horrific act. Standing there at their front door with a microphone jammed in their face, I remember thinking, "There's no way they could still love their sons after what they had done." They had brought shame upon their family. They were brutal, murderous cowards, misguided by a flawed and evil ideology. I was surprised when I heard both parents say they still loved their sons. I just didn't understand. But now I do.

Let me be clear, what Jennair did by taking Meredith's life is an egregious, unthinkable act I have yet to forgive her for. She irreparably broke the hearts of her family, her friends and everyone who knew her and loved her, including me. But for the vengeful, hateful and heartless thing she has done to me, I have forgiven her. I had to for my own peace. And I in return asked the same from Jennair. On December 19, I wrote a letter to her.

Jennair,

It's your birthday today. I didn't plan it this way. It's just the way the timing worked out. I suppose I could wait until tomorrow to write this, but in a way, it just seems right. It was our tradition for 24 years, writing letters in our birthday cards to each other. Since you've been gone, I've been dreading this day more than most. But I owe this to you.

Sorry doesn't begin to express how I feel. I betrayed you. I abandoned you. I failed you. Both as a husband and as your friend. The pain I caused you. The fear of the unknown, making you feel hopeless and helpless. You didn't deserve it. I did this. I had no right.

And neither did you. Taking Meredith's life from her, taking her from her family, and from this earth has affected the lives and broken the hearts of so many people. Not just me. She didn't deserve to die, Jennair. And neither did you. Neither did you.

There will be those that read this and not fathom how I could possibly feel anything but disgust and hostility toward you. But they can't possibly understand the depths of the love we shared, bruised and impaired as it often was. You often told me I didn't understand, nor was I capable of unconditional love. I agreed. Surely there should always be conditions, I thought. "If you killed someone, for instance," I remember saying, "I couldn't possibly love you." Strange thing is, I still do. I still unconditionally do.

Ultimately, you did this to hurt me. It was "payback" as you said in your final letter. But that wasn't you. I know you, and that wasn't you. The real you was not capable of such a malicious and spiteful attack with heartless disregard for the value and the sanctity of life. You were sick, out of control —slowly and painfully unraveling. I didn't recognize or understand just how sick you were. There were signs and I missed them. We all did. I wish I could go back and start

over, do it differently. There are so many things I would do different-
ly.

Our last year had not been kind to us. Somehow, we rallied. We
stuck together to get through it. But it took such a toll. The jabs we
took at each other. Rolling eyes. Words too late to unsay. It all
chipped away at us for months, if not years, until it was too late. Un-
knowingly, I fell out of love with you. When? For how long? I don't
even know. I didn't begin to know until I met Meredith. I know that
hurts. And I offer no excuses.

I just wasn't "me" anymore. And I don't think you were "you"
either. I didn't know how to get "us" back. Worse, I didn't think it
was possible. I had become so different, wanting something different.
A fresh start, unencumbered by the distress, the weight that we had
become for one another. We could no longer lift each other up.

If even part of the hateful things you had to say about me in
your letter were true, then you too needed a fresh start. If I and my
faults, and there were many, kept you from your happiness, then you
too deserved to be freed.

The tragedy that unfolded has forever changed everyone whose
life it touched. It devastated me. But I refuse to let it define us. I
choose to remember the good times and the bad with sweet sorrow,
smiling, weeping, tasting the tears and letting those feelings wash
over me again. That's what defined us, what made us who we were.
In the beginning we were such kids, so in love. And we literally grew
up together, learning from each other. I will never be able to cook like
you, organize like you, or love unconditionally as you did. Those
were your gifts and I will never forget them.

We knew each other so well. The quirks, so many inside jokes:
"shit my wife says," "your big book of gum," "RAH!" We had our own
language that no one else understood. We just "got" each other like

nobody else could. You had such an uncanny ability to make me laugh so easily, especially when I needed it most. I want people to know that about you. You could be so hilariously funny. So sweet. So fucking brilliant.

Somehow we will all get through this emotional catastrophe, albeit bruised and scarred. I have to, to make up for the loss of life and the promises it offered. I have so much work to do. Huck fought his cancer so bravely, stoically, wanting to be there for me. He was a light that didn't want to be extinguished. He waited for you. He missed you. Gypsy too. They both did. If you and they are so lucky to meet again soon, please watch over them. I know you will.

I had always imagined that if you ever died before me, I would stand there by your grave on a grass covered hill, looking up at a huge oak tree, just like that scene from your favorite movie that made us both cry, each and every time. I love you, Jennair.

— Mark

It's been almost two years since the killings. And though this is the final chapter of this book, I know it's really just the beginning. In the months and years ahead I will continue to search. Not for clues. Not for evidence. But for meaning. For lessons. For the reason I was chosen to live. My friends tell me I have been given a tremendous gift. One that I need to use wisely. I hope I'm worthy.

I didn't want to write this book. I had to.

EPILOGUE

Weeks ago, after reading a completed draft of this manuscript, a dear friend reluctantly shared with me her disappointment. "To be honest, I felt gypped. I was hoping to hear how you are now, and how you have healed. I wanted to know what's next for you."

"What's next for me?" I asked. "I wish I knew. That story is still being written. Every day. Every hour."

By definition, a literary memoir (French for "memory" or "reminiscence") is a mere snapshot of time in your life. This book started as a cathartic journaling exercise, because I just couldn't stop thinking and talking about the tragic day that changed my life and the lives of so many others, and everything that led up to that day. I had to channel my pain and anguish into something to slow the bleeding from my self-inflicted wounds. Looking back, I honestly don't know how I did it some days. I only know I had to. To search my soul and bare my truth, for the hope that something positive might someday come from it. Hopefully today is that day.

If I had waited to write this book until I had completely healed and knew with certainty what was next, I don't think it would have ever been written. The truth is I have no expectations of actually healing. Life as I knew it is gone. Forever changed. And it's not coming back. And the pain, albeit less debilitating today, will always be there, a constant sobering reminder of what happened on April 23, 2018, six hundred and sixty-six days ago. And I have to live with it and a new reality. To learn from it. Every day.

Although I have read and heard the beginnings of public discourse around the importance of mental health, the stigma still remains. Too many people are afraid to admit they need help, concerned their family and friends will think they're crazy or not in control. Not me. After enduring debilitating panic attacks both in public and in private, and some days not caring if there was a tomorrow, I became scared for my mental health. I couldn't trust my own thoughts or my own heart. I knew I needed help.

There's a saying that time heals all wounds. But I've come to believe that's a fallacy. Dealing with grief and trauma alone is extremely difficult and, worse, potentially dangerous. Expecting to just get over it someday without proactively dealing with the layers and layers of emotional wreckage is like paving over a sinkhole in the middle of a busy street. I am far from over my grief but wouldn't be where I am today without weeks and weeks of intensive, difficult and often painful therapy. Yes, there are still days I just want to hunker down in self-pity and not feel anything or put up a front that I'm okay. But I know in my heart it's not that easy. So, each and every day I force myself to run through the pain, not run from it.

In addition to professional help and seeking spiritual guidance, a huge part of my own therapy has been continuing to write and share my story. After I put the finishing touches on this memoir, I honestly felt a little lost, not knowing what to do with myself. After a year of pouring every thought and emotion onto the page to the point of exhaustion, strangely I felt I still had so much to say.

As I started to think of the road ahead, I realized I had no idea where that road led. I knew I had to learn how to be me again. But first I had to rediscover, or perhaps discover for the first time, who "me" really was. So, I thought, what better way to envision a life than to write about my life and life decisions in real time. Within days I started a blog to not only share my story as it played out, but to engage openly with readers, people who had also been through trauma themselves and others who wanted to offer criticism and even tell me to go to hell. More than I ever felt possible, publicly admitting my weaknesses, my flaws and my mistakes, and truly being open to criticism has been an empowering experience. I welcome your thoughts and thoughtful criticism at **irreparablebook.com**

As the two-year anniversary nears, I have struggled these past few months with the idea of putting this book out there publicly. I know I had to write it. But sharing it with thousands of people is a whole other story. When I begin to waver, I think back to a conversation I had almost a year ago with my best friend of more than thirty years. "Well," he said, "what's the worst that can happen? How does it get any worse than what you've already been through? It's time to ride that grizzly bear off the cliff."

"Giddy up," I chuckled.

He always seemed to know exactly what to say when I needed it most. Even if it was complete nonsense to others. But Mike was right. I'd been wrestling with that grizzly bear of guilt, grief and self-loathing long enough. It was time to hop on and ride it straight over the cliff once and for all. I'll never be entirely free of it, and the grief will haunt me all my life, but I need to stop wrestling with it. I need to let it go.

There are those that will undoubtedly say it was too soon to write a book, and others that I'm living in the past, unnecessarily digging up painful memories. Sure, I suppose things might be easier if I just disappeared, never saying another word. But I'm still here. And I can't help but feel there is an opportunity to make a positive impact on people's lives by sharing the lessons of an unthinkable tragedy. I know there are thousands of people struggling with grief, dysfunctional relationships, marriages on the brink, and unfortunately, infidelity. If sharing my story saves lives or marriages, then my writing will have been worth it. It just might be saving me.

So what's next, you ask? Tomorrow. And I'll never take that for granted again.

ACKNOWLEDGEMENT

I would like to acknowledge and thank my book writing coach, Dr. Janice Harper for helping me to turn the grittiest of emotionally-charged journal entries into a cohesive story. You were always there to encourage me, to challenge me and keep me inspired. But more than a writing coach, you became my therapist and my friend. I learned more about the publishing industry from you than I ever hoped to know. Thank you for lighting the way and lighting the fire under my butt when I needed it.

To Dabs, you were the first to see my rawest of words and their potential to make an impact. Thank you, brother for all the support, the countless hours of wordsmithing and for volunteering to be my one-man social defense team. I owe you a debt of gratitude and more than a few drinks.

To my editor Janet Schwind, you dotted every "i" and crossed every "t". But more than your eyes and ears, you also lent me your heart, making my words even sharper and more meaningful. For that you have my respect and my friendship for life.

To my therapists: Sam, Dawn and Charlie. You have seen and heard me at my lowest. I don't know where I would be without your guidance, your kindness and your patience. I owe you for my sanity and for giving me the courage and the tools to work towards a better day.

And finally, to my dearest group of friends: Mike, Romi, Adrienne, Kelly, Stephanie, Cecilia, Carol, Anthony, Susan, Tammy and countless others. When my world was crumbling, you were my rocks. You can't possibly know how much that meant to me. Then and now.

CPSIA information can be obtained
at www.ICGtesting.com
Printed in the USA
LVHW080625261022
731591LV00016B/1024